The Digest Book of

CANOES, KAYAKS, & RAFTS

By Charles J. Farmer

DBI BOOKS, INC., NORTHFIELD, ILL.

STAFF

Editor
  Kathy Farmer

Production Manager
  Pamela J. Johnson

Associate Publisher
  Sheldon L. Factor

Cover Photographs by Charles J. Farmer

ACKNOWLEDGEMENTS

Kathy Farmer, wife, partner, editor and chief researcher is my constant source of encouragement and inspiration, and to her I owe the largest debt of gratitude.

I want to thank Deane Gray, of Old Town Canoe Company, for all his help, past and present.

To the experts, whose words of advice and experience are contained within, I wish the best of river running and sincere gratitude for taking the time to help me.

For the river management agencies—local, state and federal—who so promptly and efficiently responded to my questions, I extend my thanks and appreciation for jobs well done.

Sincerely,
Charles J. Farmer

DEDICATION

To Brittany, the product of love

INTRODUCTION

THERE HAVE BEEN books written about canoeing; journals compiled about kayaking; and volumes published about canoeing *and* kayaking. But *this is the first book written about canoeing, kayaking and rafting.*

Recreational rafting, once reserved almost exclusively for guides and paying customers on commercial white water trips down (or up) the glamorous rivers of the West, is blossoming. New, safe inflatable boats in a variety of sizes and price ranges have made rafting a private, do-it-yourself adventure, as well as a thriving commercial enterprise. Compactability, light weight, manageable size and unequaled stability give these boats tremendous versatility. For these reasons, more of them are being found on rivers, streams and lakes throughout the country. They are part of a world of the proud, simple float craft along with the canoes and kayaks that give us, the lovers of streams and lakes, so much joy.

But what else can be said about canoeing and kayaking that has not been said before? A lot! New boats, new equipment and new techniques have injected doses of vitality into small craft recreation. And because float boats are affordable, uncomplicated and environmentally compatible, more and more people are turning to canoes, kayaks *and* inflatables for active, outdoor adventure. Basically hand-propelled, they keep us in touch with *nature.*

This book has a variety of uses. It can introduce the novice to *everything* he or she needs to know about canoeing, kayaking or rafting all under one cover. Here is a solid, easy to read foundation to enjoyable, safe boating. Money saving tips on how to buy the best boats and equipment are also featured.

For the intermediate or casual boater, the book serves as a re-introduction to old friends—the canoe and kayak.

Significant changes in construction materials and designs add excitement to sports steeped in the tradition of the Indian and trapper. New, modern inflatable boats can open the doors of adventure on rivers once thought too risky or impractical for canoes or kayaks.

There is something here for the serious boater too—the man or woman who craves constant contact with wild streams and frisky boats. There is adventure, new equipment and plenty of action photos.

For all, novice or expert, there is a gathering of the forces. Three great sports in one, described and illustrated in their many changing faces. Whether you are one or the other, both or ALL, the choice is yours and this book is here to help.

TABLE OF CONTENTS

PART 1
GENERAL FLOATING

Reliable Contacts

THE RIVER is a fickle lady—moody, mad, low, high, clear, confused, gentle, rough, fast and slow. Her faces are constantly changing. If there is anything at all predictable about her flowing, silver currents, it is the fact that none of them retain any degree of stability for any length of time. A delicately changeable nymph, lady river is subject to even the faintest whims of nature.

Because the spirit is basically unharnessed and the moods and faces change, the river has been a challenge to those who saddle her back with a bucking boat. Whereas winds and storms may temporarily whip the souls of lakes and oceans into frenzied bulls, rivers do not depend on scoldings from nature for their orneriness. They come by that trait naturally. Born in the mountains, with blood current in their veins and a madness to keep moving, rivers are free to create their own mischief by the sheer devilishness of their temperaments. Add to their sinewy strength the wrath of rain and snow runoff, the fall of the terrain, the burden of heavy squalls, the thirst of droughts, the purity of gin or the milky flow of stale coffee, and the rivers take on their true color—fickle.

Telephone communication can be the floater's best planning tool. It is used to obtain last minute information on water flow, stream levels and weather conditions. A phone call the day before a trip can nearly insure a reliable forecast of what the stream will look like at launch time. If the forecast looks good, plans are activated. When conditions are unfavorable, it might be best to delay the float until they improve.

Letter writing definitely has a place in pre-trip planning. Maps, river charts, access points, camping areas, fishing tips, regulations and stream characteristics can be collected through the mail. Deciding where and when to float can be accomplished at home before vacation time or weekends. A bundle of general information, the groundwork of enjoyable floats, can be researched during winter months. Then that informa-

Reliable contacts make good boating and comfortable camping possible.

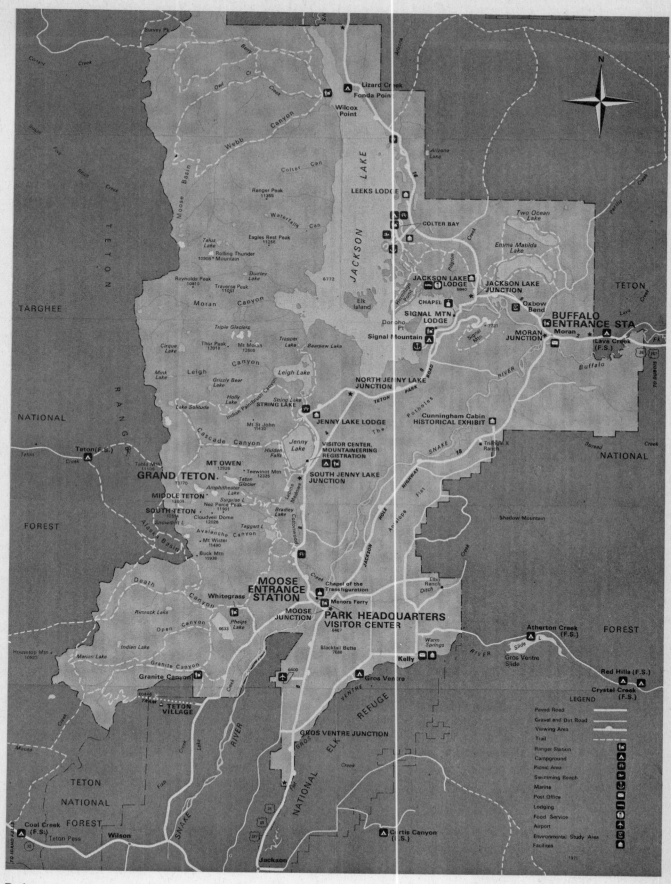

Before-the-trip contacts provide valuable information such as maps of the area to be floated.

Above—Ordinarily, the more pre-trip planning, the better the float experience. Below—Management agencies can provide information on the best times to float.

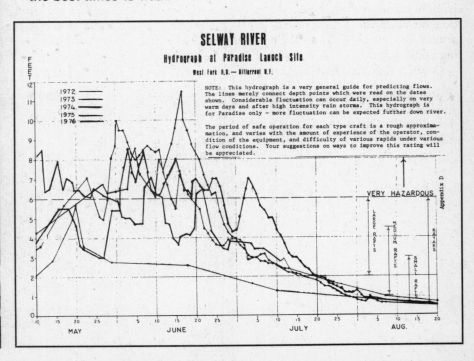

SELWAY RIVER
Hydrograph at Paradise Launch Site
West Fork R.D. — Bitterroot N.F.

NOTE: This hydrograph is a very general guide for predicting flows. The lines merely connect depth points which were read on the dates shown. Considerable fluctuation can occur daily, especially on very warm days and after high intensity rain storms. This hydrograph is for Paradise only - more fluctuation can be expected further down river.

The period of safe operation for each type craft is a rough approximation, and varies with the amount of experience of the operator, condition of the equipment, and difficulty of various rapids under various flow conditions. Your suggestions on ways to improve this rating will be appreciated.

tion can be bolstered by current phone queries to learn about variable river conditions.

Governmental agencies that administer public lands, streams and the fish within them are often excellent sources of advance letter and phone contacts. However, boaters should realize that these agencies receive large quantities of correspondence. Requests are often handled by standard printed matter. Most of the information is factual and relatively current, but may not answer specific questions. Therefore, rely on those agencies for basic information and then develop more personal contact sources for detailed information.

Agencies like the U.S. Forest Service (Washington, D.C. 20250), National Park Service (Interior Building, Washington, D.C. 20240), Bureau of Reclamation (Washington, D.C. 20240), Bureau of Land Management (Washington, D.C. 20240), Bureau of Outdoor Recreation (Washington, D.C. 20240), and the U.S. Fish and Wildlife Service (Washington, D.C. 20240) and their regional and state offices can offer good, general information, including listings of floatable rivers along with corresponding maps.

A boater determines beforehand, by consulting state recreation maps, who owns the land and the access to various stretches of river. With this in mind, the appropriate land agencies are contacted. As is often the case with prime, river bottomland, access for floating may be privately controlled. It is up to the boater to secure access permission. Often the agency that can help in pinpointing access is the state fish and game department through local game wardens and fishery personnel.

State fish and game departments are located in the capital city of each state. The main function of these agencies is to maintain and protect the state's fish and wildlife resources. Because of their close working relationship with the outdoors, wardens—the men at the grass roots level—are often the most familiar with floating conditions.

Contact fish and game departments by letter. Your letter may be forwarded to a local warden or information specialist. Or it may be sent back to you with general information and suggestions for making personal contact with an employee in your float area. Either way, local fish and game technicians can be helpful information sources. Quite often they are ardent outdoorsmen in their own right. They are aware of the floating potential of the various waters in their areas. And they can set floaters straight on public and private river access.

It is important to contact these persons in advance of the trip. As their jobs dictate, they spend a good deal of time in the field and are hard to reach at the office or at home. In an off-season letter, during winter or early spring, ask about: 1. good, floatable stretches in their area; 2. public and private access; 3. float difficulty rating; 4. length and average time of float; and 5. fishing or other tips. These questions will yield a wealth of reliable information that can be used later. If you are satisfied with the response you receive and your correspondent appears interested in helping you, request a phone number where he or she may be reached for short notice information.

State parks often provide some of the finest floating potential available. Under the auspices of state fish and game programs and outdoor recreation departments, state parks are meccas for floaters. Pertinent information about state park recreation may be obtained from fish and game departments or recreation offices at the park or state capital headquarters.

Floaters fortunate enough to have friends or relatives living near the local float scene have, perhaps, the best sources of current information.

Good, local float sources outside the governmental agency realm can also be developed. Ordinarily though, these sources produce only after a floater has visited an area once or twice and has developed some personal contacts. Possibly a motel owner or a favorite early morning restaurant cook can be the source of information.

A well-planned trip will include full information on both camping and launching facilities along with up-to-date stream conditions.

Logistics

FOR THE modern floater, landings are of great significance. Because so much prime river valley land is privately controlled, the floater, for the most part, now depends on public access points administered by the state or federal government.

There was a time when river access through private lands was fairly common and permission relatively easy to obtain. But growing recreational pressure in the last 20 years has changed that situation. There are still some areas where private access is good. But now floaters must rely heavily on land set aside by state fish and game departments, the National Park Service, U.S.

Forest Service and Bureau of Reclamation. Since boaters cannot put in or take out just anywhere, the planning of a float trip must include access considerations to and from various stretches of stream.

How does a floater find out where public landings are located? Through the state and federal agencies that administer the land. The agency may own all the land along a significant stretch of river. In that case, reaching landings presents no problems. However, more often than not, public access areas are merely easements that have been obtained specifically for the purpose of public access. The lands along the river may be

Public landings along valuable river frontage are vitally important to every floater — canoeist, kayaker or rafter. Note pickup vehicle that will be left at take-out spot.

privately owned and public access denied. This is sometimes the case even in the wide open expanses of western states.

Because some waters and the lands that border them are tightly regulated, a floater has the obligation not to violate trespass laws. In other words, fishermen who might innocently beach their boats to fish from shore or fix lunch might be trespassing. And camping is usually out of the question.

To avoid the problems associated with trespassing, the floater has the responsibility to organize floats so landing points or overnight camps are located at public access areas.

When gauging float time, take into account the float craft used, the average speed of the stretch, the time allowed for stops, wind conditions, and time allotted for water obstacles or portages.

Vehicle Pickups—Rides

One of the considerations you make as a floater is arranging for transportation before you set your boat in the water. There are several alternatives. For two-car families, one of the vehicles can be left at the take-out point. Ideally the pickup vehicle should have the capability of transporting the boat. When using inflatables, the boat can be deflated and stowed in a minimum of space. A cartop boat rack easily handles canoes and

Above—Along some stretches of river even the bicycle can be used for float transportation.

Below—Motorized bike is one means of transportation; it can be chained to a tree at take-out point.

Some resort areas that cater to floaters have pick-up shuttle services between float points.

TRAIL NO. 32E35
← ANT CANYON   4
← GOLD LEDGE FORD 5
← BULL RUN CREEK 12
← BULL RUN ROAD 13
SEQUOIA
National Forest

johnboats under 15 feet even on compact cars.

The same type of pickup arrangement can be made among fishing partners—using two vehicles; driving to the take-out point; leaving one of the vehicles there; and returning with the other to the starting point.

Another practical plan is to arrange for someone to meet you at the landing point at a pre-determined time. There are some disadvantages to this alternative. Choose a pickup driver who is reliable and has the directions straight. Decide on a fair price to pay for the service and pay part before the trip and the rest after pickup. Some river resort areas provide commercially operated shuttle service along float stretches.

Here are some other methods. Depending on the length of the float and the access road along the river, a bicycle can be used as a second means of transportation. The bike can be chained to a tree at the take-out point and used to get back to the vehicle after the float. There are limitations to this arrangement of course, but my wife and I have enjoyed this system on a multitude of short (under 6 miles) floats and find the boating and bicycling combination to be quite an adventure. A hoop rack bolted to the back bumper of our vehicle makes for a convenient bike carrier. While one person pedals

Left—Access points along float stretches are important to floaters planning trips. Maps and signs help indicate distances between points. Below, left —One way to solve logistics problem—a canoe tied to plane's pontoon.

back to the vehicle, the other person stays with the boat and equipment.

A slightly more sophisticated pickup method utilizes a small, motorized trail bike that can be transported on a frame carrier outside the vehicle. Chained at the take-out landing before the float, a motorbike provides rapid transportation back to the car and is really not as limited by distance factors as the bicycle method.

Still another alternative that can be used on some stretches of water is the addition of an outboard motor to negotiate upstream currents and get back to the starting point. This technique can be practical on slow, deep rivers.

Hitchhiking is another choice for the floater. A boater has two choices. Unload raft and gear at the starting point and have your partner wait there while you drive the vehicle to the take-out point. Then you hitch a ride back to the starting point.

A final, reasonable choice in some areas where a phone is handy is to call a friend or person who has previously consented to pick you up at the take-out point upon receiving your call.

Firm transportation arrangements after the float add to the enjoyment and peace of mind during the trip.

Enjoyment and peace of mind during a float trip are greater when transportation and pickups are arranged before the float rather than left to the end of the trip.

River Charts and Guides

River charts and guides help canoeists through new and difficult stretches of water.

RECREATIONAL boating maps are distributed by various private and governmental agencies and published by state game and fish departments. They are accurate enough to insure floaters reliable information with enough detail to pre-plan river trips. However, they are not so complicated as to require a navigation course.

Float stretches, located upstream and downstream in fairly close proximity to dams, are usually controlled by the Army Corps of Engineers (Office of the Chief of Engineers, Forrestal Building, Washington, D.C. 20314). The Civil Works Branch, more specifically, and the office of the Fish and Wildlife Section can, at times, help floaters with reliable maps and information. Division offices are located in Vicksburg, Mississippi; Omaha, Nebraska; Waltham, Maine; New York City, New York; Chicago, Illinois; Portland, Oregon; Cincinnati, Ohio; Honolulu, Hawaii; Atlanta, Georgia; San Francisco, California; and Dallas, Texas. Division offices can be contacted by letter for information and contacts at the *district* level of the Corps of Engineers where specific information can be obtained.

The Bureau of Reclamation makes river charts available for some waters. District offices are located at

Boise, Idaho; Sacramento, California; Boulder City, Nevada; Salt Lake City, Utah; Amarillo, Texas; Billings, Montana; and Denver, Colorado.

The U.S. Geological Survey (National Center, Reston, Virginia 22092) is a research agency under the Interior Department. This agency maps the nation's physical features, including water resources and can be the best source of accurate maps for the floater. The Map Information Office (U.S. Geological Survey, Washington, D.C. 20242) is the place to write for general mapping information. For float areas east of the Mississippi, write to Distribution Section, Geological Survey, Washington, D.C. 20242. Waters and lands west of the Mississippi are handled by the Distribution Center, Geological Survey, Denver Federal Center, Denver, Colorado 80225.

Maps can also be obtained from the Bureau of Outdoor Recreation in Washington, D.C., and from national, district and local headquarters of the National Park Service and U.S. Forest Service that govern waters flowing within their boundaries.

In some areas, the Coast Guard (400 7th St., S.W., Washington, D.C. 20590) can play a role in disseminat-

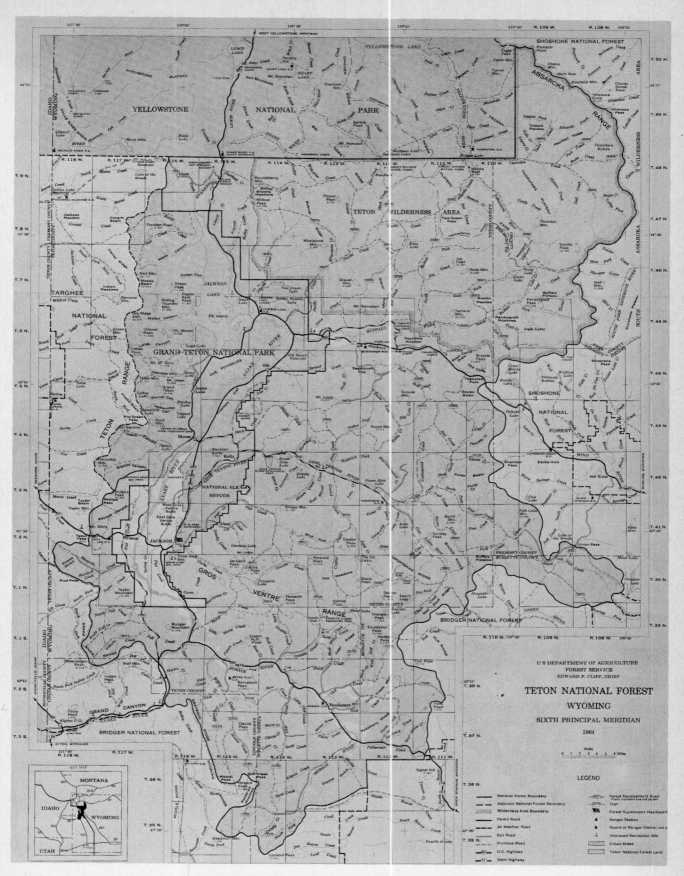

U.S. Forest Service maps show river stretches,
access points and general terrain features.

15

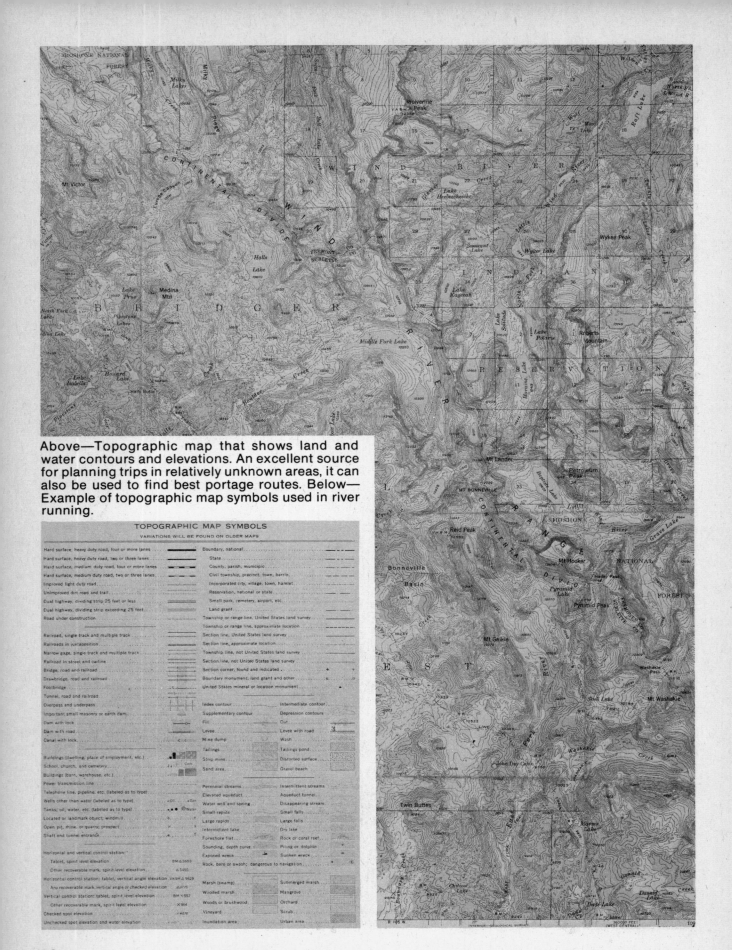

Above—Topographic map that shows land and water contours and elevations. An excellent source for planning trips in relatively unknown areas, it can also be used to find best portage routes. Below—Example of topographic map symbols used in river running.

TOPOGRAPHIC MAP SYMBOLS
VARIATIONS WILL BE FOUND ON OLDER MAPS

Hard surface, heavy duty road, four or more lanes	Boundary, national
Hard surface, heavy duty road, two or three lanes	State
Hard surface, medium duty road, four or more lanes	County, parish, municipio
Hard surface, medium duty road, two or three lanes	Civil township, precinct, town, barrio
Improved light duty road	Incorporated city, village, town, hamlet
Unimproved dirt road and trail	Reservation, national or state
Dual highway, dividing strip 25 feet or less	Small park, cemetery, airport, etc.
Dual highway, dividing strip exceeding 25 feet	Land grant
Road under construction	Township or range line, United States land survey
	Township or range line, approximate location
Railroad, single track and multiple track	Section line, United States land survey
Railroads in juxtaposition	Section line, approximate location
Narrow gage, single track and multiple track	Township line, not United States land survey
Railroad in street and carline	Section line, not United States land survey
Bridge, road and railroad	Section corner, found and indicated
Drawbridge, road and railroad	Boundary monument; land grant and other
Footbridge	United States mineral or location monument
Tunnel, road and railroad	
Overpass and underpass	Index contour / Intermediate contour
Important small masonry or earth dam	Supplementary contour / Depression contours
Dam with lock	Fill / Cut
Dam with road	Levee / Levee with road
Canal with lock	Mine dump / Wash
	Tailings / Tailings pond
Buildings (dwelling, place of employment, etc.)	Strip mine / Distorted surface
School, church, and cemetery	Sand area / Gravel beach
Buildings (barn, warehouse, etc.)	
Power transmission line	Perennial streams / Intermittent streams
Telephone line, pipeline, etc. (labeled as to type)	Elevated aqueduct / Aqueduct tunnel
Wells other than water (labeled as to type)	Water well and spring / Disappearing stream
Tanks; oil, water, etc. (labeled as to type)	Small rapids / Small falls
Located or landmark object; windmill	Large rapids / Large falls
Open pit, mine, or quarry; prospect	Intermittent lake / Dry lake
Shaft and tunnel entrance	Foreshore flat / Rock or coral reef
	Sounding, depth curve / Piling or dolphin
Horizontal and vertical control station:	Exposed wreck / Sunken wreck
Tablet, spirit level elevation	Rock, bare or awash; dangerous to navigation
Other recoverable mark, spirit level elevation	
Horizontal control station; tablet, vertical angle elevation	Marsh (swamp) / Submerged marsh
Any recoverable mark, vertical angle or checked elevation	Wooded marsh / Mangrove
Vertical control station; tablet, spirit level elevation	Woods or brushwood / Orchard
Other recoverable mark, spirit level elevation	Vineyard / Scrub
Checked spot elevation	Inundation area / Urban area
Unchecked spot elevation and water elevation	

ing information to the general public. Most often, regional Notice to Mariners and Marine Aids to Navigation are available for those waterways that share commercial and recreational boating uses. The locations of district offices can be obtained by writing to the main headquarters in Washington, D.C. Floaters can then contact regional or local branches of the Coast Guard for current, specific information about particular sections of rivers under Coast Guard jurisdiction.

Another source for maps are various Chambers of Commerce, located in towns near popular float streams. Chamber maps can offer good information. However, most of them are in need of weeding out facts from advertising come-ons.

Privately published river guides and maps are often sold in recreation areas and towns near popular stretches of river. When updated regularly, these guides can be accurate and helpful. However, be sure to look for the copyright date in the guide or on the maps. For swift, changeable western rivers especially, charts older than 3 years might be outdated to the point that they can do more harm than good. Because there is usually some desire for financial return in the commercial production of river guides or maps, a number of charts are not kept current enough to insure their reliability. It is a good idea not to depend on one guide or map as the final word for trip planning. A combination of commercially sold float guides and state or federal maps can prove valuable in double checking information and accuracy. The more time spent with several good maps of the float stretch, the more peace of mind can be enjoyed during the trip.

What should a good float chart or guide contain? In general a good float map should be broken down into various stretches. Charts should be detailed enough to illustrate all essential float information in clear, easy-to-read form. Guides containing several maps and bound in a small book or loose-leaf form are more handy. Each section of floatable water should be broken down into miles. The best charts show distances between easily recognizable man-made or natural landmarks such as bridges, dikes, rapids, feeder streams, dramatic bends in the river, signs or campgrounds. By knowing the number of miles traveled the floater can determine whether the pace should be quickened to reach the final destination at the specific time.

Topographic maps, available from the U.S. Geological Survey, give an accurate picture of a river. Distances can be measured fairly accurately by the natural and man-made features symbolized on the "topo."

River charts should show, through various signs and symbols clearly printed on the map, the location of dikes, levees or falls. Rapids of any significance are

A good river guide will indicate what stretches are suited for beginners.

Even canoe races require foreknowledge of river conditions through the use of proper maps and guides.

usually represented by solid bars on the map overlaying the stream. The more prominent features that are indicated on a map, the better a floater can determine distance covered. Picnic areas and campgrounds are shown on some maps. Creeks entering the main stream are named. Trails and portages are well defined. Obvious hills, mountain peaks, bluffs and meadows are indicated. Bridges that cross the stream or roads that parallel its course are marked. Ranches or farmsteads that can be viewed from the river are listed. Public landings, of course, are well defined.

Some maps go beyond normal information, listing such highlights as best fishing spots, historic points of interest, and gravel bars. Streams of rare, year-round stability are sometimes defined by in-stream boulders, fallen logs, riffle areas or common trouble spots. These excellent beginner streams are in the minority though. Most rivers because of their fluctuating water levels are not defined by their in-stream watermarks for obvious reasons, and ordinarily only the most prominent of trouble spots are indicated.

Some maps have some helpful notations like "difficult turn in high water" or "log obstacle during low water" or "tricky rapids with rocks all year." These "extras" are fine for some stretches and some streams. However, water safety experts have discovered that some boaters rely too heavily on charts that pinpoint trouble spots. They tend to let their guards down and often run into unexpected snags or rocks.

Some river guides also go into brief descriptions of the river and then evaluate each stretch. This gives the beginning floater or newcomer to the river an overall idea of what to expect. It's smart to keep in mind, though, that most recreational charts are merely aids. They can help the floater immensely. But their accuracy, dictated by the moods of the river, cannot compare, let's say, to the always predictable road map that seldom changes. In addition to good charts and guides then, a floater must combine boating skills and sound, common sense.

Your Legal Right to Float

"As long ago as the Institutes of Justinian, running waters, like the air and the sea, were things common to all and property of none." *(United States* v. *Gerlach Live Stock Co.)*

And then man discovered the power of water control.

The Massachusetts Bay Colony Ordinance of 1641-7 provides:

"Sec. 2. Every inhabitant who is a householder shall have free fishing and fowling in any great ponds, bays, coves and rivers, so far as the sea ebbs and flows within the precincts of the town where they dwell, unless the freemen of the said town, or the general court, have otherwise appropriated them . . .

"Sec. 4. And for great ponds lying in common, though within the bounds of some town, it shall be free for any man to fish or fowl there, and may pass and repass on foot through any man's propriety for that end, so they trespass not upon any man's corner meadow."

There have been, even in the earliest days, laws to help define public waters and access to them. In the course of time, the laws, naturally, have become more complex and harder to define with a multitude of different meanings. To say that one needs a lawyer to decode modern day water laws, as they pertain to river floaters, would be a gross understatement. It is nearly impossible for the layman to obtain a clear understanding of his water rights without the help of an attorney.

I have personally passed up some fine looking float water because I was unsure of its status. But, knowledgeable floaters can gain a command of how to interpret water laws or where to go for clarification. Research can prevent the floater from being "bluffed out" of a float trip by the harsh words of a landowner or intimidated by warning or trespass signs that could be illegal.

An attorney is a reliable source of information about water laws. I contacted my good friend, Timothy J. Bommer, an attorney of excellent reputation as well as an ardent outdoorsman from Jackson Hole, Wyoming. Bommer lives in the heart of floating country, with the Snake, Green, Henry's Fork and New Fork Rivers

Even in vast lands of the West, access is becoming difficult.

nearly at his doorstep. Tim displayed a sincere and enthusiastic interest in my query about legal floating rights, forewarning me, "The question you ask involves a complex area of the law."

Why All the Confusion?

According to Bommer, most laymen assume that all "navigable" waters of the country can be legally floated by the public. "The word, 'navigable,' is not a clearly defined word," said Bommer, "and herein lies a reason for the confusion. All surface water throughout the United States is generally subject either to federal or state jurisdiction. There continues to be a raging controversy between the United States and state governments as to the ownership of water in the states."

In other words, states define their navigable waters one way, and the federal government may define them another. Bommer poses a question, "Should the Green River (a magnificent, blue-ribbon trout and floating stream in Wyoming) be impounded at three locations to provide hydroelectric energy for Los Angeles? If the Green were determined navigable, or affected navigable waters controlled by the United States, the federal government could then make the decision of what would happen to Wyoming's water and build three dams on the Green River. But on the other hand, should the state of Wyoming be allowed to determine that more benefit would be derived through recreation and agricultural uses? It's complicated."

A few points to remember: 1. The most highly developed body of federal water law is in relation to navigable waters. 2. Since the national powers are supreme, the United States government's action in reference to a navigable river is not subject to state laws which, on the surface, seem to apply to all waters. 3. In *Arizona* v. *California,* the Supreme Court declared that the power to dam and store the water of a navigable stream gives the power to distribute the water to states in such shares as Congress or its delegate may determine.

That's a brief overview of the federal/state water law problem. Now down to state level.

Where Does Your State Stand?

Navigable waters of the various states are defined by the states themselves. Some states have apparently made no attempt to create a definition of "navigability" or "public waters." These states are: Arizona, Arkansas, Colorado, Connecticut, Delaware, Florida, Hawaii, Kansas, Kentucky, Maine, Maryland, Nebraska, Nevada, New Jersey, North Carolina, Pennsylvania, Rhode Island, Tennessee, Washington, and West Virginia.

Court decisions in Missouri, New Mexico, Wisconsin, and Wyoming have placed varying degrees of emphasis on state constitutional declarations when establishing a broad foundation for recreational surface uses. New Mexico and Wyoming appear to have taken the strongest position on this point. The New Mexico Constitution states: "The unappropriated water of every natural stream is hereby declared to belong to the public."

The Wyoming Constitution provides that the water of the state belongs to the state and therefore belongs to the public. In the rather unique *Day* v. *Armstrong* case, the decision holds that even if a particular stream is "nonnavigable" the water flowing through that stream is a public easement, and can therefore be used by the

Some states declare that the shoreline is public. . . .

public. The decision went one step further in allowing the public to reasonable trespass across private lands in the event of an obstruction in the water course.

The Wyoming Constitution further states, "Persons and their property may only float by boat, canoe or raft for any lawful purpose down that part of any stream in the State of Wyoming where the records of the state engineer for the ten years preceding such floating show that part of the stream to have had an average flow of water for the month of July exceeding 1,000 cubic feet per second."

The Wisconsin Constitution provides, "The River Mississippi and the navigable waters leading into the Mississippi and St. Lawrence, and the carrying places between the same, shall be common highways and forever free, as well to the inhabitants of the state as to the citizens of the United States, without any tax, impost or duty therefore."

The Texas definition reads this way. "All streams so far as they retain an average width of thirty feet from the mouth up shall be considered navigable streams."

California and Illinois represent the legislative patterns in which navigable waters are defined in a commercial context, essentially limited to transportation uses.

Historical overtones permeate the Mississippi provision. "All rivers, creeks, and bayous in this state, twenty-five miles in length, that have sufficient depth and width of water for thirty consecutive days in the year, for floating a steamboat with carrying capacity of two hundred bales of cotton, are hereby declared to be navigable waters of this state."

A product of the Land and Water Law Review of 1971 is a passage drafted which is an attempt to codify the common law concerning rights in public waters—a nearly impossible task. It reads, "A river, stream, creek or channel which, during any stage, including the ordinary high water stages, has been or is being used or is capable of being used in its natural and ordinary condition for floating any boat, canoe, skiff or craft with at least one person aboard, or for floating products for transportation purposes, is declared public."

Floaters Can Find Answers

You can see, by the various examples of water laws, why some landowners have gotten away with illegal obstacles to "navigable" or public waters. Confusion and lack of definition have been on their side. As recreational river use increases, more attempts to close or block certain waters are being made. It is important for you, the floater, to know the laws in your state. And it is wise, even to the point of sounding ridiculous, to carry a copy of those laws with you when floating. You can take steps beforehand to insure that your public water rights are not violated or threatened.

1. At least one month before your trip, write to the Attorney General of the state in which you live or wish to float for the laws pertaining to the ownership and use of the water within that state. Carry a copy of these laws with you when you float.

2. Check with your local fish and game department to determine what waters can and cannot be used by the public in accordance with the laws of the state.

3. No matter what the law states, always make inquiries as to the floatability of unfamiliar waters. Some landowners can be hostile, regardless of the law. Certain stretches can be dangerously blocked. A few floats may not be worth the battle.

. . . .other states have trespass laws that prohibit even a hand from contact.

Wild and Scenic Rivers

EVERY FLOATER should cultivate a sincere and unyielding interest in the *National Wild And Scenic Rivers System*. It is by far the most important law affecting streams, rivers, lands and the people who love them. Authorized by the Wild and Scenic Rivers Act (Public Law 90-542) on October 2, 1968, and amended by Congress (Public Law 93-621) to include 29 additional rivers for study, the System is a product of beauty. Despite its vulnerability to politics and big money, the System lives and works. A remarkable tribute (in a time of relentless energy demands, commercial water hoarding and inflated land prices) to the men and women who fought to preserve the water roots of America.

The National Wild and Scenic Rivers System

The Wild and Scenic Rivers Act declares: " . . . Certain selected rivers of the Nation which, with their immediate environments, possess outstandingly remarkable scenic, recreational, geologic, fish and wildlife, historic, cultural or other similar values, shall be preserved in free-flowing condition, and that they and their immediate environments shall be protected for the benefit and enjoyment of present and future generations. The Congress declares that the established national policy of dam and other construction at appropriate sections of the rivers of the United States needs to be complemented by a policy that would preserve other selected rivers or sections thereof in their free-flowing condition to protect the water quality of such rivers and to fulfill other vital national conservation purposes."

How the System Was Implemented

Congress established the National Wild and Scenic Rivers System and designated all or portions of eight rivers as the initial components of that system to be administered by the Department of the Interior or the Department of Agriculture. Those rivers designated were the Rio Grande (New Mexico), Saint Croix, Wolf, Eleven Point, Middle Fork of the Feather, Middle Fork of the Clearwater, Middle Fork of the Salmon and the Rogue.

The 1968 Act designated 27 other rivers for detailed study as potential additions to the National System. On January 3, 1975, the Congress amended the Act, adding 29 rivers for study. In addition to the original eight rivers, the Snake (Idaho), Rapid, Lower St. Croix, Chattooga and New River are now included in the System and administered by the federal government. The Little Beaver, Little Miami and Allagash, also part of the System, are currently being administered on a state or local basis, but also have federal protection. Under certain conditions, the Secretary of the Interior can add a select state or locally administered river area to the National Wild Scenic Rivers System upon application of the governor.

Criteria for Inclusion

All rivers in the National System must be substantially free-flowing and have water of high quality or water that could be restored to that condition. The river and adjacent lands must also be in a natural or esthetically pleasing condition and possess outstanding scenic, recreational, geologic, fish and wildlife, historic, cultural or other similar values.

Because all rivers are different and some have been altered in varying degrees, there are three classifications for inclusion in the National Wild and Scenic Rivers System. These are Wild River Areas, Scenic River Areas and Recreational River Areas. Basically, the Wild River Area is the most primitive, inaccessible and unchanged. It is managed to preserve and enhance the primitive qualities. A Scenic River Area can be accessible in places by road and is managed to preserve and enhance a natural, though sometimes modified, environment and provide a modest range of facilities for recreation. Recreational River Areas may have undergone some development and impoundment or diversion in the past. They are managed to provide the visitor with a wide range of readily accessible recreational opportunities which may reflect evidence of man's activity, yet remain esthetically pleasing.

Because of the wisdom of people who were willing to fight for and defend free-flowing rivers in the United States, canoeists, rafters and kayakers will benefit. Not

Because of concerned persons and wise legislation, some rivers and streams will be kept free and unchanged.

Some rivers are not protected by Wild and Scenic River regulations—the results are self-evident.

only will we enjoy a variety of streams in their natural or semi-natural state, but so will our children and their children. However, the fight is far from over. Complacency threatens progress already made and deters the inclusion of other qualified rivers into the System.

The Wild and Scenic Rivers Act does not prohibit the construction of roads or bridges, timber harvesting and livestock grazing or "other uses that do not *substantially* interfere with full public use and enjoyment." Mining and related mineral activities must be conducted in accord with the provisions of the Wild and Scenic Rivers Act.

While these activities may not be disastrous in themselves, past performance demonstrates the need for caution. Unnecessary road building, timber sales allocated to unscrupulous clear cutters, overgrazing and strip mining all affect existing Wild and Scenic Rivers and can block the inclusion of rivers under consideration.

Any floater who feels protective about the stream that affords so much floating, fishing, camping, nature, or photographic pleasure can contribute, in some way, to monitoring and safeguarding her wild and scenic virtues. We can support legislation aimed at adding more rivers to the System.

For our efforts, we are richly rewarded. The privilege of public access to waters and lands of remarkable beauty and quality is but part of the bounty. Floating a Wild and Scenic River is a personal matter—a special communion between floater and river. It is a testimony: here lies a stream forever saved from the complexities of modern man. Clean water, fish, trees, meandering courses, birds, animals, stillness, canoes, kayaks, and inflatable boats—that's what a Wild and Scenic River is.

RIVER MILEAGE CLASSIFICATIONS FOR COMPONENTS OF NATIONAL WILD AND SCENIC RIVERS SYSTEM

River Present Units — National System	Administering Agency	Miles by Classification Wild	Scenic	Recreational	Total Miles
1. Middle Fork Clearwater, Idaho	USFS	54	—	131	185
2. Eleven Point, Missouri	USFS	—	44.4	—	44.4
3. Feather, California	USFS	32.9	9.7	65.4	108
4. Rio Grande, New Mexico	BLM/USFS	51.75	—	1	52.75
	(BLM)	(43.90)	—	(0.25)	(44.15)
	(USFS)	(7.85)	—	(0.75)	(8.60)
5. Rogue, Oregon	BLM/USFS	33	7.5	44	84.5
	(BLM)	(20)	—	(27)	(47)
	(USFS)	(13)	(7.5)	(17)	(37.5)
6. St. Croix, Minnesota And Wis.	NPS	—	181	19	200
7. Middle Fork Salmon, Idaho	USFS	103	—	1	104
8. Wolf, Wisconsin	NPS	—	25	—	25
9. Allagash Wilderness Waterway, Me.	Maine	95	—	—	95
10. Lower St. Croix, Minn. and Wis.	NPS	—	12	15	27
	Minn. & Wis.	—	—	25	25
11. Chattooga, N.C., S.C., and Ga.	USFS	39.8	2.5	14.6	56.9
12. Little Miami, Ohio	Ohio	—	18	48	66
13. Little Beaver, Ohio	Ohio	—	33	—	33
14. Snake, Idaho and Oregon	USFS	32.5	34.4	—	66.9
15. Rapid, Idaho	USFS	31	—	—	31
16. New, North Carolina	North Carolina	—	26.5	—	26.5
	Total	**472.95**	**394.0**	**364.0**	**1,230.95**

Important Roles for River Lovers

We can take active roles in initiating new legislation or safeguarding the existing Wild and Scenic River System. A most important point to remember is that river lovers, like yourself, are responsible for preserving many of our beautiful streams. Action was no doubt initiated at water level, by common, ordinary citizens who witnessed the pollution of our nation's waterways and were sickened by it.

First of all, thoroughly acquaint yourself with the Wild and Scenic Rivers Act by obtaining a copy from the Department of the Interior, Bureau of Outdoor Recreation, Washington, D.C. 20240; or Department of Agriculture, Forest Service, Washington, D.C. 20250. From either of these two agencies you can obtain a copy of the Act and pamphlets *Wild and Scenic Rivers* and *Guidelines for Evaluating Wild, Scenic, and Recreational Areas* along with a map of current and proposed rivers. Then you will have the facts as they stand.

Under the System, rivers are listed in various categories, such as: existing components of the System; studies completed; and studies in progress. Studies must be completed by law on specified dates. A significant portion of the river candidates have studies still in progress. Here is where your voice and actions can be heard and felt. Investigate the study. Is the time consuming research legitimate and necessary to the total criteria of a certain river or is there lack of interest, political red tape and strong opposition by powerful money interests?

The Wild and Scenic Rivers Act encourages state and local governments to participate in the program. Local and state representatives and senators should be contacted. Remember, there is strength in numbers. Join a canoe club, a sportsmen organization, or a state or national conservation group. Letters, phone calls, petitions and personal visits all work. It is your governor who has the option of applying for inclusion in the national Wild and Scenic Rivers System. When it comes time to vote, find out how your representatives and gubernatorial candidates feel about Wild and Scenic Rivers. Getting the job done involves some politicking.

The Environmental Protection Agency, Corps of Engineers, State Water Pollution Control Agency, State Engineers Office, and Fish and Game Department are offices that wield powers over the future of our float waters. Know their addresses. Write letters when you have questions regarding local or national problems. Attend public hearings. Monitor water pollution with simple water-quality sampling techniques. When we take active roles in guarding the streams we love, and preserving their future, then we realize the full meaning and responsibility of floating a wild and scenic river.

Hard fighting on the part of river lovers preserves streams for future generations.

River Management

THE MIDDLE FORK of the Salmon River in Idaho, the Rogue River in Oregon, and the Colorado and Arkansas Rivers in Colorado are four extremely popular river running challenges. The recreational management of these rivers by the U. S. Forest Service, State Marine Board, and Division of Parks and Outdoor Recreation is also a challenge—one that is growing every year as more and more floaters take to the rivers. Here is an insight into how these rivers are managed and some of the problems currently encountered.

Middle Fork of the Salmon River

When and why did a permit system go into effect for the Middle Fork of the Salmon River?

Sam E. Warren, Middle Fork District Ranger, Challis, Idaho gives this reply:

"Trip permits were first required for outfitters in 1972. Beginning in 1973, trip permits were required for noncommercial trips but no reservation system was used. 1974 was the first year of complete reservation and permit system. These regulations were made necessary by the increased use of the Middle Fork.

"The Middle Fork is a nice 5- or 6-day float trip. It made a very convenient trip to launch on Sunday or Monday and come off at the mouth of the river on Friday or Saturday. This allowed a day of travel on each end of your float trip. Consequently 80 percent of our use on the Middle Fork was launching on Sunday and Monday. Since most parties floated at the same speed a large group of people floated down the river together. This caused a loss in some of the wilderness values involved as well as complications and overcrowding at the campsites. It was necessary to distribute this use evenly throughout the week and throughout the season if we were to utilize the recreation potential of the Middle Fork as well as maintain its value as a Wild River."

Does the permit procedure effectively limit the number of people who want to run the river?

"I feel that our permit and reservation system does give us a definite limit on users. Whether our capacity figures are correct or not is another question. Determining the capacity of a campground is relatively easy. A capacity of a river system or a wilderness is a much more complicated procedure.

"I think that our capacity of seven parties launched per day on the Middle Fork is the correct amount. We may find that future conditions warrant some adjustment. Whether our party size of 30 people for commercial outfitters is too large for a wilderness type trip, I don't know. This depends on each person's value system and wilderness aesthetics and beliefs. Our regulations work and are enforceable at least to the extent the river and its ecology are being protected. There are some people who manage to beat the permit system in one way or another, but this is a very minor amount.

Guides and trip leaders have to be qualified. PFD's (life preservers) are a must.

Our law enforcement procedures are designed as an education and management tool rather than a crime and punishment type situation. In this context our regulations are enforceable."

How many noncommercial boat permit applications are granted each year?

"In 1976, almost 300 noncommercial reservations were granted. Approximately 150 requests for reservations were turned down. Almost all of these were turned down because the date or dates requested were not available. There were still unused launch slots available after the 20th of August. The Middle Fork is still floatable at this time but is not as "desirable" as it is earlier in the season. An interesting point along this line is that out of the almost 300 reservations issued, approximately 30 percent of the parties did not show up to start their trips."

How many accidents and fatalities occur on the Middle Fork of the Salmon?

"There have been 5 fatalities connected with boating accidents on the Middle Fork of the Salmon River since

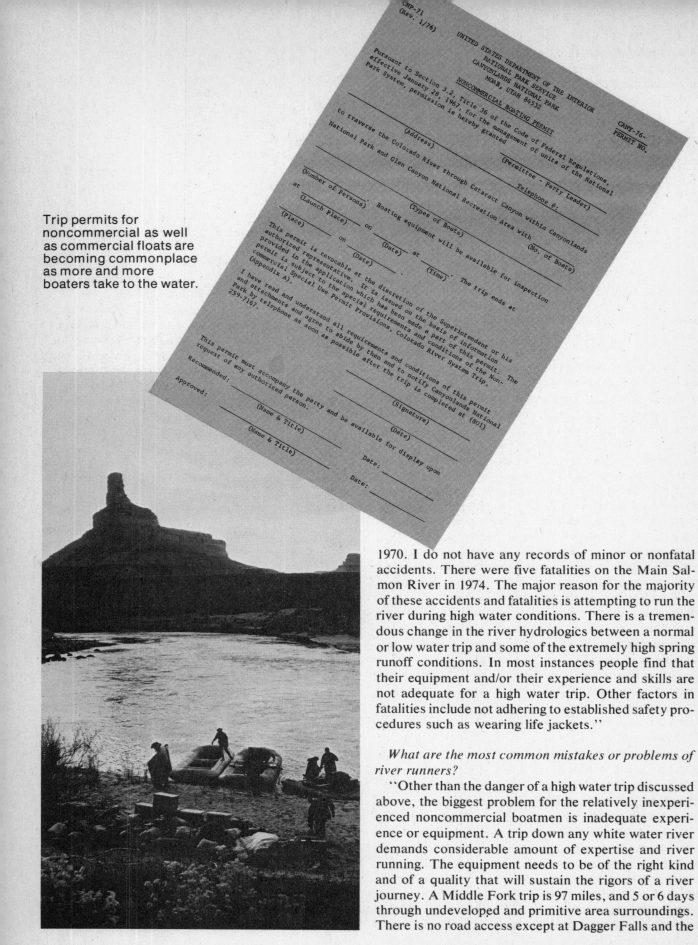

Trip permits for noncommercial as well as commercial floats are becoming commonplace as more and more boaters take to the water.

1970. I do not have any records of minor or nonfatal accidents. There were five fatalities on the Main Salmon River in 1974. The major reason for the majority of these accidents and fatalities is attempting to run the river during high water conditions. There is a tremendous change in the river hydrologics between a normal or low water trip and some of the extremely high spring runoff conditions. In most instances people find that their equipment and/or their experience and skills are not adequate for a high water trip. Other factors in fatalities include not adhering to established safety procedures such as wearing life jackets."

What are the most common mistakes or problems of river runners?

"Other than the danger of a high water trip discussed above, the biggest problem for the relatively inexperienced noncommercial boatmen is inadequate experience or equipment. A trip down any white water river demands considerable amount of expertise and river running. The equipment needs to be of the right kind and of a quality that will sustain the rigors of a river journey. A Middle Fork trip is 97 miles, and 5 or 6 days through undeveloped and primitive area surroundings. There is no road access except at Dagger Falls and the mouth of the river. Help, radio telephone communications, and airstrips are few and far between so that any minor accident can become a serious problem.''

Rogue River

When and why did a permit system go into effect for the Rogue River?

James Hadley, Director of the State Marine Board in Salem, Oregon gives this reply:

"The permit procedure for the Rogue River became effective in 1975 and was prompted by increasing use of a Federal Wild River which is also an Oregon State Scenic Waterway.''

Does the permit procedure effectively limit the number of people who want to run the river?

"The rules, presently under revision, have effectively limited increases to commercial river running operations, work reasonably well and are enforced.''

How many noncommercial boat permit applications are granted each year?

"Up to this time, noncommercial use of the river has not reached capacity. Thus, permits are issued without limit at Grave Creek, the ingress point.''

How many accidents and fatalities occur on Oregon white water rivers?

"Fifty-seven (57) accidents have occurred on Oregon white water rivers in the past two and one-half (2-1/2) years for which we have available data, and 27 fatalities have occurred. While accidents happen to the highly qualified and well prepared, it is the neophyte and ill-equipped who most often become statistics according to our data.

"White water boating requires unique skills and abilities not attained overnight. It also requires an extraordinary ability to 'read' a river's characteristics, always new and different, and the good sense to scout all riffles and rapids before boating them. River guides (booklets and maps) are always valuable aids which should not be ignored.''

What are the most common mistakes or problems of river runners?

"White water river runners should always use good boats, whether 'hard' or 'inflatable,' and of a type suitable for the particular river. The boatman has to have knowledge of the capabilities and limitations of his boat, as well as unadorned knowledge of his own skills.

"Life jackets should be available for all persons aboard, of an appropriate type and size, and worn in all potentially dangerous waters. Once again, scouting rapids and studying maps and river guide books are an absolute necessity. Persons with physical limitations or chronic illnesses, such as heart or lung diseases, should avoid this extremely physical sport.''

Colorado River

When and why did a permit system go into effect for Colorado white water rivers?

Pat Hatch, Boat and Snowmobile Coordinator for the Colorado Division of Parks and Outdoor Recreation in Littleton, Colorado, gives this reply:

"At the present time, user permits are not required to run any of the rivers in Colorado except for the portions of the Green and Yampa rivers within Dinosaur National Monument. Applications for permits on these rivers can be obtained by contacting Dinosaur National Monument, P.O. Box 210, Dinosaur, Colorado 81610, (303) 374-2216.

"White water boating, especially river running with inflatable rafts, is becoming extremely popular in Colorado. River use permits will undoubtedly come about in the future, however, agencies having responsibilities of river management in the state agree that use permits are not needed at the present time. When the time does come that user permits will be required, I would expect the two agencies mainly responsible for river management in the state, the U. S. Bureau of Land Management and U. S. Forest Service, to set up a user permit system similar to that used in Utah.''

How many accidents and fatalities occur on white water streams in Colorado?

"Colorado has been somewhat fortunate in that during the past 3 years we have had only seven fatalities due to white water accidents. They are as follows:''

YEAR	RIVER	FATALITIES	CAUSE OF ACCIDENT
1974	Colorado	1	Kayak overturned (inexperienced operator)
1975	Uncompahgre	1	Inflatable raft upset
1975	Clear Creek	1	2-man inflatable raft upset (victim was not wearing PFD)
1975	Arkansas	1	2-man inflatable raft upset (victim was not wearing PFD)
1975	Colorado	1	Canoe upset (victim was not wearing PFD)
1975	Arkansas	1	Kayak upset (victim washed into log jam—died later of injuries)
1976	Colorado	1	Inflatable raft upset (victim was not wearing PFD)

What are the most common mistakes or problems of river runners?

"I would say that the most common mistake of river runners, especially beginners, is that they underestimate the force and power of the river and overestimate their own ability. Also in the case of many beginners, they are totally unprepared in both river knowledge and river equipment. Our advice to the beginner is to first take a trip with a commercial outfitter or with someone who has sufficient river running experience before attempting to strike out on his own.''

The Rules of the River and Why

MAJOR float rivers, as well as lesser known streams, are experiencing heavy use from commercial and private floaters. It is doubtful whether this trend will ever take a reversal. The rivers that were once governed only by a few common sense rules and regulations are now flowing under tighter control.

Some argue against river running rules, limitations and permits. "Rivers belong to everybody. It's not right to limit the number of floaters."

Despite the fact that few stream lovers enjoy seeing a wild, free river managed under a maze of rigid restrictions, most foresighted river runners see the need for regulations. It takes but a few days on a major river to witness firsthand the abuse that commonly occurs. The majority of floaters are river lovers. But there is an alarming increase of boaters who seek the thrill of a strong current without respect for the wilds from which it flows. They like to brag about the rivers they have "tamed." The "rugged" landscape reflects their "toughness" and stamina. But they rebel against rules.

Aside from those who openly violate nature and the rules of the river, there are also newcomers to the sport who, because of insufficient knowledge and skill, and inferior equipment, must also be guided by regulations.

The 1976 River Running Operational Requirements and Conditions for the Colorado River in Grand Canyon National Park may not typify rules for the majority of the streams across the country, but they are a sign of the times.

Environmental Protection and Sanitation

"All cans, rubbish and other refuse MAY NOT BE DISCARDED IN THE WATER OR ALONG THE SHORE OF THE RIVER. This shall also apply to any side-canyon, trail, escape route, or any other portion of the canyon. All burnable material must be completely burned or carried out. Liquid and wet garbage attract red ants, flies and animals which dig up the refuse, as well as resulting in smelly beaches.

"Liquid garbage such as coffee, soup or dishwater should be drained into the river (not on shore); wet garbage such as egg shells, leftover solid food, bones, grapefruit peels, melon rinds, should be carried out. Grease should be burned or carried out. The trip leader should make sure that participants are aware of proper disposal of pop-tops and cigarette butts. The use of biodegradable soap is restricted to the Colorado River

Large groups of floaters on today's rivers make rigid regulations necessary.

Rules on many major rivers require the use of portable toilets.

Where open fires are prohibited or restricted along some river stretches, the portable gas or propane stove is the only means of preparing a hot meal.

only. Use of soap in side streams or their confluence with the river is prohibited."

Portable Toilets

"All trips shall carry portable chemical toilets or other means for the concentration or containerization of human waste for burial. The containerized waste should be carried, by boat if necessary, to an area not normally used for camping. Burial shall be in a hole at least 2 feet deep, 6 feet above the high normal river fluctuation, at least 50 feet from the river bank and at least 200 feet from any area normally used for camping. It is recommended that toilet paper be kept separate and burned in the burial hole prior to dumping the toilet. During the day (whenever the toilet is not set up), toilet paper should be burned away from vegetation or carried back to the raft and placed with other refuse. Waste shall be deposited and buried away from areas of visitation. Powdered toilet deodorant disinfectants containing zinc do not decompose and are not recommended."

Fires

"Gas stoves and sufficient fuel must be carried due to diminishing driftwood supply along the river. If open fires are to be built, only charcoal briquets or driftwood may be used. Gathering wood from trees, dead or alive, is prohibited. Violators will be prosecuted. Fires must be contained in a metal fire pan to prevent spread of ash and charcoal over beaches. Fires should be allowed to burn out as much as possible and remaining ashes deposited in the main current of the river. Such deposits must be cleaned of all non-burnable materials as indi-

cated in the section above. It is recommended that fire pans be elevated to avoid scorching sand and to prevent severe burn injuries. The kindling of open fires using gathered wood, charcoal or similar fuels is prohibited when away from beaches. Gas stoves are required for overnight trips away from the river."

Incident Reports

"Any incidents resulting in personal injury requiring a physician's attention or property damage of $100 must be reported to Grand Canyon National Park. Incident forms must be given to a National Park Service Ranger at the time of evacuation. Incident forms will be supplied by Grand Canyon National Park and carried on each trip."

Helicopter Evacuation

"In the event of an emergency requiring helicopter evacuation, and rescue by a trip leader or guide, arrangements will be made for the rescue by Grand Canyon National Park, who will notify the outfitter as promptly as possible of the incident. The outfitter will be responsible for the cost of said rescue if appropriate arrangements cannot be made between the passenger and the helicopter company. Requests for helicopter evacuation of a passenger by someone not on the trip will be made through Grand Canyon National Park. Responsibility for cost of such evacuations will be decided following consultation with the outfitter and the requestor prior to the evacuation."

Qualifications of the Trip Leader

"The trip leader is a person whose character, personality and capabilities qualify him as a responsible leader in charge of each river party. He must have made at least three additional river trips through the portion of the Colorado River to be traversed, all as a guide running the entire trip. He must hold a current first aid certificate, indicating the holder has satisfactorily completed the equivalent of an American Red Cross Advanced First Aid or Emergency Medical Technician course.

"He must be knowledgeable and capable of giving a suitable orientation talk to all passengers throughout the trip. This required orientation will cover life preservers, boating safety, swimming, hiking safety, drinking water, sanitation, and human and natural history of the Grand Canyon."

What's Been Said?

The initial reading of Grand Canyon National Park's Operational Requirements and Conditions tends to irritate an accomplished outdoorsman and boater. However, because of the large number of people using the river, the black-and-white do's and don'ts of river use boil down to pure and simple law and order. Besides attempting to preserve the environment, these rules also are reliable guidelines for the inexperienced river runner.

Where Has The Romance Gone?

The passenger accompanying a commercial float trip down one of the major float rivers will find a smattering of romance. None of which can match the satisfaction of a do-it-yourself float. Big rivers, big boats, and the attitude of letting someone else "do all the work" has been glamorized in magazine articles, brochures, and television. If there be one pitfall that a prospective river runner frequently runs into, it is the introduction to the sport through a commercialized experience. Good outfitters keep the experience as natural and as personally satisfying as they can. The poor ones run an assembly line, and you can tell it by the taste of the food, the faces of the guides, and the feeling you have when you leave the river.

The Rules

The rules of the river leave no room for individual consideration. As one can imagine, within the vast courses of river, enforcement is frequently inadequate. But the rules are there, and most of us would obey them even if they were unwritten. You can find the romance on an individual basis. You can heed the regulations without making an issue of them. We can learn to live and float with rules—maybe even improve them.

Should an emergency arise in an isolated area, the helicopter may be the only means of evacuation.

Timetables and Rating Systems

MORE FLOATING experiences have been dampened by inaccurate or false float time information and difficulty ratings. Stories about "spending the night on the river" and "doing enough paddling to last a lifetime" travel fast in floating circles. Difficulty ratings have scared away some boaters too, especially the tales of supposedly flat, smooth "beginner" stretches of river that turned into frothy white water, sucking currents, and an obstacle course of rocks.

The blame, I suppose, could be traced back to the floaters themselves for not digging into the river structure a bit more thoroughly. But unfortunately, the river challenge for one may not be the same for another. The float speeds of different river boats vary. Wind conditions are factors. High and low water levels definitely make a difference in float speed (travel time from one point to another). And then there is the simple case of bad or outdated information.

Unless times and distances are recorded in writing by those actually floating the river and exact river and weather conditions noted, information can vary considerably. River guide and navigation books can virtually be deemed useless (and sometimes a hazard in themselves) when they are not accurately updated each year. Some rivers, especially the untamed giants of the west, are constantly changing their course. While obstacles, like fallen trees, dead-end water braids, and fences may disappear during one season, others take their place seemingly overnight. New channels develop; old ones lead to time-devouring portages.

What is the best floating timetable to follow?—your own. Start with rough estimates. Take careful precautions on a new stretch and add more time than is prescribed. After the float, log your findings according to: 1. time started; 2. number and duration of stops; 3. float craft used (canoe, johnboat, inflatable); 4. water conditions (high, medium, low); and 5. stream difficulty (fast, moderate, slow). A small, pocket-size notebook can serve as a handy journal for your particular craft and pace. That's the best guide for you.

Here are some facts to remember. Canoes and kayaks can be classified as *fast* float craft. The ma-jority of published timetables for various floats are set according to the float speed for recreational canoeing and not necessarily for fishing and floating. Canoes and kayaks are the least affected by winds, and they handle well in long, flat stretches of water.

Aluminum, fiberglass and wooden johnboats, rowboats, prams, double-enders and McKenzie boats can generally be considered *average* speed floaters. Most guides and fishermen base their times made with these craft. They are considerably slower than canoes and kayaks and more affected by head winds. During long, flat stretches of water, the boats can be burdensome.

Rubber inflatables, because they feature built-in water drag, can be classified as *slow* float boats—often a blessing to fishermen working swift streams where drag allows more time to hit likely holes where lunker fish hide. The slightest head wind will slow a rubber boat down considerably.

Some rivers become treacherous during high water levels.

River ratings are proportional to water temperature. As the temperature drops below 50 degrees Fahrenheit, the difficulty rating for a given stretch of water goes up by at least one class.

Difficulty Ratings

A more reliable guide, and one that is more generally accepted as a reference for float fishermen and canoeists alike, is based on a rating system table from one to six; the larger the number, the more difficult and dangerous the stream.

Ratings are based on criteria consisting of current speed; water obstacles; grade or fall of the water (from flat stretches to rapids and white water to dropoffs and falls); stream course (relatively straight or meandering); portages; diversion dams; or low water areas.

There are very few rivers whose entire length can be categorized under one classification. In other words, correctly defined, most rivers fall under several different ratings.

When considering river difficulty rating, evaluate your ability and the worthiness of your craft. Try to avoid the mistake of accepting the information of unknowledgeable sources as final criteria for going ahead with a float. Check as many information sources as possible for current information; take a guided scenic or fishing float on the stretch before making your own; or personally inspect known trouble spots by car or foot before putting your boat in the water.

A difficulty rating system is only as good as the agency or individual who rates it. Make sure the rating variables fall in line with your skills and equipment.

The American White Water Affiliation has established a couple of different river rating systems that can be used as general references. It is widely known that most accidents occur when boatmen attempt to negotiate water that is more demanding than their skills, knowledge and experience can justify. Most of us, however, are quick to accept a challenge, and sometimes we are "blinded" by pride in our boating and outdoor skills. Canoeists, kayakers and rafters should learn to frankly and honestly evaluate their own skills as well as the difficulty of water to be floated.

Generally speaking, Class I and II rivers can be run in open canoes. Some Class III rivers are suitable for open canoes if time is allowed for emptying water from the boat. Any class of river may change according to the amount of river runoff and the depth of water. Water temperatures below 50 degrees Fahrenheit should be considered at least one class more difficult because of the potential hazard in event of capsizing.

Class I—Very Easy stretch for the practiced beginner. Waves are small, regular and passages are clear. Usually gentle sand or dirt banks, with some possible artificial difficulties like bridge abutments or a few small riffles.

Class II—Easy stretch for intermediates. Rapids are of medium difficulty. Passages are clear and wide. Some low ledges. Spray covers might be useful. Some maneuvering is required.

Left — In addition to difficulty ratings for streams, there is an ability rating for boaters. Below left — Rapids are gauged according to swiftness and obstacles. Below right — A timetable is established by the type of craft, river speed and how many stops will be made.

Class III—Medium difficulty stretch for experienced boaters. There are numerous high, irregular waves. There are rocks, eddies, and rapids with passages that are clear, though they can be narrow and require expertise in maneuvering. Inspection before making the run is necessary in some areas, and spray skirt or splash cover is necessary.

Class IV—Difficult stretch for highly skilled boaters with several years of experience. Should be with an organized group of boaters for this run. There are long rapids and powerful, irregular waves. Dangerous rocks and boiling eddies are common. Passages are difficult, and inspection is a must. Powerful and precise maneuvering is required, and spray skirt or splash cover is essential. Conditions along these stretches make rescue difficult in case of trouble and *all* kayakers should be able to Eskimo Roll.

Class V—Very difficult stretch that is run by teams of experts. There are extremely long, difficult and violent rapids that follow each other almost without interruption. Plenty of obstacles, big drops, violent current and very steep gradient. Shore scouting and planning is essential, but extremely difficult because of the terrain. Because rescue conditions on this stretch are extremely difficult, mishaps can and do often lead to death.

Class VI—Extremely difficult stretch that is run by teams of experts. Nearly impossible stretch to run and very dangerous. Even for teams of experts, favorable water levels and close study and careful planning are needed for success.

At various times of the year, and different water levels, either through natural conditions such as rain or snow runoff or dam (impoundment) water releases, difficulty ratings can change on various stretches of

Class VI Rivers should be run only by teams of experts in appropriate craft.

river. These variances should be considered, in addition, to the classifications already listed.

L (Low)—Less than acceptable level for satisfactory paddling.

M (Medium)—Normal for rivers of slight gradient, but less than enough water for good passage in a steeper river.

MH (Medium High)—Higher than normal. Enough water to provide passage over ledges and through boulder gardens. This is the best level for some of the more difficult river sections.

H (High)—The river is full, and the water heavy. Covered boats are necessary on most rivers; some large rivers are at a dangerous level.

HH (High-High)—Very heavy water makes for complex and powerful hydraulics. Even rivers of moderate gradient can become dangerous.

F (Flood)—Abnormally high water. Extremely powerful effects with debris on the surface. Not for boating of any kind.

Rate Yourself (Honestly) as a Paddler

Some boating clubs have various rating systems for members so that members can be matched to various stretches of water. This is a good, general guide to follow in rating your own abilities.

Class I—You are a beginner who knows all the basic strokes and can handle a boat competently in smooth water.

Class II—You are a novice who can effectively use all basic white water strokes in the kayak, or in both bow and stern areas of a canoe. You can read water and negotiate easy rapids with confidence.

Class III—You are an intermediate who can negotiate rapids requiring complex maneuvering. You know how to use eddy turns and basic bow-upstream techniques. In the bow or stern of a double canoe, single canoe or kayak you are skillful in moderate rapids.

Class IV—You are an expert who has the proven ability to run difficult rapids in all boats and you are skillful in heavy water and complex rapids.

Class V—You are a trip leader with expert boating skills, wide river running experience and good judgment for leading trips on a river.

Note: Rafters are by no means ignored by rating systems. Although the above systems were designed primarily for canoeists and kayakers, rafters can rate streams and themselves accordingly. It should be acknowledged that *good* inflatable boats allow for certain mistakes that could prove trouble for canoes and kayaks. However, inflatable boats are better suited for heavy treacherous water, and they are commonly found in waters that might be "suicide" for canoeists and kayakers. The same skill is required for canoeist and rafter alike.

How to Read the River

READING A RIVER means choosing the right course and is probably the most important skill canoeists, kayakers and rafters can develop. The ability to correctly and efficiently read the river's current and character comes from experience. It is the combination of clever reading ability and strong stroking techniques that make good river runners.

Any new stretch of water is first *read* by seeking the information found on *current* printed river guides. Learning the overall character of the river is the most important step in floating. By doing that you will learn *generally* what to expect.

In the *Snake River Guide*, by Verne Huser and Buzz Belknap (Westwater Books), an opening paragraph sets the character of the Snake River as it flows southward from Yellowstone Park.

"River channels change frequently, sometimes overnight. Stumps, overhanging trees, log jams and sand bars may suddenly be laid in or washed away. Inquire locally, secure permits where necessary and inspect your proposed course before undertaking any Snake River trip in your own craft." Later on in the book, describing a particular stretch, "Although there are no rapids in this section, the current is swift and even a small obstruction (a rock or stump) can quickly capsize the inexperienced or careless boatman. Route finding can be a problem. The Snake sends numerous channels braiding their way through the glacial gravels of Jackson Hole (Wyoming); many of these are often blocked by shallow riffles, fallen trees—or even a bull moose."

The character of the Snake River in the vicinity of Jackson Hole is deceptive and ever changing. And it has fooled many people, including myself. Supplemental information can be obtained from the National Park Service, U.S. Forest Service, and Game & Fish Department personnel. Sort the facts from conjecture. Remember, river classifications and difficulty ratings are personal matters. No two rivers are alike. Boating skills vary. Never take a river evaluation as gospel but merely as an aid to support your own skills and knowledge.

Water temperature is a very important consideration to advance river reading information. During spring, summer or fall, for instance, the Snake River runs alarmingly cold. When you pre-read the Snake, you will know not to base your true course entirely on published guides or recommendations. You know the river is basically unpredictable and that few if any mistakes can be made because of the immobilizing water temperature. River charts and topographic maps will help to some extent, but it is your on-river reading skills that will get you through the surprises. Successful river reading depends on keen downstream observation, alertness and pre-trip tips.

Picking the Right Channel

Some streams have more channels or braids in them than others. Certain stretches of the same river are characteristically open and straight; others, narrow and meandering. It is often the narrow, meandering stretches that are more fun. They present the greater boating challenges.

During high water, most common in the spring, channel selection can be difficult because all waters are running fast. Normal water level obstacles may be covered over, and the wrong channel can be easily taken. Novices or intermediate floaters should consider normal water levels when planning a trip. Float when waters have receded, generally in midsummer or early fall. At normal levels, the best channel to take, provided there are no obstacles, is the deepest, fastest waterway. Faster water commonly washes obstructions away and does not allow a bottom build-up of debris. Successfully and safely running the fastest channel depends on good strokes and a reflex skill of how and when to use them. Skill comes with practice.

A Slip of the Tongue

River running is full of variables, but a common rule of thumb is to always follow the *tongue* of water. It has a smooth, glistening flow to it, because water is funneled from slow flat water to a fast current at the head of a chute or drop. Follow the tongue because of the unlikelihood of obstacles in the funnel. At the bottom of

1. Here's a downstream ledge. Could be tricky; however, major current flow on right indicates passable spot and tongue.

2. Viewed from above, this ledge looks impassable, and for some it would be best to get out and portage or line the boat. However, where current is strongest and water whitest, a tongue would allow safe passage of canoe or inflatable.

3. In center background is a side eddy. Opposing currents separate the eddy from current and slipping in and out of the eddy can be tricky in canoe or kayak. Note hump of rock to the left and resultant haystack.

4. View upstream shows ledge to the right which would be poor course choice; while slick at left is more favorable. Best course might be right in the middle of the drop, as there are rocks indicated to extreme left of passage.

5. Impossible course? No. Experienced canoeist or kayaker, using full choice of strokes and techniques, could work his way through top center tongue; turn right (going downstream) and drop over chute.

6. Long chute or slick, near rock, is best passage. However, note presence of rocks by churning white water at left. Ledge at right, however, is too risky. Boiling water indicates severe drop.

7. An overall view of above chute or slick (photo #6). Passage near boulder, of course, would be safest.

8. An obvious rock hump and churning white water. Hump is very prominent, not smooth or molded. That means rock is very near the surface and there's a good chance here of snagging or capsizing if rock is hit. Either side of the rock provides safe passage.

Get into good position ahead of time for such obstacles as bridge abutments. Current here could suck the boat into bridge. Amazingly enough, bridge abutments cause a large share of accidents.

the tongue and drop where the gradient flattens, there will be standing waves—the height and force are dependent on the gradient drop, current force, and width of the tongue. Follow the standing waves, as they line out in succession from the chute. You'll get a pretty good ride, but the water is deepest there.

On braided rivers with more than two channel choices, water speed is hard to distinguish. Look for the biggest waves downstream if you can see them. If you can't, take the braid that drops before any of the others. The reason for this is that you can see the drop. Despite the fact it may be shallow, you have "a bird in hand." Those that you cannot see could be obstructed downstream.

How to Spot Rocks

Some rocks are very obvious; parts of them can be seen above the water. Amazing as it seems, there are a significant number of boaters each season that run into exposed rocks. Negligent downstream observation is usually the cause. Sometimes strokes and techniques are begun too late to steer clear of the obstacle.

Submerged rocks, on the other hand, cause more problems because they are not as obvious and usually feature standing waves immediately downstream of their position. Novices, seeing the waves, do not realize that the upstream rock is the obstacle causing the wave. Sometimes a maneuver is not made in time.

A hump in the water, difficult to see under certain lighting conditions and in choppy water, usually indicates the presence of a rock. There will be times when the hump will not be sighted until you are almost upon it. A quick draw stroke must be taken. Often the hump is spotted with plenty of time to spare. Plan a right or left course around the obstacle instead of waiting until the last few seconds. Where an obvious hump is sighted, there are likely to be others. Scrutinize the water for other possible rocks. Downstream observation and planning is a matter of careful concentration, taking nothing for granted.

Flow patterns over rocks vary with water depth. Shallow water depth over a rock is indicated by a foaming, spitting eddy. As the depth increases over rocks, there is more of a haystack pattern. The latter may not be the best route, but it is ordinarily forgivable; while the former does its best to grab and dump you.

Fallen Trees Can Be Your Worst Enemies

My wife and I tangled with a beaver-chewed tree at "Spruce's Ditch" in the Snake River one cold day and have never forgotten the incident. Rocks can be forgiving. Fallen trees, with current flowing into them, usually are not. They are traps that can dump, maim and kill. Stretches with downed trees should be carefully read and negotiated. There are times when it might be best to avoid them altogether and portage.

Despite the fact that river rangers commonly patrol popular float stretches looking for dangerous obstacles, fallen trees can occur overnight. High winds, rotted trees, and beavers can change the difficulty rating of a

Above — River channels can change every day. Beaver felled trees can make a safe channel a hazardous one. Right — Water fluctuation from dams is important in understanding the river.

stretch in a mere instant. An "easy" rapid can be changed to an impossible one when a tree falls across the channel.

Take it for granted that when a downed tree is spotted ahead, the current will take you into it unless you take the appropriate actions. Begin maneuvers well ahead of the obstacle by gaining good upstream position so that strokes can be used to avoid it; sticking to the middle or inside bend of the river; or getting out and looking the situation over. In a strong current, a middle position may not be safe enough. Stick further to the inside. When the situation looks too risky or impossible, line the canoe downstream or portage it. That's the better choice than ruining the entire trip.

The Bend of the River

A bend in the river calls for tactics executed well in advance of the turn by heading the bow sharply toward the inside of the bend while paddling forward. This can be easily accomplished when the bend is sighted in plenty of time. Backpaddling techniques can also be used, holding the stern to the inside bend (setting) and backpaddling around the bend. This is the favored technique when a sharp bend appears suddenly. Backpaddling strokes should be strong and smooth. This is a tough maneuver for beginners to master because proximity to the mouth of the bend can be an unnerving feeling unless paddlers have confidence in their strokes and boat.

Bridge Abutments

Although rarely talked about, bridge abutments are dangerous. Bridges often signal put-in and take-out points of a river cruise. When boaters put-in slightly upstream of a bridge, they may not have the maneuver-

ing time to get into good position to miss the supporting pillars anchored in the water. At the end of the float, weariness and carelessness near the take-out point can account for colliding with abutments.

Abutments are deceivingly treacherous water obstacles, especially if there are several of them stretching across the stream. In swift water, they produce peculiar currents, and the boat not positioned carefully between the pillars could be in for trouble. Abutments also catch logs and debris during high water, and a boater may not have much room to pass through. Bridges located just downstream of sharp bends in the river can produce problems if paddlers are not aware of them. Upstream positioning is important for middle-of-the-abutment passage.

Low Bridges and Fences

Some streams have an abundance of low water bridges. Fortunately fences are not common. A low water bridge will commonly allow passage of a canoe, raft or kayak to float under it, but that's all. In order to spot such bridges or barbed wire fences, downstream observation is vital. The boat can be beached upstream and lined underneath the obstacle or portaged if that is more practical. Attempting to remain inside a canoe while floating under a low bridge can be extremely dangerous.

Take-Out Points

It is easy to miss a take-out point unless it is identified by landmarks or signs. Begin take-out maneuvers (paddle rudder or back rowing) well in advance and try to beach the boat in still water or back eddies rather than in swift currents. Remember to hold onto the boat after getting out.

Dressing for the Occasion

Guide, Paul Crittenden, wears heavy-duty rain jacket, woolen shirt and sweater, waders and cowboy hat to protect against the elements on an early spring float.

DICK LUDEWIG, a friend from Cody, Wyoming, who is a superior and dedicated outdoorsman and an excellent guide, once sent me a list of "essentials" that were being mailed to all persons preparing for a week long wilderness boating-camping adventure on the southeast arm of Yellowstone Lake.

Ludewig's epistle, here in abbreviated form, is a classic.

"You feel clean in clean underwear. Bring enough so you can change each day on the trail. Throw in an extra pair for good luck. Women note—riding horseback for hours WITHOUT BRA may lead to pain not in keeping with your outdoor experience. What about long underwear? You probably won't use it unless as pajamas. (Editor's note: It's great for preventing chafed knees, thighs and buttocks on horseback trips.) However, if you feel better knowing they're along, bring a pair. Include one (1) pair of socks for each day out plus one extra pair.

"In the backcountry, we look at our shirts and slacks as protection from the elements, from insects, scrapes and snags—and as part of the system for keeping warm. Color is pleasant. We like to change shirts as the temperature climbs. When choosing your backcountry wardrobe, consider durability and comfort first. Whatever you do, don't choose the threadbare pair of cast-off slacks you use for gardening or scrubbing floors. Imagine the seat coming out 4 hours down the trail! Deep colors stay fresh appearing longer. And you won't have room to carry a change of clothes for each spatter of mud or drop of coffee."

Most commercial float outfitters, unlike Dick Ludewig, assume you know how to dress for the outdoors. It is up to you to determine the type and number of clothes to wear and pack.

Canoeing, kayaking and rafting demand sensible and appropriate clothing. A full wet suit is important for cold water or cold climate canoeing and kayaking. It is relatively cheap insurance (about $120 dollars worth) against hypothermia in case of accidental dunking.

Dressing in wool and breathable nylon according to the layer principle is necessary for early and late season boating. During the summer, however, and depending on the climate, wool can be too hot. Loose-fitting cotton is a good alternative. Wear long pants, long-sleeved shirts, and a wide-brimmed hat. Pack a pair of cut-offs or swimming suit for a mid-day dip. However, bring more clothing than you think you will actually need. Cover the body with comfortable slacks and shirts. Pack along rain gear (pants and parka) just in case and extra shirts and jackets for early morning and late afternoon when temperatures, especially on the water, have a tendency to drop fast.

I'm not going to make a list. My friend Dick Ludewig said it all. Dress for the elements. Go over-prepared. Today's good outdoor clothing is warm, practical and good looking.

Spray skirts and canoe splash cover keep paddlers dry and help prevent hypothermia.

Small day packs (below) can store extra clothes. Larger packs (left) are fine for extended float trips. A life preserver is part of proper dress.

There are times when shorts or a bathing suit permit a refreshing dip.

Float Fishing

THERE IS A brand of fishing that truly relaxes the body and spirit. Float fishing. More than a tonic though, float fishing just may be the most effective method of freshwater fishing known to modern day anglers. Why? It is the technique that counts.

The floater, whether loafing down a placid Ozark stream or riding the back of a bucking western river, has several distinct advantages over conventional fishermen. The number of good holes that can be fished in a half-day or whole day of floating, as compared to wading, is increased to such a degree that the catch rate rises accordingly. Where a fish might be spooked or "put down" by a bad cast at one hole, a floater only has to wait a few minutes until the next chance. Float fishing is a forgiving sport. For if we fail at one hole, there is always the next eddy, the next undercut bank, the next rock or log. The floater commands sheer power of variety and accessibility, regardless of the stream or the species of fish. The floating technique is charged with high potency. It is no wonder, in a time of increased fishing pressure, that more anglers are turning to the float craft to get where the action is.

Another obvious advantage the floater has is access to fishing waters that might otherwise be posted or blocked by impassable obstacles. Public access areas receive the brunt of fishing pressure, and permission to fish private stretches of water, often leased by private fishing clubs, is getting tougher to obtain. Floaters, however, putting-in and taking-out at public access points, can legally float and fish stretches of water bordered by private lands.

Whether the float craft be a canoe, inflatable, or johnboat, the float fisherman has the advantage of quiet stalk. Even the stealthiest of waders spook fish as they approach on land or move through the water. A floater, on the other hand, becomes part of the stream. From good casting position near the middle of the river, where fish are not likely to be, a good caster can hit the deep pool pockets along the banks where big fish hide. When fishing from shore or wading, these same pockets are often spooked out or bypassed. Because of over-hanging vegetation or brush, some of the best fish holding lairs are impossible to reach except by boat. A floater has the best angles, the most opportunities to see the "hidden" holes, and short, accurate casts do the job.

Popular Float Fishing Craft

There is a reasonably good guideline to follow for choosing a float boat to match your brand of fishing. Keep in mind there is not a perfect boat for all types of waters and all types of fishing conditions. However, there are boats that are very well suited to particular conditions.

The canoe is best suited for slow-to-moderate current speeds. It also has a place in white water fishing streams where significant stretches of slick or slow water separate rapids and riffles. A canoeist fishes the slicks and concentrates on boat operation through the fast water. Only skilled canoeists can handle both jobs effectively.

It is possible for one person to fish a slow stream effectively. And a few experts can work the white water streams alone and do well. But for the novice or average canoeist who wants to enjoy good fishing *and* good floating, it's best to share a canoe with a partner. Over extremely slow stretches two anglers can work a given shoreline with not much concern for maneuvering the boat. But, because a canoe is extremely responsive, even sluggish currents demand considerable attention to boat operation to maintain favorable casting distance from canoe to bank and comfortable angles for casting to likely spots.

Fishermen can actually dim their chances of scoring by fishing "two at a time" even through slow water. Boat position is important. Take turns running the boat and fishing. That way, each person receives a full and uninterrupted share of fishing and canoeing. There's a lot of satisfaction of "guiding" your partner into just the right position for a good cast and big fish. And that is one of the real joys of silent, swift canoe float fishing.

Inflatable boats, because they have more built-in drag, are more popular on moderate and fast current rivers. They can slow the float speed down on swift rivers so anglers can cast to the back eddies and land fish off the main current. The inflatables have good stability and make excellent fishing platforms. The inflatable with a wide margin for error is a bit more popular than a canoe for all-around float fishing in fast current streams. A boat rigged with a rowing frame and good oars can be maneuvered by one person as the other fishes. The roles can then be reversed for the thrill of enjoying both aspects of float fishing. On slow streams, rubber boats are burdens—hard to maneuver, sluggish and victims of the wind. On fast fishing water, they shine.

The johnboat is a float fishing tradition in the Ozarks of Missouri and Arkansas and definitely has a place on slow to moderate streams. It is flat-bottomed, stable, and lightweight, and fairly responsive with room for a lot of gear. In fast water its float speed is faster than the

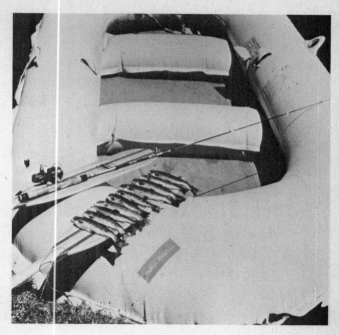

A limit of brook trout taken from an inflatable.

Oar-equipped canoe is fine for working lakes.

inflatable boat and doesn't give casters much time to hit the holes. Having limited freeboard, due to its low, flat design, it takes in much more water than a canoe or inflatable in rough water. Some extremely light, aluminum johnboats require constant attention in moderate currents and can be overpowered by strong whirlpools and currents.

Fishing from a kayak is impractical. However, the kayak, when loaded properly, can be used as a tool to gain access to good fishing waters along public stretches of water or private sections where permission has been obtained. Other specialty float craft, like McKenzie, Rogue River and various styles of wooden double-enders all have a place on the river. Most of us, however, will choose a canoe, inflatable or johnboat for our float fishing fun.

Planning a Float Fishing Trip

Regardless of the craft, the success of the float fishing trip, aside from how cooperative the fish are, is good pre-planning. State fish and game departments along with local sportsmen and boating clubs can give reliable information as to the difficulty rating of a given stretch; how long the average float takes; and the quality and type of fishing. The most common mistake novice floaters make is biting off more than they can chew on maiden voyages. Oftentimes, they wind up floating in the dark which is extremely dangerous. Gauge rest stops, on-shore fishing, and lunch breaks carefully. It's best to get off the river too early than too late. Begin with half-day trips and work up to full day affairs. Most

landing points are easily recognizable, but some are not. Be certain you know where your pickup ride is located or where the pickup vehicle is parked. Another good reason for getting off the river before dark is the likelihood of your missing the take-out point.

Pack along rain gear, warm clothing, a jug of drinking water and plenty of snacks. You may be floating through a primitive area or roadless or impassable terrain. A waterway can be a wilderness experience, and it's best to be over-prepared.

Special Gear

Float fishing has no boundaries. Spin fishermen, fly rodders, bait casters, cane polers and trot liners all seem to share the same enthusiasm for river floating. All fishing methods work well. Depending on river conditions and time of year, some work better than others.

Generally speaking, spring is a time of high, roily rivers. Fishing will probably be at its lowest ebb for most species. Fishermen using cut bait or worms usually have the best success. A platter full of catfish fillets, served with hush puppies and steamy biscuits endears springtime fishing to the entire family.

Late spring, early summer is a time of receding rivers and clearing waters. This can be a highly productive time for big fish. Work spinners and spoons slow, deep and close to the bank and to logs, brush, rocks and eddies. There may be so many good holes along a stretch that a floater has to be selective. Keep one eye downstream for the likeliest spots and plan your casts

Guide maneuvers boat so float angler has best angle for cast.

Above — Fisherman portages around rocks and riffles to new holes. Right — Author displays chunky brook trout taken from stream.

ahead of time.

Fishing for trout, bass and panfish in the summer and fall when rivers are low and water is clear is a time for the fly fisherman or ultra-light advocate. Popping bugs, tiny lures, dry flies and slow, careful water stalking, early and late in the day, can make this the most pleasurable of times on the river.

Good timing is vital to good floating. Heavy rains, prolonged cold spells and significant river level fluctuation can dampen the fishing. Call ahead to tackle shops in the area or contact fish and game offices for current information. Float fishing is the ultimate fishing experience.

The Nature Float

HARNESS the stream to your spirit. Take to your heart the flavor of living current. Inhale into citified lungs the rich aroma of bottomland vapor. You are alive. And the stream is a silver thread that curls its way through a magic land. The forest glitters. The oaks stand naked. The pines are forever green and overbearing.

When you communicate with nature from the silent, motorless drift of a float boat, you are on equal terms with her. Part of the river; part of the land that borders her. You need neither rod nor reel for true joy. There will be enough of that. And the quest for white water with its instant thrill of tumultuous ecstasy is not of immediate importance. You are alone with a peaceful river, and the world is full of things natural and wild. There is special river joy. For in the world of diminishing natural purity, every floating river is naturally pure. And you, the nature floater, are equally and bountifully blessed.

Natural water is, and always will be, a magnet for nature and wildlife. As the desert oasis draws animals, birds and vegetation, so does the float stream. Even those great rivers that bear the crowded cities of today retain a wildness about them that countless civilized pressures have failed to suffocate. The degree of wildness, the quality of nature, varies considerably. But it is there for those who seek it—from the often harassed Ohio to the dammed, once-free Snake. The serpentine courses roll on and as long as they do, we can garner their natural treasures.

Canoes, inflatables, johnboats, and wooden double-enders serve the nature floater well. And for the sheer thrill of floating "through" nature, kayaks do the job. Consider current speed when choosing a suitable craft. Canoes are great for slow to moderate currents. Inflatables, with built-in water drag, are better suited to moderate and fast water. Johnboats are fine in moderate current speeds.

Choice of craft is a matter of taste and individual needs. However, stability, maneuverability and safety are important considerations. A boat that demands constant attention may not be the best for nature obser-vation. A boat that speeds a floater through an area with little or no time to study the surroundings could be the wrong choice. Or a boat that is sluggish and hard to paddle or row on long, smooth stretches can be more work than fun. There is no perfect boat for all waters. Choose a float boat according to the type of water you will be floating most often. A good way to find out which float craft is the best for your needs is to rent several different types before buying.

With a float craft, you have the foundation for exciting, close nature observation. Basic equipment can be as simple as your eyes, ears, nose and hands. That's really all you need. But you have the option of making your communion with nature as simple or as complex as you see fit. Add a pair of binoculars, and the views of nature can be intimate. You can record findings in a small notebook. Field guides to birds, flowers, trees, insects, reptiles, and mammals aid in identifying your sightings. Select field guides that are localized to your area or geographic zone.

Nature or wildlife photography is a wonderful bonus to nature floating. Regardless of whether the camera gear is simple or elaborate, the floater has several distinct advantages in capturing good nature shots on film. Most shots can be taken directly from the float craft. Birds and animals are spooked less by floaters than they are by persons approaching on foot. Animals and birds are concentrated along rivers which fill their water, food, and shelter requirements. Because of the silent approach, floating photographers often catch deer, raccoons, squirrels, and waterfowl in natural, undisturbed moods. And this aspect alone makes the difference between good wildlife shots and great ones. Quite a few of today's top-notch professional wildlife photographers use the rivers and float boats to get their best shots.

The 35mm SLR (single lens reflex) system is probably the best all-around camera body and lens combination for float boat photography. Equipped with a normal (55mm), wide-angle (21 or 28mm), or telephoto (200mm, 300mm, or 70-210mm zoom) lens, the photographer can handle almost any photographic situation

Left — Boaters can be treated to doe/fawn scenes like this. Below — Common sight along float rivers — waterfowl of all kinds.

Above — Many streams are clear enough to permit underwater observation. Right — Quiet float brought close-up of moose.

Above — Nature surrounds the floater who takes the time to look and appreciate. Right — Ideal protection for camera is foam-lined and compartmented Shutterpack Case.

49

along the river. Perhaps the most versatile lens would be a telephoto zoom. However, the distinct disadvantage to the system is that it is not waterproof. Within a securely closed plastic bag, the system can be protected from moisture damage. But, by keeping the camera locked in such a bag, good shots are often missed.

There are several alternatives. A nature floater, interested more in capturing good photos than in a fast, thrilling ride, can choose the more stable inflatable or johnboat as opposed to the less stable canoe. But a good canoeist is less apt to take a dunking and can with confidence pack along an expensive SLR system. For the average floater, photography and canoeing blend together best in slow to moderate currents.

Another alternative is the underwater camera housing. Adjustable to fit a variety of camera bodies and lenses, it can be used not only for underwater photography during a float but also as a precautionary measure when the chance of tipping or taking in water exists. The special waterproof housing, of course, can be rendered useless if the camera is lost in murky or deep water. A short shock cord, secured to camera housing and boat, prevents accidental loss. For more information on waterproof camera housings write: Ikelite Underwater Systems, 3303 North Illinois Street, Indianapolis, Indiana 46208.

The Nikonos II is an underwater 35mm camera with a special housing that makes it waterproof. Light and compact, it can be worn around the neck for quick shots. The addition of an elastic belly or chest strap, that you make yourself, holds the camera comfortably in place when paddling or rowing. In the event of a dunking, it keeps the camera safely against the body. The Nikonos II takes lenses of 15mm, 28mm, 35mm and 80 mm. The disadvantage to the system for wildlife photography is the limitation that the 80mm lens puts on the photographer. For wildlife close-ups, a 200mm is more suitable. Equipped with the 80mm lens, the photographer has to work harder for an action shot that is relatively routine with the 200mm. The Nikonos II is a good choice though, and close-ups are possible through careful, quiet floating where the photographer stalks and surprises wildlife.

Whether the photographer employs the instant photography of a Pronto SX-70 (which is a fun camera on a float trip) or the compact simplicity of an Instamatic, packing a camera along, despite the chance of accidental dunking, is always worth the effort.

Nature Along the Banks

Trees, shrubs, plants, wildflowers, insects, and reptiles are found in abundance along most rivers. Observation of these smaller, less obvious forms of nature on the river banks may not be as dramatic as the sighting of a deer, heron, or turkey. But by taking the time to stop, observe, and investigate, new information and surprises emerge. Even a few unexpected bonuses, like the joy of discovering a patch of scrumptious morel mushrooms or a floating bed of tangy watercress, are fairly common to unhurried floaters.

Observing Aquatic Life

With or without the use of an underwater face mask, the floater, depending on water clarity, has a chance to observe fish life, aquatic insects and plants, muskrats, beaver, otter, frogs, turtles and water snakes. All the activity is by no means confined to the banks. While the best on-land observation is usually in the early morning hours when wildlife is on the move, the finest underwater viewing comes when the sun is straight up and filters like a torch through the water. The slower the pace, the greater the opportunity of observing aquatic life—often the most interesting forms of nature.

Tracks, Signs, and Calls

The float stream attracts all forms of wildlife to its banks. Even though observation of birds and animals is a special treat, the tracks, signs, and calls of wildlife that may not be in view of the floater make for fascinating study themselves. A majority of wildlife is nocturnal, hunting, feeding and watering under the protection of darkness. There is a special thrill involved with investigating and determining the freshness of the tracks of a raccoon that came to the water's edge during the night in search of snails. Equally as exciting is spotting the velvet rub of a whitetail deer on a tree trunk or rock in late summer.

The sounds of nature, during the stillness of a quiet float, take on distinctive meaning. The throaty call of the bullfrog. The delicate peeps of mallard ducklings. The cry of a red-tailed hawk. All these calls are magnificently clear and thrilling on the river. There are good books available on track, sign, and call identification. The *Peterson Field Guide Series* is excellent. *A Field Guide to Animal Tracks* by Olaus J. Murie is another fine book.

Best Seasons and Times

In nature, May and June are months of birth, rebirth, and renewal, which are fascinating times to ride the river. But heavy snow or rain runoff during spring or early summer can make floating impractical and often dangerous. Low runoff and a dry spring make for ideal floating conditions for exploring the river world and new, fresh nature.

In terms of the nature float, summer is a fine time, but autumn is better. Nature is preparing for the winter ahead, and creatures are busy. Fall colors are breathtaking. Where rivers do not freeze, winter floating can be beautiful and completely different from mild-weather river running. Early morning and late afternoon hours are best for wildlife observation. Whatever the time, the nature float is extremely satisfying and the slower the pace, the more memorable it can be.

Hunting from Canoes/Inflatables

IF YOU ARE a hunter and delight to the silent, swift stalk for game birds and animals, perhaps there is no finer, more relaxing way to hunt than by boat.

Canoes and inflatable rafts make excellent hunting boats because they blend in with the natural scheme of the river. Both types of craft are light enough to be portaged or carried, launched and taken out almost anywhere.

The Hunting Spirit

Canoeing or rafting enkindles the hunting spirit. The magic of a misty October river sets the mood. More than the shooting, the spirit and tradition of float hunting attracts river hunters. The ingredients of both sports settles deep in the minds and bodies of persons steeped in outdoor tradition. Feel the mist on your stubbled beard. Smell the perfume of damp October leaves as they lie still and soggy beneath clusters of pecans and black walnuts. Dip the paddle into still, gray water. Look to the russet leaves and breathe in pure river spirit. Gone are the things of city worry. Are you really reborn? No doubt. Look at the worn stock of your river gun. It has given you so many good hours. And the boat. Watch it knife through the morning river as if knowing full well that game waits around the next bend. This is where you want to be, and you hope that both the day and the feeling never end.

Hunting From Canoe or Raft

Canoes or inflatables are access tools for hunting. They can take the hunter comfortably and silently through lands where game abounds and on waters where ducks and geese may be resting. Boats open up areas that may otherwise be inaccessible because of the lack of roads or lands that are blocked by private holdings.

The boat hunter has several things in his favor. He is able to float and paddle into good areas without spooking game. Foot hunters, on the other hand, unless they are capable stalkers and have moist ground and the wind in their favor, often spook game before they see it. It is often possible to get within good shooting range,

Large concentrations of geese congregate along rivers and marshes in some areas.

both for shotgunning and rifle, by keeping a low profile and drifting as naturally as a log floating downstream.

Game on and Along the River

Rivers are magnets for certain species of game because they provide water, food and cover for game birds, animals and migratory waterfowl. Quite naturally then, a lot of game can be concentrated along certain stretches of river. This gives the boat hunter an advantage.

The congregation of ducks, geese and huntable shorebirds is dependent on the type of river and its proximity to major and minor flyways and resting areas. The season and weather conditions are also important factors. Waterfowl ordinarily use potholes, marshes and ponds for food and cover before freeze-up

and utilize rivers later on in the season. However, in heavily hunted refuge areas, ducks and geese use rivers as resting areas throughout the season. The closer the river to the shooting area, the better the chances for boaters. Rivers are used as minor flyways early and late in the day. Small ponds, back eddies and sloughs off the main river are likely spots for jumping ducks and geese. Boaters can often spot good areas from the river, beach the boats and proceed on foot.

Hunting for gray and fox squirrels can be excellent along midwestern, southern, north central and eastern streams where squirrels have plenty of cover and likely food sources. Oak, hickory and beach trees are squirrel favorites. Both gray and fox squirrels can be extremely wary. Beaching the boat and sitting still for 15 or 20 minutes, while watching a promising oak or hickory

Left — The canoe can get you into prime hunting areas fast. Above — Deer is a prime target for silent, careful stalker.

patch, will often turn up plenty of squirrels. However, slow steady drifting through likely areas can yield good close shots from the boat too.

An extremely effective method of hunting whitetail deer in the East or mule deer in the West is floating for them early in the morning and late afternoon. They water at least once a day, and if a floater is quiet and motionless, good shots under 50 yards are possible. The slow, silent stalk by boat is a tremendous advantage because bucks are taken off guard. A boat may be the most practical and efficient way of hunting dense cover where on-land stalking would only drive deer to another area.

In states like Wyoming, Alaska and the Canadian provinces, boat hunting can be very successful for other species of big game such as elk and moose.

Hunters should check the hunting regulations for boat hunting in their state. Waterfowl, for instance, can be hunted from boats in most states provided the boat is not propelled by a motor at the time of shooting.

Ordinarily, a canoe can be used for safe, practical hunts on streams of slow to moderate currents. Inflata-

Quiet floating for big game often produces close shots at deer.

Left — Hunter and dog have sights set on waterfowl. Above — the Canada goose, a favorite target of river shooters.

Boats painted dull brown or green colors are fine for waterfowl.

ble boats are better suited to swifter streams where greater stability is desired. Generally speaking, the slower streams are better suited for waterfowl and squirrels. Consequently, a canoe would be the best choice—far easier to propel and maneuver through the long, flat stretches.

Canoes can be purchased with a brown or "dead grass" color that camouflages them when floating or used as blinds for ducks and geese. Rubber boats in gray or black are better than bright colored rafts for hunting. However, any canoe or inflatable can be fitted with a camouflage cover that can be made at home and custom fitted to the boat. Camouflage netting or nylon material can be purchased at military surplus stores or sporting goods departments and used to make a quick, effective floating blind. Paddles and oars can be painted dull colors for further camouflage effectiveness.

Special Precautions

Cold weather and water temperatures are likely to prevail during most hunting seasons. A wise added precaution is a wet suit. Worn under loose fitting outer garments, the wet suit not only provides warmth, it is extra insurance in the event of capsizing. Canoe hunters in northern climates should consider the wet suit standard equipment.

Shooting from canoes or inflatables is not as tricky as it sounds, provided a low center of gravity is maintained. The shooter should be well anchored and have adequate control over his shotgun or rifle. As with hunting from a duck blind, shooters must swing and shoot only in their area of fire. In a boat, be especially careful of your partner in the bow or stern.

Keep shotgun or rifle within easy reach and protected from moisture, sliding, falling and banging by a tarp or piece of inch-thick foam that can be used to cushion it. Problems often develop when guns are out of reach and game is sighted. Desperate efforts to get to the gun in time for a shot could result in a dunking. *Never should the hunter keep a shotshell or cartridge in the chamber.* Ammunition can be stored in the magazine of the rifle or shotgun safely or carried in an easy-to-reach pocket for quick loading.

Clothing

If it is cold in your neighborhood during hunting season, chances are it will be a bit cooler on the river. Rowing and paddling produce warmth. If you are not paddling, and a good duck hunting day is upon you (wind, rain and/or snow), be glad that you brought along more clothes than you thought you really needed. Extra jackets, sweaters, socks, gloves and caps can be stored in a small rucksack.

Foul weather gear, consisting of rain parka and pants (usually camouflaged for waterfowl hunters), is standard hunting equipment and should never be left behind even on days that start bright and sunny.

I have found one of the best all-around *boat hunting* boots to be the Maine hunting boot, sold by mail order from L.L. Bean, Freeport, Maine 04032. With rubber bottoms and leather tops, the Bean boot is lightweight and very comfortable. Two pairs of woolen socks can be worn or a sheepskin-leather inner-sole can be ordered extra from Bean. Keeping the feet warm is vital to the warmth of the entire body and enjoyment of the hunt.

Plenty of hot drinks and food, in addition to warm clothing, replenish energy and spark the spirit. There is no finer outdoor adventure than using a canoe or inflatable to get where the game is.

Food and Water Rules

WHEN I FIRST received a packet of rules and regulations from the National Park Service at Canyonlands National Park in Moab, Utah, I was somewhat skeptical. "Why all the fuss?" I mumbled to myself. "There's enough paperwork here to run the army."

A request for *information* regarding boating information on the Colorado River through Cataract Canyon brought an overwhelming list of rules covering everything from personal hygiene to what food to pack along. I was miffed. "Doesn't Big Brother give us credit for any intelligence?"

It wasn't until I floated tricky sections of major western rivers and saw for myself the foolish mistakes that a lot of people made that the Park Service Rules and Regulations began to make sense. I studied accident and fatality reports which are sad testimonies to the serious consequences of "small" mistakes. Inadequate boating skills and inferior equipment were responsible for most of the unfortunate occurrences, as they are on other streams and rivers. But within the guidelines posted for major float areas in national parks across the country, a less obvious, but equally serious threat to safety and enjoyment, kept cropping up. Guidelines for the correct handling of food and water, for 2-day to 10-day trips, were constantly brought to my attention.

Whether the stream be a raging, western white waterway or a gentle, meandering Ozark stream, particular care and attention must be focused on food and water, which can be just as important as skill and good equipment for overnight or extended trips. Rafters, canoers and kayakers should be equally concerned. Improper food selection and handling or poor treatment of water can turn the best planned, best equipped river expedition into an uncomfortable mess. Bad food and water can seriously impair the physical and mental well-being of boatman, paddler and crew. Good judgment is affected. Mistakes are made and dangerous mishaps can result.

There are varying degrees of discomfort associated with the effects of bad food and/or water. But one thing is certain. Even the mild effects of diarrhea or stomach cramps weaken a person physically and detract from the enjoyment of the trip. A simple, basic knowledge of food handling rules and water treatment techniques can eliminate all problems of illness caused by bad food or water. Most of these rules are common sense guidelines that we learned as children and carry throughout our adult lives.

With helpful information supplied by the National Park Services, here is a guideline for food and water handling that can be easily followed.

Hand Washing

Yes, out on the river hand washing is a bit more inconvenient. There're a lot of chores to be done or the fish are biting and someone forgets to put a pot of wash

The success of a float and sandbar camp is based on good food and water.

Above — Food should be kept in soft or rigid coolers and eaten before spoilage. Right — Water, even from a crystal-clear stream, should be purified.

water on the fire or stove for heating. The cook merely dips his or her hands in the stream to wash the sweat and dirt off from a day's paddling. The fishermen and tent setters, having been called to dinner, find no hot water and soap and conveniently rinse their hands in the river. No hot water, no soap—totally inadequate preparation for killing germs or preventing the spread of disease. A real gamble when river running.

Shigellosis, like other types of dysentery, is transmitted fecal-orally. Hands inadequately washed, or not washed at all, can spread disease to others in a group. Food, water and equipment contaminated by infected persons are potential means of spreading disease.

Hand washing for *all* members of a float party should be established routine practice before any food is handled, before eating (including snacks), and after going to the bathroom. If these rules seem more stringent on a float trip than they do at home, they are meant to be. At home, the bathroom, a bed or medical attention are conveniently available. Not so on the river.

Hands should be washed with hot water and soap and dried with a paper towel. A good camping practice, as well as a good floating rule, is to keep a big pot of wash water available at all times to be heated on stove or fire. Water is transferred from the kettle to a wash pan for individual use. Wash water can be discarded away from camp, preferably dumped on sandy soil or dirt, away from the river bank.

Pre-Trip Illness

If illness like diarrhea, hepatitis or flu is diagnosed before a trip begins, that person, rather than risking the chance of infecting other floaters, should not make the trip.

Food Handling

The Park Service says the less food that is handled, the better. Trip cooks, or those persons alternating as cooks, should do the food handling and only after they have thoroughly washed their hands.

All foods should be wrapped in suitable, non-absorbent material, except canned or prepackaged items. Plastic wrap or plastic bags qualify. Some foods, like lettuce for instance, are not usually cooked and can harbor disease. Lettuce and other vegetables should not be allowed to lie for any length of time out of the cooler or directly in the ice melt at the bottom of the cooler.

Ice should be safe to use in drinks. It should be made at home or purchased from a licensed ice manufacturer or commercial-type ice maker.

Fresh meats are likely to spoil when not chilled and pork or chicken are the most vulnerable of the meats. Beef is better to use. Frozen food should not be thawed at temperatures in excess of 45 degrees Fahrenheit.

Refrigeration

There are many good ice chests or soft ice bags on the market that feature sturdy insulation and nonabsorbent interior shell material. On extended floats you may need several ice chests—one for meats and produce, another for beverages, and a third for storing extra ice and fish.

Ice chests and bags should have drainage plugs to minimize ice melt in the bottom of the chest. And they should be easy to clean. Perishable items like mayonnaise, fish products, and sandwich spreads are better purchased in small containers so they can be used in one or two days.

Paper Plates, Bowls and Cups

There are arguments pro and con for the use of disposables. Some call them a waste of natural resources. For float tripping, single-service eating/drinking gear is extremely handy, eliminates dish washing, and in the case of poor washing or rinsing, safeguards against the chance of uncomfortable cramps or diarrhea. Plastic knives and forks are also recommended. Disposable items should be burned completely, where burning or fires are permitted. Otherwise they should be packed out in large, heavy plastic garbage bags.

If stainless steel or aluminum dishes and utensils are used, clean them in a chlorine solution in which 2 teaspoons or one capful of chlorine bleach is added to each gallon of wash water. Completely immerse dishes and utensils for at least 60 seconds in the solution and allow to air dry after removal.

Disinfection of Drinking Water

Using household chlorine bleach, add 8 drops to each gallon of raw water. Iodine from a first aid kit can be used, mixing 20 iodine drops with a gallon of raw water.

Cooking fresh foods over open fire insures good spirits and a happy camp.

When halazone tablets are used, follow the directions on the label. Or, boil water vigorously for at least 2 minutes.

Whether chlorine or iodine is used, mix the water and drops thoroughly by stirring or shaking. Let the water stand for 30 minutes before drinking. Chlorine is a gas and after it has done its job will dissipate in about 30 minutes, giving little or no taste.

Water Storage

Water storage containers should have a closed top that can be tightly sealed. The container itself should be smooth and clean. Commercially sold water jugs or 5-gallon plastic containers can serve the purpose for water storage.

When to Purify Water

Even the most remote waters of the country are subject to some kind of contamination or pollution. Major float rivers, not coming directly from the untampered high country, contain water that needs to be purified.

Unless packing your own water from home, it's a good idea to purify *all* water, regardless of how pure or clear the stream appears. Purification can be done in advance so that quantities of water are ready for drinking, cooking or washing.

First Aid on the Water

BEHIND THE subject of first aid and first aid kits lurks the suspicion that too much emphasis is wasted on preparing for the negative. Why not simply look forward to the good things surrounding an outdoor adventure?

I can get boyishly excited over the prospects of floating a new stretch of river or the thought of deep, mysterious trout holes downstream. But adhesive tape, gauze, snake bite kits, calamine lotion and all the itching, scratching, swelling and pain that accompany these tools of pessimism never stir me much.

After all, first aid kits are boxes that you never can find when you need them. They always work their way to the bottom of the boat where they become filled with water and coated with grime. When the need for the first aid kit arises, opening the lid of the box often reveals a hopelessly soggy mess of bandage, gauze and punctured ointment tubes. Which just goes to prove the utter uselessness of first aid kits.

From a practical viewpoint, the first aid kit is a box of *insurance*. Good ones are rather heavy and take up precious storage space. Small kits get lost. So does it pay to carry a lot of insurance? The answer is *yes*. The fanciest first aid kit is only as good as the working condition it is in and the ability of its owner to find it quickly and be able to effectively use the tools and medicines contained therein.

When to Pack a First Aid Kit

The idea that first aid kits are only needed on extended float trips or through difficult stretches is a foolish one. Whether the trip be a 3-hour fishing trip or an overnighter, the very nature of river floating is reason enough to have a good, working first aid kit on board.

It is not so much the idea that a lot of bad things can happen on float trips, but rather the degree of isolation associated with floating. Even near metropolitan areas, the meandering course a stream takes can be quite inaccessible to roads, highways, houses and help. Some rivers are characterized by high canyon walls along their courses which prohibit access to areas

where help can be sought. For this reason, distance or difficulty rating should not be the sole determining factor in first aid consideration and preparation. The fact that immediate first aid can be given when needed can prevent discomfort and possible serious consequences later on. With some basic preparations, float trips that might be otherwise spoiled by minor ailments or injuries will only be temporarily interrupted.

The Best Kit for Your Float

The size of your boat with its space and weight restrictions dictates the type of first aid kit you will have on board.

In a survey conducted by the National Park Service and the Interagency Whitewater Committee, which includes river managers and guides, various first aid kits were reviewed and evaluated. Major and minor first aid kits varied from area to area, with the degree of isolation being the apparent reason for the size of kits. Major kits ranged in size from 15 to 40 items; minor kits, from 10 to 15 items; and standard kits ranged somewhere in between these extremes.

The size of the kit is not as important as its contents. The inclusion of the necessity items is vital for major, standard and minor kits alike. The geographical characteristics of the river, along with inherent insect or reptile pests, and such nemeses as poison ivy, oak and sumac should also be considered when determining sufficient quantities of various medications.

Basic Kit Instruments

A pair of medium size *scissors* is needed for cutting tape. A *razor* with extra blades is handy for removing hair before taping. *Tweezers* remove splinters. *Safety pins* can be used for mending and securing triangular bandages. A package of *cotton swabs* can be used for cleaning lacerations, eyes, and ears. For long trips an *inflatable splint* can be added.

Dressings

A supply of *Band-aids* in medium and large sizes for lacerations should be kept in their own container inside

Minor injuries, requiring basic first aid attention can occur on the water or in camp.

the kit. *Butterfly Band-aids* in various sizes help close lacerations. An *elastic bandage* 2 or 3 inches wide is needed for sprains. Be certain to follow the wrapping instructions that come with the bandage to guard against blocking circulation. A couple of rolls of 2-inch *adhesive tape* secures *sterile gauze pads* or flats for large and small wounds. And several rolls of 2-inch *roller gauze* hold the gauze pads in place before taping.

Medicinal Relief

Aspirin, or aspirin substitute, relieves pain or headaches. *Antacid tablets* alleviate indigestion. A bottle of *calamine lotion* soothes poison ivy or insect bite itching. Some sort of *pain killer* is advisable on long trips.

How to Prevent Problems

A good first aid kit can solve a multitude of discomforts and minor injuries. That's why commercial floaters ordinarily carry kits that include not only basic gear and medicines, but also other items to cover almost any "field treatable" discomfort or injury in the book.

Most problems on a float trip can be prevented. Here's how. *Insects*, including mosquitoes, chiggers, bees and wasps can cause aggravating discomfort. Regardless of the season, pack along enough insect repellent to ward off insects before they swarm. New bugproof repellent jackets have proved effective, along with several brands of repellent lotion that is applied to

exposed skin. Long pants, long-sleeved shirts and jackets are natural repellents. Headnets and gloves may be required in some northern areas where mosquitoes and flies are ferocious biters, and chemical repellents are ineffective.

Chiggers, especially bad in the Midwest and South, can be discouraged by liberally dousing powdered sulphur on skin areas where clothing is snug, such as ankles, waist, armpits and knees.

For overnight float camps, tents with sewn-in floors and nylon screening can prevent bites. Camp away from the water and if possible at a higher elevation to eliminate some insect problems.

Although a few bee and wasp stings are unavoidable, use some care when stopping for shore lunch or camp. Exercise caution and be alert for beehives. Look before sitting down on the ground. Floundering around at dusk or in the dark for firewood is a good way to pick up insect stings and bites.

Snakes can also be avoided by using caution along water areas where rattlesnakes or water moccasins (cottonmouths) are known to reside. Canyon areas bordering rivers can be especially lively with rattlers during spring, summer and fall months. Walk with care, especially during the early morning and late afternoon of summer days. Be careful where you place feet and hands. Carry a good snake bite kit in your first aid kit and know how to use it. By wearing leather hiking boots that cover the ankle or waders when fishing, the lower

Below — Headnets prevent annoying and serious bites from insects—sometimes they are the only means of relief. Right—Prevention eliminates many problems—such as drying your sleeping bag to avoid spending the following night in a damp bag.

leg, most often hit by poisonous snakes, can be protected. Be especially careful while gathering firewood not to probe in brush or under logs with your hands. Instead, use a long stick to shake brush or roll the log over first. Never trust a rock or log in snake country.

An overnight or extended float trip is no place to begin the sun tanning process. *Sunburning* often results and nothing can be more aggravating than rowing or paddling with painfully hot arms. Resist the sunning temptation or limit yourself to an hour. For face and arms, apply suntan lotion or zinc oxide sun screen. A sunburn relief lotion, like Solarcaine, can help but why let the problem develop in the first place? Mild to severe sunburning is one of the most common first aid problems on float trips and results in a wide range of discomforts from nausea and diarrhea to chills, burning skin and blisters. Sunburning ironically is the easiest problem to prevent.

Food and Drink Intake

Proper food and drink handling is a habit that seasoned floaters get into early. Severe stomach cramps, nausea, vomiting and diarrhea are especially uncomfortable symptoms on float trips. Whether on your own float or on a commercial float, never take it for granted that the food and water are "alright." Check on it.

Hats, Rain Gear and Sleeping Bags

Hats and rain gear are indeed first aid tools. They prevent a good number of on-stream ailments. Wide-brimmed western hats or baseball caps, for example, cut the glare of reflected sun, which can "burn" the eyes. They also prevent sunburned face and scalp. As a result, headaches and eye soreness can be reduced significantly simply by wearing hats that shield the sun.

Sudden rain squalls drench clothes and skin without the protection of *rain jackets and pants*. Chilling and colds result. Pack rain gear at all times and have it handy on board. Much of the need for aspirin or antihistamines can be reduced by wearing rain gear, warding off wet or damp clothing and staying warm.

Some commercial float outfitters provide sleeping bags upon request. It is better to bring your own *warm* bag with its own stuff sack and protective plastic covering (plus the outfitter's waterproof boat bag) and keep the bag dry. Cold or wet bags lead to insufficient rest, colds and bad attitudes.

How and Where to Store First Aid

Store first aid instruments, medicine and ointments in a single container made of wood, aluminum or heavy duty plastic that is waterproof and equipped with strong latches for positive opening and closing. There are a number of good places to store the kit—fishing tackle box, food bag, clothing bag or flotation-cargo bag. With a piece of masking tape, mark the bag where the first aid kit is located. Keep the kit handy near the top of the duffel.

Good Reading and Information

BOOK AND magazine days are those wintry times not fit for man or canoe. Nestle in front of fire or heater and bask in the adventures of others. If you love river floating and are eager to learn and if you delight in words of advice and relish the adventures of others, prime your mind through reading for that first, delicious day in spring before runoff when you and your boat will make the first trip of the season. There is no perfect book for everybody. And not every author will say what you want to hear. Sift through the good and the mediocre and garner treasures that will make you a better floater and outdoorsman who appreciates what nature has to offer. There is a world of floating adventure in books, magazines and booklets:

Paddling

Best Canoe Book Ever (Davidson and Rugge). First-hand adventure.

Boatbuilder's Manual (Walbridge). How to build your own fiberglass canoes and kayaks.

Canoeing (Michaelson & Ray). Information on equipment with good instruction.

Canoeing and Kayaking (Ruck) All aspects of canoeing and kayaking.

Canoeing for Children (Malo).

Canoeing Wilderness Waters (Heberton Evans III). Covers the essentials.

Canoe Poling (Beletz). Comprehensive study of the subject.

Guide to Paddle Adventure (Kemmer). Beginner's manual for paddling.

Kayaking (Evans & Anderson). Covers all phases of kayaking—the "bible."

Pole, Paddle and Portage (Riviere). How-to book on techniques.

River Running (Huser). Comprehensive guide for river running with inflatables.

Survival of the Bark Canoe (McPhee). With sketches.

Whitewater Canoeing (Sandreuter). Complete white water instruction.

Wilderness Canoeing (Malo). A good how-to manual.

Canoeing and Camping

Campground Cooking (Farmer). Good food ideas for boat and trail camping.

Camper's Digest (Bauer). Covers every phase of outdoor adventure.

Canoe Camper's Handbook (Bearse). Complete outdoor adventure.

Malo's Complete Guide to Canoeing & Canoe Camping (Malo).

Fishing and Photography

Backpack Fishing (Farmer). Lightweight, compactable techniques for boat and trail.

Fishermen's Digest (Bauer). Everything a fisherman needs to know.

Hunting With a Camera (Bauer). How to stalk game with lens from land or boat.

Outdoor Photographer's Digest (Bauer). Real adventure in outdoor photography.

The ABC's of Fishing (Zwirz). From novice to expert.

Trout Fishermen's Digest (Richey). How and where to catch big trout.

Nature and Wildlife

Birds of North America (Robbins, Bruun, Zim & Singer). Good identification book.

Outdoor Lore (Ormond). Covers *all* outdoor lore and techniques.

Reptiles and Amphibians (Zim, Smith). Easy guide for quick identification.

Sand County Almanac (Leopold). Puts nature and environment in perspective.

Wildlife Illustrated (Ovington). 240 American game birds, animals and fish.

Booklets

Basic Canoeing (Hasenfus-American Red Cross). The "bible" of canoeing.

Good books are now available on the techniques of white water rafting.

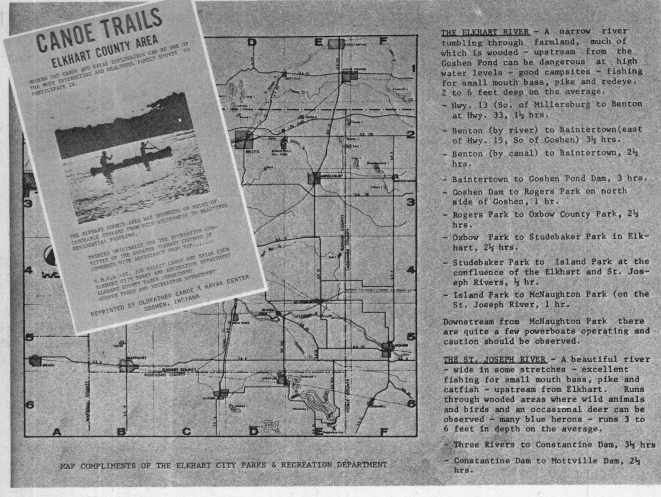

CANOE TRAILS
ELKHART COUNTY AREA

MODERN DAY CANOE AND KAYAK EXPLORATION CAN BE ONE OF THE MOST INTERESTING AND HEALTHFUL FAMILY SPORTS TO PARTICIPATE IN.

THE ELKHART COUNTY AREA HAS HUNDREDS OF MILES OF CANOEABLE STREAMS FROM WILD WILDERNESS TO BEAUTIFUL RESIDENTIAL PADDLING.

PRINTED ORIGINALLY FOR THE RECREATION COMMITTEE OF THE GREATER ELKHART CHAMBER OF COMMERCE WITH ASSISTANCE FROM THE.....

Y.M.C.A.–ST. JOE VALLEY CANOE AND KAYAK CLUB
ELKHART CITY PARKS AND RECREATION DEPARTMENT
ELKHART COUNTY PARKS DEPARTMENT
GOSHEN PARKS AND RECREATION DEPARTMENT

REPRINTED BY OLDFATHER CANOE & KAYAK CENTER
GOSHEN, INDIANA

MAP COMPLIMENTS OF THE ELKHART CITY PARKS & RECREATION DEPARTMENT

THE ELKHART RIVER – A narrow river tumbling through farmland, much of which is wooded – upstream from the Goshen Pond can be dangerous at high water levels – good campsites – fishing for small mouth bass, pike and redeye. 2 to 6 feet deep on the average.

- Hwy. 13 (So. of Millersburg to Benton at Hwy. 33, 1½ hrs.
- Benton (by river) to Baintertown(east of Hwy. 15, So of Goshen) 3½ hrs.
- Benton (by canal) to Baintertown, 2½ hrs.
- Baintertown to Goshen Pond Dam, 3 hrs.
- Goshen Dam to Rogers Park on north side of Goshen, 1 hr.
- Rogers Park to Oxbow County Park, 2½ hrs.
- Oxbow Park to Studebaker Park in Elkhart, 2½ hrs.
- Studebaker Park to Island Park at the confluence of the Elkhart and St. Joseph Rivers, ½ hr.
- Island Park to McNaughton Park (on the St. Joseph River, 1 hr.

Downstream from McNaughton Park there are quite a few powerboats operating and caution should be observed.

THE ST. JOSEPH RIVER – A beautiful river – wide in some stretches – excellent fishing for small mouth bass, pike and catfish – upstream from Elkhart. Runs through wooded areas where wild animals and birds and an occasional deer can be observed – many blue herons – runs 3 to 6 feet in depth on the average.

- Three Rivers to Constantine Dam, 3½ hrs
- Constantine Dam to Mottville Dam, 2½ hrs.

Each area has its own local float guides and tips booklets. They are very helpful provided they are current.

Basic Sailing (American Red Cross). All-around guide applicable for canoe sailing.

Fundamentals of Kayaking (Evans). Teaching guide for kayaking.

Group-Camping by Canoe (Grumman Boat Co.). The basics of trip logistics.

Grumman Book Rack (Grumman Boat Co.). Complete list of books and guides for canoeists.

Rent-A-Canoe Directory (Grumman Boat Co.). Canoe rentals coast-to-coast.

White Water Handbook for Canoe and Kayak (Urban). Good all-around guide.

Magazines

Camping & Backpacking Journals (Davis Publications). Camping techniques and some floating articles.

Canoe (American Canoe Association). Complete canoe, kayak and poling coverage.

Canoe News (U.S. Canoe Association). Canoeing news and adventure.

Down River (edited by Eric Evans). Covers white water river sport.

Whitewater Journal (American Whitewater Affiliation). Whitewater running.

State and Regional River Guides

Nearly every state in the country that has a significant number of floatable waters within its boundaries produces state or regional guides to floatable waters and best techniques for running them. Some guides are published by the state or county, National Park Service, U.S. Forest Service or Bureau of Outdoor Recreation. Others are published on a commercial basis. A *good* state or regional guide can be the best source of reliable information—provided it is current. You can inquire at libraries and bookstores for locally published information. The combination of accurate, current, local guides and maps and good river skills, add up to happy, safe float trips.

Basic Boat Knots

CANOEISTS, kayakers and rafters can avoid lost boats, broken fingernails and lost tempers if they learn a few basic knots. Unlike the square knot, the following knots hold boats securely, are easy to tie and loosen and do not jam.

Bowline

The best knot for making a loop that won't slip or for tying two ropes together. Form a loop in one hand, pass the free end through that loop, around the standing part, then back the loop through, as illustrated.

Sheet Bend

This knot joins ropes of different sizes and materials. The form of the Sheet Bend is identical to that of the Bowline. Form a loop with one end of a rope. Take the end of another rope through that loop and tuck the end of it under the form where it came through, making sure to cross over both parts of the opposite rope.

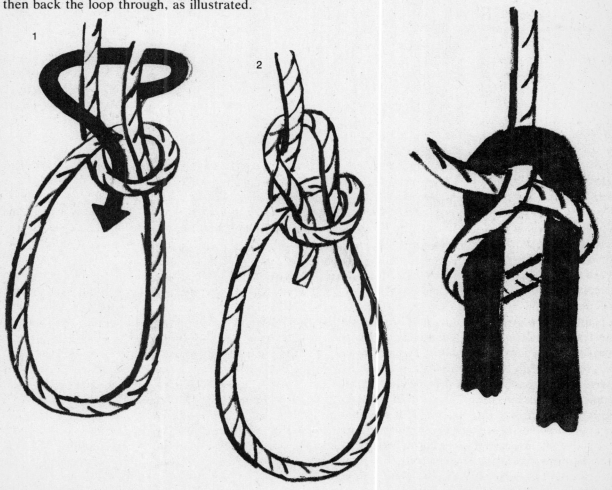

Clove Hitch

A good knot to use for securing bow and stern lines to moorings. Bring the end of the rope over or around the mooring post. Bring the end down, under, and up at the left side of the standing part. Cross the end over the standing part, make another turn down around the post, bringing the end up again, and under its own loop to the right of the standing part of the rope.

Butterfly Noose

This is a loop knot that won't jam and can be used for hand holds in pulling. Twist a loop and then fold the lower part of the loop and pull it through the center.

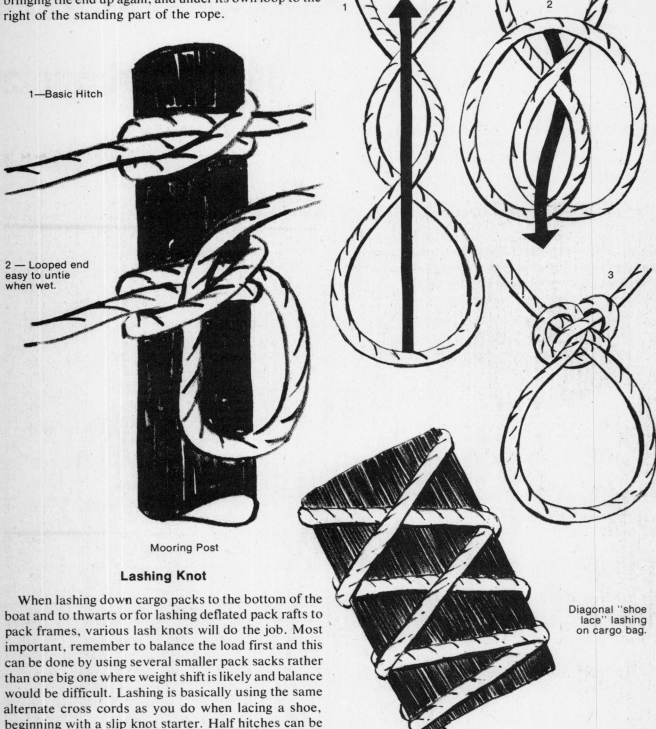

1—Basic Hitch

2 — Looped end easy to untie when wet.

Mooring Post

Diagonal "shoe lace" lashing on cargo bag.

Clove Hitch loop finish.

Lashing Knot

When lashing down cargo packs to the bottom of the boat and to thwarts or for lashing deflated pack rafts to pack frames, various lash knots will do the job. Most important, remember to balance the load first and this can be done by using several smaller pack sacks rather than one big one where weight shift is likely and balance would be difficult. Lashing is basically using the same alternate cross cords as you do when lacing a shoe, beginning with a slip knot starter. Half hitches can be used to retain tension on the lashing and to tighten diagonal rope twists. Finish lashing off with a clove hitch that is easy to untie, even when wet.

PART 2
CANOEING

A History of Canoeing

SKY, THE TREE RIDER

HIS PEOPLE, dwellers of the mountain caves, called him Sky, and his place and reputation were prominent. For it was Sky, at that time having accumulated 16 years on earth, who first rode the tree.

Broad chested, bow-legged Sky was watcher of the river—a job of considerable importance. He gauged rising waters, forewarning his people of imposing floods. During periods of low water, Sky discovered safe crossings to the other side of the river. There in late summer and early fall, his people could feast on the bounty of wild fruits and berries.

Sky was a river man. He knew the moods of the current. Not knowing how to swim according to our standards, he was an excellent floater and paddler,

imitating the movements of the trout, beaver and otter. Sky was a water creature, and he would ride the current like a nymph hatched from it. But his rides were short, not like that of the river otter, and this often depressed him. The water of the river, born fresh from the high peaks, was wonderfully clear and pure. But it was also so frigid that Sky's limbs would turn numb and blue, even on the warmest days.

Simple minds, attuned to living with nature did not, of course, pre-plan feats of great significance. It was just another day for Sky, who, for some instinctive reason, latched his muscular arms around the trunk of an uprooted floating tree. And he floated with the tree. His hands, arms and part of his shoulders were above the water surface, out of reach of the aching numbness of icy water. Sky shouted to no one in particular. He

rode the log and felt the touch of current under his body.

The moon had burned its light. In darkness Sky discovered after many cold wet rides that by carefully mounting the log in shallow water, "gripping" the log with his inner thighs and paddling slowly with his feet, that he could ride the current for longer periods of time without rolling off the log. His rides became longer and longer. And by using his arms, he found he could change direction.

The dark phase passed, and the new moon came. It was time for Sky to show his people the riding tree. In his excitement, he rolled off the log with his first try and from the people came spontaneous moans and chattering. They drank the water from the river but had never floated in it like Sky. Some of them left. Again Sky mounted the log, this time more carefully. He floated toward the main current and then out of view. Some friends wept uncontrollably. Others ran along the banks and stayed with Sky and the floating log. He taught them to ride the log, and soon the tree and the river became tools.

Many, many moon phases passed before Filo, a man of high reasoning power, became disenchanted with the riding tree. He was often rolled off the log and drenched in the swift waters that typified his people's area. In the cold climate, where people wore loin cloths and capes of hide, the feet and legs of tree riders would ache with numbing pain. The very act of sitting on a round log was one that took skill, and it was nearly impossible to stand on most trees. Many baskets of fruit and roots had been lost in the river.

Filo selected three, beaver-felled logs of similar length. The logs, much smaller in diameter than the single tree boat, were old and partially rotted. Because thistle down and dried leaves floated high on the current, Filo reasoned that old, light logs would do the same. With strips of bark and simple knots, he lashed the logs together, front and back. Sitting on the log platform, he hand paddled into the mild current and was carried downstream. The precise balancing needed for the tree boat ride was a thing of the past. With feet propped on the two outside logs, he stood up and was amazed that the boat did not roll over.

With a long pole of poplar, Filo steadied the boat and guided it in any direction. The rest of the tribe copied Filo's discovery. Eventually custom accepted a new test for manhood—guide the lashed-log boat down the fastest water and ride the waves without losing balance.

The poplar pole was useless in deep water where the pole could not reach bottom. Then boats whirled in eddies and careened out of control, losing both men and craft. One day while observing the beaver, Filo became entranced by the broad, flat tail that propelled the beaver through the water. For two days he searched for a pole that flattened near the end. He further flattened the root end of the pole with a large rock, smashing the wood fibers into a shape much like the beaver's tail.

With the flattened pole, Filo sped through the rapids. Despite poor balance, crashing into a rock, and nearly upsetting his boat, Filo led the others through the raging torrent. Before long, all the boaters adopted the flattened poles. Filo won no more races. And the men soon found they could carry baskets of fruit and berries on their boats without fear of losing them to the angry river. The beaver logs became more efficient tools.

Fire had been sparked and men made warmth and cooked food for themselves. Inso, a strong youth of the valley people, was hunting for roots when he came upon a tree that had been charred by a great flash from the sky. After examining the blackened tree closely, he found it to be a great deal lighter than the logs used for tree boats or lashed-log boats. With a piece of bone, he easily scraped the charred wood from the felled tree. By the second day, Inso had carved a depression in the log, nearly deep enough for him to sit in. Inso gathered his family together to show them what he had done. Had the tree god taken away Inso's legs? They laughed when they realized Inso was sitting inside the tree. What a joke. Each took a turn sitting inside the silly tree seat.

A multitude of years passed before a descendant of Inso's tribe discovered the charred tree half buried in the sand. Like Filo, Tol was a reasonable man. People from many tribes sought Tol's advice. Despite its rough appearance, the carved-out tree intrigued Tol. He had long detested the often uncontrollable, slippery, wet lashed-log boats that were often at the mercy of the current. Besides the wind blowing them aimlessly about on the ponds and lakes, skins and kindling often became waterlogged when carried on unprotected lashed-log boats.

Tol recalled watching a chunk of cottonwood bark drift down the river. Used to scoop water from the river, cottonwood bark retains its rounded tree shape. The vision of the dugout came to life. Like the rounded sides of the bark, the dugout canoe would have enclosed and uplifted front and back, designed to slice through the water.

Finishing the job that Inso started, Tol and a helper lit small fires on the charred tree, further carving and hollowing out the trunk. With crude axes and scrapers, they shaped the dugout to a design and profile similar to today's canoes and kayaks. For the first time, men could sit or kneel inside a boat. They could be protected from current or wind-blown water. Their food and trading goods stayed dry. Flattened paddles, honed with stone and bone tools, would enable them to glide through the water.

Not too long ago, dugouts were equipped with outriggers for greater stability. Or two canoes were joined together by securing a platform between them. The double canoes, often equipped with sails, were the forerunners of the modern catamaran.

The giant cedar trees of the Pacific Northwest provided Indian tribes with the material to build dugouts, some of which were 60 feet long and were used for hunting whales.

Man progressed in boat building. Planks were placed edgewise and secured to the gunwales to make drier boats. The additional freeboard made larger loads possible.

In recent times in treeless regions canoes were constructed of wooden frames and covered with animal skins. The Plains Indians of North America built a circular canoe of buffalo hides. But the Eskimo kayak is the finest example of the covered frame canoe. Sealskin is stretched and sewn over a driftwood frame, leaving a small cockpit for the paddler. Kayaks are extremely seaworthy.

The skeletal frame of wood with a watertight cover of birch bark was perfected by the North American Indian. The birch canoe was light, fast, maneuverable and built in different sizes for various needs, from one-man boats to war canoes. Explorers using the birch bark design with minor modifications played a vital role in shaping the early history of the white man in North America. For about 200 years the canoe was the chief means of travel to remote and unexplored areas.

From birch bark the canoe progressed to the all-wood canoe in 1879, followed by the wood-frame, canvas-covered models. Plywood, pressed aluminum, fiberglass and plastic have taken over. The canoe is still very much with us. Thank you Sky, Filo, Inso and Tol.

Above—Pictographs along the Green River are a part of canoeing history. Below—If only the originators of the first canoes could see this.

Is the Canoe for You?

ASIDE FROM all the basic realities of life, like family size, economics, portaging weight, available waters and special uses, I think most of us who choose the canoe as a lifelong friend have a bit of trapper blood in us.

Seldom do I dip the paddle into stream or lake, whether fishing, hunting or floating for the sake of floating, without dreaming a bit of the buckskin men who used the canoe and waterways for trapping and exploration. I am one of those men. Sometimes for scarcely a minute the spirit engulfs me. Other times, an entire day of canoe kinship passes before I realize the days of river trapping and pioneering are over. Or are they? Not as long as the canoe spirit lives. And live on I believe it will because this simple watercraft has gracefully endured the progressive stings of a sometimes venomous civilization. Motors just can't seem to drown out the slurp of a paddle slicing water. And the canoe, the boat of simple adventure, thrives in greater number now than it ever has. Break out the buckskins and glide.

The Family Canoe

Ideally, canoeing is a two-person sport with paddlers in stern and bow for a well trimmed boat. The narrow beam of the craft, in comparison to other boats, is best suited to one person in the bow and one person in the stern in the sitting or kneeling paddling position.

Depending on the length of the canoe, with an average range of 12 to 20 feet, extra passengers are possible. A 17- to 20-foot long canoe can safely carry a family of four. However, to believe that any canoe has the stability of a rowboat or johnboat is foolish. A canoe with two passengers or four is safe only when the manufacturer's recommended weight capacity is followed and all passengers retain a low center of gravity. The kneeling paddling position is favored by skilled canoeists for this reason. Stability is increased, and paddling strokes can be used more effectively.

Where a kneeling or sitting position can be comfortable for paddling adults, the positions may not be favorites of the kids for any length of time. Canoe back rests

and chairs, especially made to fit in the bottom of canoes for low center of gravity, can help relieve the fidgeting and cramped feeling that children get. The best technique, however, is teaching children why they must remain low and how their efforts can better balance the canoe. With short trips up to an hour in duration, there is usually not much of a problem. However, longer trips do pose problems that confront even the most patient parents and willing children. A canoe is just not the kind of craft where kids or adults can get up and stretch their legs. Periodic shore breaks help. But the best overall solution is to admit that, except for carrying small children, two canoes are better than one for the family of four or more. With good basic instruction, 10-year-olds and older can paddle their own canoes. Canoeing is meant to be a participation sport and few persons enjoy spectator roles.

The Lone Canoeist

For the single man or woman, a canoe can be a good choice. Nothing can beat the feeling of a solitary float down a quiet, misty stream in early fall. Paddling from a position in the middle (amidship) of the canoe, the lone paddler can enjoy good boat control, even on relatively swift streams.

A good command of canoe strokes and sound understanding of stream navigation and water currents are necessary for the lone canoeist. If canoeing partners exhibit a good command of techniques, the single floater should be able to demonstrate them even better. Mild streams, ponds or lakes usually pose no threat to the lone paddler. However, common sense dictates that two paddlers are better than one in some situations, and there is safety and help in numbers. The most important decision the floater makes is correctly evaluating a certain stretch as safe and knowing that if something does go wrong he or she can get out of the jam.

Another minor consideration for the solitary boater is the weight of the canoe for portaging and cartopping. With help not always readily available, choose a canoe you can handle.

Canoe Advantages

A canoe has *shallow draft*. What that means simply is that it does not take much water to float a canoe. Where heavier, deeper boats with prominent, protruding keels hang up in shallow water, canoes with one or two paddlers on board can skim through. Canoes require water only a foot deep. Most canoes weigh under 90 pounds. Thus, the volume of water displaced (the weight of the displaced fluid being equal to that of the displacing body) is slight compared to heavier boats. As a result, the canoeing fisherman, hunter, camper, nature observer and photographer can glide over shallow back waters that would be impassable for conventional boats. Shallow draft also makes the canoe an ideal stream craft during low water periods in summer and fall. There will be times and places where dragging or portaging a canoe is necessary, but only when the riffles are barely trickling over the stream bed.

When compared to other boats, canoes are *light*. A 15-foot aluminum, Grumman Canoe of standard weight (they also come in lightweight models) weighs 69 pounds and is 35⅛ inches at the beam (width of canoe at widest part). An Old Town Carleton fiberglass model of 16 feet weighs 79 pounds and has a beam of 36 inches. While an Old Town wood and canvas Guide model 18 feet long weighs 85 pounds and beams at 37 inches. Most adult men, acquainted with the techniques of lifting and leverage, can handle these weights without assistance when loading and unloading from cartop.

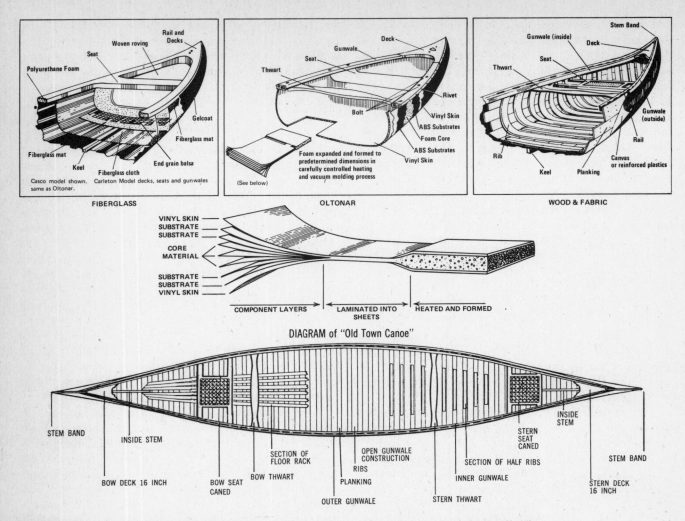

FIBERGLASS

Polyurethane Foam
Seat
Woven roving
Rail and Decks
Gelcoat
Fiberglass mat
Fiberglass mat
Keel
Fiberglass cloth
End grain balsa

Casco model shown.
Carleton Model decks, seats and gunwales same as Oltonar.

OLTONAR

Deck
Gunwale
Seat
Thwart
Bolt
Rivet
Vinyl Skin
ABS Substrates
Foam Core
ABS Substrates
Vinyl Skin

Foam expanded and formed to predetermined dimensions in carefully controlled heating and vacuum molding process

(See below)

WOOD & FABRIC

Stem Band
Gunwale (inside)
Deck
Thwart
Seat
Gunwale (outside)
Rail
Canvas or reinforced plastics
Planking
Keel
Rib

VINYL SKIN
SUBSTRATE
SUBSTRATE
CORE MATERIAL
SUBSTRATE
SUBSTRATE
VINYL SKIN

COMPONENT LAYERS — LAMINATED INTO SHEETS — HEATED AND FORMED

DIAGRAM of "Old Town Canoe"

STEM BAND
INSIDE STEM
BOW DECK 16 INCH
BOW SEAT CANED
BOW THWART
SECTION OF FLOOR RACK
RIBS
PLANKING
OUTER GUNWALE
OPEN GUNWALE CONSTRUCTION
STERN THWART
INNER GUNWALE
SECTION OF HALF RIBS
STERN SEAT CANED
INSIDE STEM
STERN DECK 16 INCH
STEM BAND

Diagram of a canoe and the different types of construction and materials available.

The sport canoe by Grumman takes motors and is a stable compromise between canoe and rowboat.

Average 3-foot beams make storage, even in limited apartment dwellings, possible. Two canoes can be carried on a standard size vehicle and compacts can easily handle one canoe. Portaging, with the aid of a homemade or commercially manufactured carrying yoke, can be handled by a man of average strength with little difficulty for distances up to a mile. And some canoeists swear it is easier to portage a canoe by themselves, on their own back, than sharing the load with a partner. Either way, canoes are light enough to be easily handled by one or two people, without the aid of a special trailer, hoist or winch.

Modern canoes, made of aluminum, fiberglass or plastic, require *little or no upkeep*. Interior and exterior finishes can be protected and kept nice looking with occasional applications of paste wax. Canoes should be stored under some kind of shelter on racks or boards that keep them from contact with the ground. Wood and canvas canoes, still manufactured commercially by the Old Town Canoe Company, Old Town, Maine, require more upkeep. They must be protected by varnish or paint. The beauty, tradition and workmanship inherent in the wood-canvas canoe often instills a strong sense of maintenance pride in its owners. Upkeep then, for some, is a matter of personal satisfaction and the true worth of the canoe increases with age and use.

Excellent quality canoes, from 12 to 20 feet in length, fall into a general price range extending from $200 (for a

Above—The canoe makes an excellent lake craft—easy to paddle. Right—Family size may dictate that two canoes are needed. Below—The lone paddler uses small 12-footer to fish from and portage.

Above—Sailing rigs can be purchased as canoe option. Right—Some canoes have Styrofoam flotation strips on the exterior. Below—This 15-footer is fine for two persons. It's made of polyethylene.

used model) to $500 for 18- or 20-footers. Good paddles of ash, spruce or maple cost $10 to $30. More expensive paddles are required for white water. Coast Guard approved personal flotation devices (P.F.D.s) for each canoeist and bow and stern ropes round out the basic gear. Good cartop carriers can be purchased for under $30. Nothing is really cheap these days, but it is reassuring for prospective canoeists to know that most modern canoes are high quality products. A canoe can last a lifetime. Considering the enjoyment and adventure a canoe can give, the initial investment (most often under $400) seems small in comparison. Add to these facts. the beauty of swift, gas-less, paddle propulsion, and we

have a craft that is cheap to run and maintain. The canoeist does have a gas or electric motor option. Canoeing can be truly simple and uncluttered and that's the joy of it.

Because the canoe is silent, because it does not need fuel for propulsion, and because it seems to fit into the natural scheme of things outdoors, it is *the* ideal sport of streams and lakes. For the peaceful fisherman who gauges his success on a quality experience, for the stalking hunter steeped in the tradition of trapper times, for the camper who craves solitude and river spirit, and for the nature observer and photographer who likes natural contact still and up close, the canoe is for you.

How to Choose the Right Canoe

EVALUATED on their own merits, there are few, if any, "bad" canoes—most name brand craft are quality products. However canoes can be classified according to stability, construction, safety features, and maneuverability. They can also be judged on how well they perform certain functions. For instance, one brand or model might be better for lake or pond use rather than for white water.

As a novice canoeist in the initial stages of canoe buying, all boats might look basically the same. But closer investigation begins to turn up differences. And as small as those differences might be, they can be important. After some simple, basic research, the prospective canoeist soon discovers that the type of keel on a particular model, for example, better suits the boat for lakes rather than for rivers.

Canoes, though basically simple in design, often have subtle features that account for the hows and whys of boat performance. As a prospective buyer, the secret to sound buying is to look closely. Avoid fancy frills, and expect sound, definite answers to all your questions. Reading several canoe manufacturers' catalogs in advance of actual shopping can help. Here's a general guideline.

Brands

Canoes reach brand name status by producing good quality products for a number of years. Some companies have a multitude of years under their thwarts; others, because of demand, innovation and good advertising have earned fine reputations in relatively few years. However, do not choose your canoe solely on the reputation of the boat builder, rather purchase a canoe that meets *your* personal needs. Some name brands you will come across are Old Town, Grumman, Lund, Sawyer, Mad River, Lowe Line, Alumacraft, Sea Nymph, Michi-Craft and Smoker-Craft. Some companies specialize in certain materials for building

Aluminum canoes are durable and require little upkeep.

Above—Some aluminum canoes can be ordered painted in a variety of colors. Right—White water canoes have shallow keels and extra ribs. Below—Small, 10- and 12-footers are fine for portaging and pond use.

Above—Folding kayaks for two or one solve transportation and storage problems. Left—Some canoes and kayaks can be easily converted to sailing rigs. Below—Square end canoe has transom designed to easily mount an outboard motor.

New synthetic plastic canoes are durable and light.

their products like aluminum, fiberglass, plastic or wood and canvas. New multi-laminates, like Kevlar and Oltonar are becoming increasingly popular for canoe hulls. Your choice of canoe depends somewhat on the type of material used for its construction.

Hull Materials

Aluminum canoes are rugged. They will stand up to a good deal of abuse and require relatively little or no upkeep. They are subject to denting and, under moderate to heavy white water use, when pinned in the current by rocks or logs, can bend in two beyond repair. Some "thin-skinned" lightweight canoes, not really recommended for heavy white water use, are also susceptible to puncturing by rocks. Certain aluminum hulls have rough edges which could prove dangerous in a hasty exit. Aesthetically speaking, the unpainted silver hull has not been awarded any beauty prizes. They also have been described as "loud" because sound is easily carried through aluminum. Several manufacturers offer color options at prices ranging from $30 to $50 extra. The average weight of a 17-foot double-end aluminum canoe is 75 pounds.

Fiberglass canoes are durable and require little or no upkeep. They are more susceptible to river running abrasions and cracking than quality aluminum boats are. Contrary to popular belief, fiberglass boats are not generally lighter than aluminum ones. On the contrary, depending on the model, length and construction, the average fiberglass craft weighs a few pounds more than an aluminum one of comparable size. Fiberglass canoes are "softer" and "quieter" than the rather harsh aluminum ones. They do not conduct cold or heat as aluminum canoes do nor do they have the rough appearance and edges of aluminum. Built from molds, they do not have rivets and therefore appear more "finished" than aluminum. Colors are softer and richer in appearance due to impregnation of pigments into fiberglass resin. The average weight of a 17-foot double-end fiberglass canoe is 80 to 85 pounds.

The Old Town Canoe Company still makes high quality **wood and canvas** canoes. As Old Town puts it, "Wood and canvas is for those special people who believe in tradition and appreciate the beauty of wooden craft and the skill that goes into their construction." Enough said. The sight of a wood n' canvas makes me drool. However, they are more than double the price of good aluminum or fiberglass craft. Lighter than fiberglass, they are ideal for lakes and slow streams and aesthetically cannot be touched by any other canoe, but they are susceptible to rips, cracking and warping when not properly cared for. They are a dream to paddle—soft and quiet. Old Town makes five different wood and canvas models. An 18-foot "Guide" model by Old Town weighs 85 pounds and is a graceful creature.

The Synthetics—ABS plastic, polyethylene, Kevlar, and Oltonar—are new canoe materials. They are super tough substances that excel in many ways. They are virtually indestructible, unsinkable and, when trapped in currents of heavy force, they do not fold or crack. Extremely heavy blows may cause dents, but these can be removed with application of heat. There is no up-keep or maintenance, save an occasional washing for the sake of cosmetics.

I recently put a 15-foot Pelican by Eskay through the paces on the Snake River in Wyoming; its 60 pounds could be easily portaged, and it was as tough as a boot. On the average, the synthetic boats weigh from 10 to 20 pounds less than aluminum and fiberglass canoes of the same size. They have the smooth, molded form appearance and retain a variety of colors well. The addition of wood trim and seats should give the synthetic boats special appeal and a bright future.

Length Dependent on Use

There are short canoes (10-14 feet.), mid-length (15-17 feet), and long canoes (18-20 feet). Short canoes weighing 30 to 50 pounds are fine for kids or for solo paddling. They are easy to launch, paddle, portage, and are good for one-man fishing floats. For camping, their load-carrying capacity is limited.

The mid-length canoes are good all-around canoes for general family use, lake or pond fishing, and stream running. Ideal for two people, there is moderate load space to handle fishing gear and camping equipment. These canoes weigh from 55 to 80 pounds.

The long canoes may weigh 85 to 120 pounds, on the heavy side for an inexperienced portager. However they make excellent expedition canoes for extended camping and fishing trips. Ample cargo space provides room for the necessities as well as a few luxuries. Generally speaking, the longer the canoe, the faster and the better it tracks. The long canoes are good for big lake travel and for running wide, swift rivers. Use in tight white water, filled with rock gardens and logs, is limited because of slow maneuverability and length.

However, the longer canoes cannot necessarily hold more passengers. More cargo, that can be carefully stowed for good trim, yes. Two people per boat is ideal. For family use, consider two mid-length canoes rather than one long boat. The mid-length canoes and especially the 17-footers are certainly the best all-around choices

Choice of Keels

A keel, the reinforcing ridge down the center of most canoes, comes basically in two different styles. A standard keel enhances the forward tracking stability of a canoe, particularly in crosswinds. If most of your canoe travel will be on lakes or on long, deep river trips, the standard keel is for you.

There are also flat, shoe (or shallow draft) keels that give some tracking stability yet do not significantly affect side-to-side maneuverability. (Side-to-side maneuvering is seriously hampered by standard keels which offer lateral resistance to the water.) The shallow draft keel, or no keel at all, is for paddling in moving water or white water running. It is less likely to catch on shoal obstructions and provides more protection to the bottom of a canoe than a narrow, deep keel. The flat shoe or shallow draft keel is about ⅜-inch deep.

Folding Canoes or Boats

Boats with wooden frames and special canvas or hypalon skins that fold or pack for storage, comprise a special category of canoes. They display similar characteristics to rigid hull canoes. Details on some of those folding boats, and manufacturer's address are listed elsewhere in this book.

Things to Do Before Canoe Purchase

1. Rent as many different types of canoes (constructed of various materials) as possible.

2. Collect brochures of leading canoe manufacturers and compare statistics and features.

3. Determine what your intended use is and select a craft that fits your needs.

4. Make sure rivets are well secured, of good design and properly spaced on aluminum canoes.

5. Ragged edges and sharp metal on aluminum canoes are signs of inferior workmanship.

6. Compare canoe warranties. Lifetime warranties, under normal use, are standard.

Canoe Equipment

CANOEING IS simple sport in its purest form. Besides the boat itself, paddles and Coast Guard approved flotation devices are the only equipment necessary.

Canoeists themselves, though, differ extensively in tastes and desires, needs and skills. As a result, canoe equipment manufacturers produce a broad variety of items that can add comfort, convenience, safety and enjoyment to the sport. In evaluating equipment, consider your own needs. What may be considered a gimmick by some, may be a necessity to others.

Paddles

A variety of paddles are available to canoeists. Construction and material determine whether a paddle can be rated poor, fair, or good. Single blade paddles are most commonly used, while double blades are fine for solo cruising against rather consistent strong winds and waves. Top grade wooden paddles are made of selected pieces of spruce, ash or maple. Sections are glued to-

Below—T-handle fiberglass paddle and wooden canoe paddles. Right —Synthetic paddles.

gether with the grain of the wood kept flat in the blade. The wood grain in the shaft is placed at right angles to the blade. This arrangement strengthens the paddle and increases its durability.

Inexpensive paddles, often advertised as "bargain" items, are usually mass-produced from a single piece of wood and are heavier than composite wood paddles. Some are made of spruce, but, more commonly, soft woods like pine, cedar and fir are used. Hardwood paddles can withstand much contact abuse in shallow water, whereas softwood will chip, splinter and crack. Quality hardwood paddles are your best buy. A good spare paddle should always be carried.

Wooden paddles sometimes are fiberglass or aluminum tipped for extra protection against bottom contact. Also, the shaft of the paddle can be fitted with a leather or fiberglass chafing collar near the throat.

Besides wood, paddles can be made of fiberglass, aluminum, ABS plastic and Kevlar, and various combinations of these materials. Such paddles are better choices than inferior wood paddles for most canoeing needs. They require no upkeep and have strength and durability. Paddles with some built-in flex, whether wood or synthetic, are favored over stiff paddles. The only way to discover various degrees of flex in paddles is to try out as many different brands as possible. The flex quality will not be as obvious to a novice canoeist as it will be to an experienced paddler, but it is important for good feel and satisfying rhythm on extended cruises or lake paddling.

Personal Paddle Fit

Rules of thumb: The distance from the paddler's nose to the ground measures the approximate length of a proper paddle fit. Or, the length of the paddle should span the outstretched arms with the fingers curled over the tip of the blade and the end of the grip. Give or take an inch or two, these two rules produce similar results.

Cartop Carriers

For the transportation of one or two canoes, the cartop carrier is standard equipment. Canoes are light

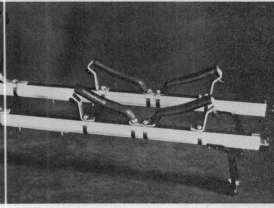

Above left—Most standard size passenger vehicles can easily handle two canoes. Above right—Cartop carrier of aluminum with attachments for carrying canoes on edge. Right—Foam block type carrier clamps on boat's gunwales, holds firm.

enough and have a narrow enough beam to be transported easily on the roof of a vehicle—a trailer is unnecessary. It is important to select a cartop carrier that fits the car securely. An ill-fitting carrier, poor tie-downs, and faulty lashing techniques can cause dangerous shifting of the load and possible loss of the craft.

Basically there are about three different types of carriers. For vehicles without rain gutters, rubber pads or suction cups grip the roof while vinyl-covered clamps fasten to the door frame. Another type clamps or screws down into the rain gutter. A new model, by Grumman, called the CanoeTopper, consists of four sponge vinyl blocks that snap onto the boat's gunwales. With two lines and four side hooks the canoe is tightly secured to the car's roof with a minimum of wind resistance.

Carriers have extruded aluminum or wooden cross-bars on which the canoe rests. Old Town Canoe Company has a contoured boat rack available as an option that fits on their carrier.

A few things to remember about cartopping: Always try to obtain help in putting the canoe on and taking it off the rack. Boats are always topped upside down or bottom up. And tie-down lines from each end of the canoe should be tightly secured to the car. In addition to the rack itself being clamped to the car, vertical tie-downs attached to one side of the rack, stretched over the canoe and secured on the other side of the rack complete cartop rigging. Commercially made tie-downs hold boats securely fore and aft and eliminate time wasted in tying and untying knots. Shock cords, because of stretch, do not qualify for fore and aft tie-down material. Quarter-inch cotton or Dacron line does the job best. It's a good idea, on long trips, to check carrier clamping systems and tie-down ropes periodically.

Trailers

A variety of flatbed or stacked rail trailers are used to transport one or more canoes. Persons with bad backs, those canoeing alone, or where help is usually not available for cartop loading and unloading often choose simple, two-wheel trailers. A trailer is especially nice if it can also be used for purposes besides canoe transportation. Trailers made especially for hauling several canoes or racks custom-built of steel can be purchased commercially. They are especially suited for scouting groups, canoe outfitters, and expeditions. As with cartopping, canoes must be secured tightly in racks for safety and to prevent damage. For short hauls, some

Conventional boat trailer can be used to haul canoes.

Specialized trailers can carry group canoes.

pickup truck beds adequately handle one or two canoes. Too often, though, the canoe extends over the tailgate, thus requiring special care to cushion and tightly lash the boat down to tarp hooks and bumper.

Motor Brackets

Outboard motor brackets for gasoline or electric powered engines are made of metal and wood and clamp to the gunwales of most double-end canoes without any structural changes. Most canoe manufacturers have their own brackets that are especially designed and fitted to their boats. The addition of a motor may be handy for covering large stretches of lake or flat river water and for fishing.

Aluminum canoe equipped with lateen sail, rudder, mast and leeboards.

Sailing Rigs

Most canoes can be converted to sailing rigs with a minimum of structural changes. The addition of a sailing rig can add a new and exciting dimension to your canoe. The Grumman Canoe Company offers a convenient sailing package that fits their factory prepared canoes. Either 45-square foot lateen or 65-square foot gunter rigs can be used. Aluminum mast, boom, sail, leeboards, spreader bar, rudder, and adapter and rigging lines come in the package. A screwdriver and pliers are the only tools required for converting the canoe into a sailboat.

Rowing Attachments

Some manufacturers offer optional rowing attachments that clamp to the gunwales. Other rowing attachments can be custom-made. Rowing rigs are not meant to replace paddling as much as to add speed and power to long flat lake trips and for solo fishing from a canoe. Oars about 7 feet long are used with most canoe rowing rigs.

Carrying or Portaging Yokes

Carrying yokes of wood or metal with cushioned pads that rest on the shoulders can make the difference between miserable and fairly comfortable portaging. Although life preservers, rolled up jackets and shirts can make the job easier, the yokes are far more stable and comfortable. Available from some manufacturers or home-made, they can be mounted on center thwarts. Wooden crossbar yokes are far more comfortable than metal.

Kneeling Pads

Without a cushioned pad, kneeling is uncomfortable in a canoe. Pads should provide some type of ventilation at the point of contact. Kneel pads or protectors sold in sporting goods stores are adequate for short runs. Large cellulose sponges are good and so is raw foam rubber, at least 4 inches thick or doubled for added cushion.

Seats or Backrests

Metal, or even better, wooden seats and backrests are sold by manufacturers and make sitting much more comfortable for passengers. Floors of aluminum canoes especially can become very cold and sometimes wet. Besides being built for comfort, good seats encourage a low center of gravity.

Cargo Bags

Waterproof, watertight bags of heavy-duty plastic keep gear safe and dry. Some feature canvas or nylon interior or exterior linings. Look for sturdy construction, carrying handle, and strong lash loops.

Canoe seats, seat back, carrying yoke and outboard motor mount.

Portage Packs

Nylon rucksacks or cargo bags with sturdy backpack straps (padded for loads over 10 pounds) can keep hands free when portaging. Food, extra clothing, first aid kit, camera, and fishing tackle can be packed in portage packs.

Canoe Caddies

Rather large, lightweight rubber tires and frame with bicycle-type spoked wheels strap or clamp to the canoe for portaging or transporting over short distances. Handy in permanent or semi-permanent camp or landing areas where solo portaging is the rule rather than the exception.

Add-on Pontoons

Foam pads clamp on to the gunwales for additional stability and flotation in rough water or when carrying heavy loads. Not a bad precaution when carrying small children as passengers. Some canoes are manufactured with foam strips attached to the hull. They are not to be confused with the accessory pads.

Anchors

Any anchor up to 5 pounds of either a folding or mushroom type holds a canoe in calm water or slow currents for fishing or photography purposes. Vinyl covered anchors are quiet and eliminate rough edges.

Poles

Wooden, fiberglass or aluminum poles, 12 feet long, propel a canoe in shallow water either upstream or downstream. Until recently, poling was somewhat of a lost art.

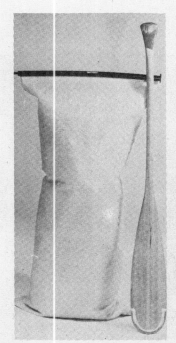

Left—Expedition cargo pack. Below—A canoe camping pack. Both are waterproof.

Canoe Strokes

AS WITH most sports requiring knowledge and skill, there is a right and a wrong way of paddling. Novices, first introduced to canoeing, ordinarily do what comes naturally. Whether in the bow or stern position, they jab the paddle into the water, close to the canoe and pull the blade towards their position in the boat. Not bad, really, for this simple stroke will propel them in adequate fashion. If bow and stern paddlers are fairly synchronized—which is possible after a bit of practice—strokes can be smooth and some fair distances can be covered. Hopefully, this practice session is conducted in a pool, pond or lake. The absence of even mild currents enables the canoeists to track in a relatively straight line to a given destination or turn on a desired course. For some novices that's the extent of paddling skills, especially if they are limited to lakes. Beginners feel the "jab and pull" to be all that is needed to propel a canoe.

When introduced to stream cruising, it becomes dramatically obvious that there is more to canoe paddling than meets the eye. The addition of a current, however mild, makes instruction necessary. It's like the skier who without instruction has the strength and agility to "work" a small hill. But, presented with a significant grade, a long run, and a few trees to negotiate, the novice using muscle alone usually meets with disaster. It is not until the skier learns the moves, edges, angles, and harnesses the down grade to skill and knowledge that the mountain can be mastered. The same with canoeing. Stroking is more than pure muscle. It is harnessing the current to the paddle—getting the angle, the edge, the course of most or least water resistance.

There is a distinct type of stroke for nearly every type of current situation and to enjoy the full thrill of canoeing, and save a lot of needless "pure muscle" work, learning the full complement of strokes is worth the effort. It is reassuring for women and children, who may lack the pure physical strength, to realize that the

The foundation to good stroking is the kneeling position and a good, low center of gravity.

Here is proper grip on paddle displayed by author's wife.

knowledge of stroking and the currents can put them on nearly equal stream-running terms with men.

Strokes can be learned from books and from the guidelines that follow here. But, the fastest, most practical way to learn them is from qualified instructors in a canoe safety program. The American National Red Cross, through their Small Craft Safety program, is one such organization that offers basic instruction. Men, women and children can participate. Families can enroll in the same course for added enjoyment and a solid canoeing education for the future.

10 Basic Canoe Strokes

Depending on terminology, there are basically 10 canoe strokes that should be learned and practiced until they become nearly reflex actions. Precisely, when and where to use the various strokes takes on-stream practice—because rivers and currents are different, strokes will also vary. Canoeists soon find that various strokes can be modified to fit particular water and weather conditions.

Forward and *backward* strokes, executed in the same way but in opposite directions, are counted simply as one stroke. The *J-Stroke, Steering* or *Rudder, Draw, Cross-draw, Cross-backstroke, Scull, Pry, Sweep* and *Inverted Sweep* are the techniques to learn.

Strokes are made with one hand cupped on the grip of the paddle and the other on the shaft several inches above the blade. A general rule to follow for the distance between grips is the distance from the paddler's armpit to the tips of the fingers. When the distance is right, a paddler can usually *feel* good power and some paddle flex when strokes are made. It is a good idea to practice strokes both right- and left-handed as this will

increase proficiency and stamina. When not making strokes, hold the paddle horizontally across the gunwales in the "ready" position or keep it in the water as a keel for stability in rough stretches.

Possibly one of the best habits you can develop is learning the basic strokes from a kneeling position (use cushions or knee pads while learning). Not only will your center of gravity be lower, affording more stability, but the kneeling position is highly recommended for running any kind of white water. Since modern canoes have to be ordered special *without* seats, most of us, when learning paddling strokes, assumed that everything done in a canoe is from the sitting position. More power can be put into strokes from the kneeling position because of more efficient and easier torso movements. In the kneeling position, rest your buttocks against the thwart or the edge of the seat. This low kneeling position is a good brace for extra stability and for absorbing impact with obstacles in the river. Strokes should be practiced and learned first in lakes, ponds, or flat stream water.

1. FORWARD AND BACKWARD STROKES

Forward and backward paddling strokes should be made parallel to the gunwale with a solid bite or catch of the flat blade with a smooth continuous stroke. At the end of the stroke, the bottom hand will be about even with the hip with all the power having been applied at that point. Both arms are then relaxed and the blade is withdrawn from the water at a "feathered" angle to the water for a smooth, nearly dragless recovery, and the stroke is repeated. Backstrokes for backward maneuvering alone or for stopping or moving backward with a partner, is done in the same way, with the blade feathered out upon the forward recovery.

2. J-STROKE

The final part of the basic pull stroke, an outward curve or "J" counteracts the push of the forward stroke, enabling a lone canoeist to hold a straight course. The more vertical the stroke (that is, not angled but using the hips and back for placement), the more effective it will be for keeping course. Some canoeists execute this stroke so well, an observer would swear there's an invisible bow paddler helping to keep the boat on track.

3. STEERING OR RUDDER STROKE

This is the stroke that looks and feels good, especially for a novice sternsman in swift water. It's easy to make because the blade of the paddle is held firmly in the water at the stern for a rudder. However, the steer-ing stroke should be used for only minor course changes since it slows headway considerably (sometimes desir-able) and is best applied when approaching landings. A bow rudder can also be used to move the bow sharply toward the paddle side when the paddle is angled about 20 degrees from the bow. There will be a lot of water pressure on the bow blade in this stroke so it is advis-able to brace the paddle shaft on the gunwale.

4. DRAW STROKE

The draw stroke accomplishes movement to the side the paddle is working on. Start the stroke as far out from the gunwale as you can reach, with the blade facing the gunwale, and draw the paddle towards you. In this stroke, you are actually pulling the canoe to the paddle. In swift current, where sideways maneuverability is

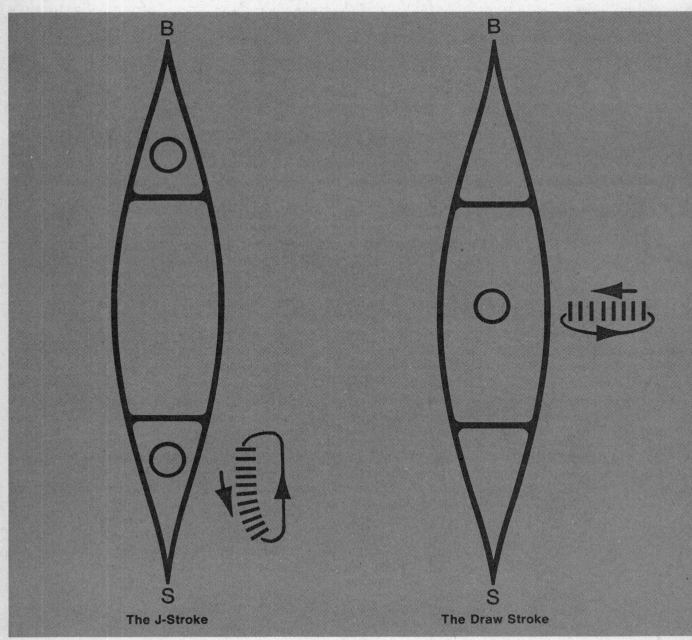

The J-Stroke **The Draw Stroke**

vital, the draw is the most important and powerful stroke in canoeing. It can be modified to a variety of angles. Bow and stern paddlers draw together on the same side to maneuver the canoe directly sideways or on opposite sides to execute a pivot turn.

5. CROSS-DRAW

This stroke is performed more efficiently at the bow than stern or amidship. The paddler pivots at the waist and swings the paddle over the canoe to make a draw stroke on the opposite side of the canoe without shifting his grip. This stroke enables you to pull your end of the canoe to either side.

6. CROSS-BACKSTROKE

This stroke permits back paddling on either side

without changing the grip. It is similar to the cross-draw but differs because the stroke draws from the stern toward the bow.

7. SCULL

An alternative to the draw strokes, sculling is used for movement to the side. As in a draw, the paddle is away from the hull. The blade is then worked in a forward-backward manner, alternating blade angle as the paddle is pulled steadily toward the boat. The blade action puts pressure on the blade face nearest the canoe and draws the canoe toward the paddle. The action is reversed to move the canoe away from the paddling side. In sculling, a paddler leans somewhat on the paddle for effective stroking.

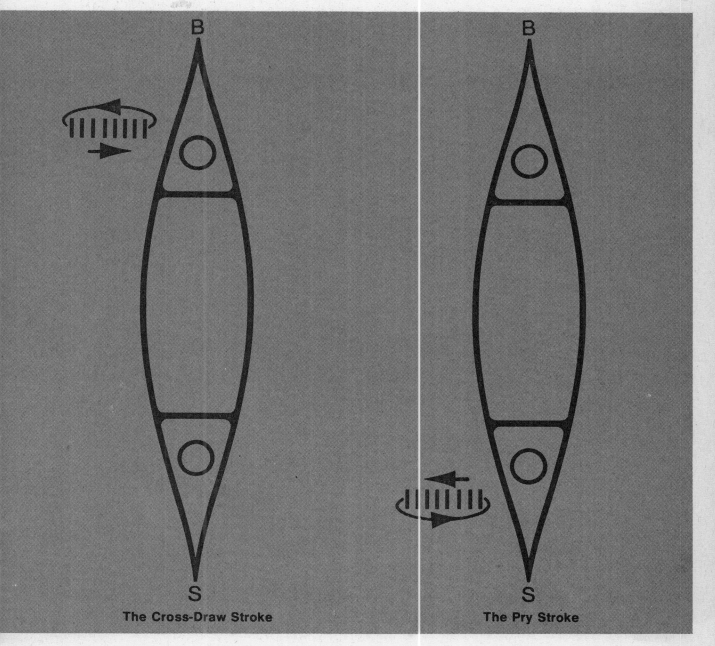

The Cross-Draw Stroke   The Pry Stroke

8. PRY

This is an effective stern stroke for side movement or turning because the blade has powerful leverage. A strong outward motion is necessary for making this stroke effective. It is a good stability stroke since a paddler need not change sides in heavy water. It is, however, not as powerful as the draw stroke. Because of the angle of the paddle and stroke, it can capsize a canoe if paddle and rock or limb make contact in shallow water.

9. SWEEP

This is a wide arc stroke used for power and turning. Single paddlers, near amidship use the sweep of a 180-degree arc, well out from gunwale to a finish near the boat, for sharp canoe turns. A stern sweep traces the forward path of an arc, beginning close to the gunwale and ending away from it to complete the arc. A back sweep, in bow or stern, is the reverse of the forward sweep.

10. INVERTED SWEEP

The stroke begins like a bow draw, then blossoms into a sharply hooked J-stroke while sweeping next to the gunwale at midpoint in its arc. This is a good stroke to use for turning sharply toward the paddle side when paddling from the center of the canoe.

At first, strokes should be thought-out techniques to match the type of water. But it does not take long for them to become second nature.

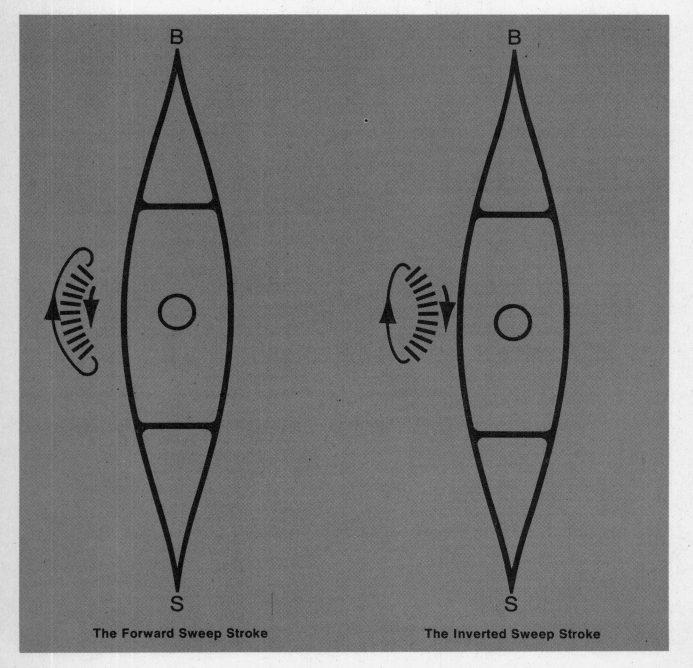

| The Forward Sweep Stroke | The Inverted Sweep Stroke |

Left—The real enjoyment of canoeing comes with knowledge of proper strokes. Note follow-through on sweep. Above—Here's the start of the forward sweep stroke. Below—Bow paddler starts draw stroke and stern paddler changes sides. The dog is dog-paddling, obviously.

Canoe Safety

An overloaded or improperly trimmed canoe is an open invitation to capsizing or swamping.

DIFFERENT brands and styles of canoes have varying degrees of stability. "Goosey" might be one word to describe the raw stability of canoes. And, what manufacturers and avid canoeists describe as "good stability" may reflect instead the skill and knowledge of the canoeist. Stability is, in reality, a low center of gravity, good trim, smooth proficient stroking, and common sense. Increased canoe stability is directly proportional to increased canoeing proficiency. It is the inherent quality of the craft that begs to be balanced, controlled and made stable. A good canoeist makes a canoe good.

Because stability and balance are a challenge, like the difference between *riding* a bicycle and *operating* a car, there comes with canoeing special considerations for safety. Consider a few points.

Swimming Ability

Can a person really enjoy canoeing if he or she cannot swim? Yes, provided that person's inability to swim has not resulted from a fear of water. Swimming, dog paddling, or back floating should be mastered before attempting to canoe. In addition, each canoeist should learn how to negotiate currents if the boat should capsize. That is, by floating on the back with legs up and out, facing downstream. In event of spilling, the canoeist should assume this position as soon as he hits the water. Like downhill skiing, the best practice is falling down. For canoeing, dunk yourself in the water first and get the feel of the current.

Canoe Instruction

Take it! There's a wide variety of clubs, civic groups, sportsmen's organizations, Boy Scouts, Girl Scouts, Red Cross, YMCA, YWCA, camps, city and state agencies that offer canoe lessons free or for a nominal charge. Lessons prevent bad habits, help overcome fears and guide novices through decisions about buying equipment of their own. Many beginner classes develop into enduring canoe clubs. And good canoeing streams are often located through classes and clubs. Instructional pamphlets and books are fine, but nothing beats the firsthand learning process with fellow novices who share a common interest and goal.

Life preservers have added some style. Most boating vests are U.S. Coast Guard approved and can be worn comfortably at all times.

Life Preservers

Life preservers live up to their name. They save lives. Today preservers are also known as flotation jackets or vests, flotation devices, life saving devices, life jackets, competition vests, canoe vests and buoyant vests or jackets—all are labeled PFDs (Personal Flotation Devices) by the Coast Guard. Few today are *not* Coast Guard approved (for example, water skiing belts are not approved "devices"), however, make sure that any you wear are stamped or labeled "Coast Guard Approved." Also, make sure that the PFD is properly sized for the wearer: most have a weight specification included with the Coast Guard approval.

Modern vests or jackets are filled with closed cell marine foam flotation and are less bulky than the old standard, kapok or cork preservers. Quite possibly, one of the most important, yet unheralded, advances in sport boating in recent years has been the modernization of the life preserver. Why? Personal Flotation Devices are now attractive, formfitting, and comfortable. This means they can be worn at *all* times when canoeing, rather than tucked under the seats. Foam nylon shells, insulated against cold and heat, double their usefulness. They are made in men's, ladies' and child's sizes. Front zippers, side adjustments and quick release buckles make wearing vests and jackets more convenient and pleasant.

Canoe Streams and Rivers

Safety means knowing that some streams and rivers are far beyond the skills of average canoeists. Leave heavy white water, dangerous chutes and rapids to the experts who are fully aware of the consequences of mistakes. Choose streams recom-

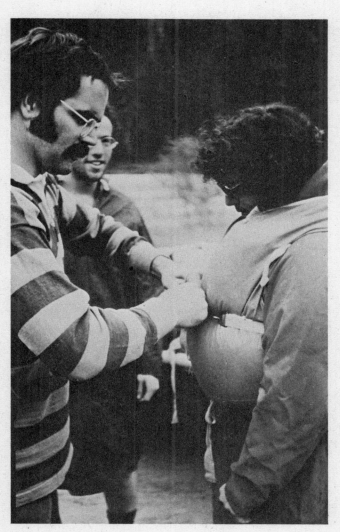

The most important canoe safety rule: *Wear properly fitted life jackets when afloat.*

Opposite page—Snags such as tree branches and rocks require preplanning moves and strokes far in advance. A good knowledge of strokes and life preservers are musts for white water running.

Above—Practice righting a capsized canoe *before* taking that float trip. Right—Even when swamped, canoes should have enough built-in flotation to prevent foundering.

mended for canoeing. Judge the difficulty of a stream not only by its course, obstacles and water flow, but by water temperature, wind and chill factors, and ingress and egress routes in case of emergency. Realize that the most notorious white water rivers in the country are negotiated mainly by large, commercially operated, inflatable rafts run by professionals.

The Tip or Hit and Fall

You will, at one time or another, tip over in a canoe or hit an obstacle that forces the boat to tip over. That's why it is good to practice falling out of a canoe in a swimming pool or in a quiet stretch on a nice warm day. Make falling out of a boat a reflex movement. Several things should be kept in mind. You may want to exit and then grab the canoe to prevent it from floating away and to use the boat for flotation. As you fall, keep your hands and arms in front of your face and head to avoid being hit by the boat or obstacles in or along the river. Roll out of the boat rather than making a panicked effort to get away from it. One of the worst things is getting a foot, leg or arm trapped inside.

Entrapment

There are more cases of fatal or injurious entrapment in kayaks than in canoes, but canoe entrap-

ment occasionally occurs. Some canoes are manufactured with cross bracing under the thwarts and seats for extra strength. However, the braces can snare a leg or foot, preventing a hasty exit. In a similar fashion, extremely low slung seats or those with shelves or braces can be death traps to a canoeist wedged or snagged underneath an overturned boat.

Sloppy bow and stern or anchor lines (the reason why good boatmen place such importance on properly coiled and placed ropes) are other hazards that can trap you under a canoe. In addition the current can cause entrapment under logs, rocks, holes and brush. If dumped from a canoe, swim or float away from obstacles that can pin you down in heavy current.

Avoid Snags

Although some boats bounce off snags in moderate to heavy currents, a canoe usually does not. Possibly one of the most difficult maneuvers that a novice or intermediate faces in a stream is being sucked by the current into dangerous snags. Shallow water snags, such as, tree trunks, branches, rocks or brush are usually not as troublesome as those found in deep, heavy water. Safety dictates avoiding such snags by pre-planning moves and strokes far enough in advance.

Stay With the Boat

There are times when lake canoeing or stream running that you can elect to stay with a capsized boat. On a lake, the boat can help you reach shore. On a stream, you can float through the riffles until you get to calm or shallow water to beach the canoe. In heavy water, it is often advisable to move away from the boat, which could hit or entrap you. Another alternative is to stay clear of the boat, yet retain a hold on the bow or stern rope.

First Step Could Be The Last

In a crouching position, with hands on the gunwales, enter a canoe carefully by putting one foot near the middle of the floor, sliding the torso over the gunwales and slowly swinging the other foot in. Have a partner steady the canoe with a paddle as you enter or exit. Exiting should also be performed in low profile, one foot at a time. Stepping directly into or exiting a canoe or small boat in an upright position without any kind of handhold usually causes a capsize and discouragement.

Proper Clothing

Dress warmly enough so that cold or chilly weather does not force you to make questionable decisions and mistakes. Cooler waterway temperatures and wind can produce cold bodies and foolish haste. Extra clothes can always be shed. Rain gear is standard equipment.

Hypothermia

Hypothermia is caused by severe lowering of the body temperature. Body heat is lost at a faster rate than the system can replace it. Cold, wetness and wind can cause it. It's a good idea to have some idea of survival times in cold water—survival time in 30 or 40 degree water is, at best, only a few minutes without proper protection. A scuba diver's wet suit is the best precaution for cold water temperatures and weather.

Canoe Camping

IT IS FALL and the leaves have turned tawny. The day is crisp and filled with an unbelievable array of satisfying smells. Somewhere downstream campers burn logs of cedar, and an ever so slight upstream breeze carries wafts of sweet scent to my nostrils. How long has it been since I smelled the perfume of an outdoor fire?

The canoe glides ahead with a mere slice of the paddle. The water is flat and sweet, eager to please. Although at times I crave the bounce of churning white, I savor the level ride. It feels good and so do I. Oaks and trunk-to-trunk black walnuts line the banks. It is damp along the river, and a thick earthen aroma hangs heavy. Wisps of camp smoke and bottomland musk unite and form a blend so pleasurable I wish the stuff could be caught, bottled, and rationed later on in the city where I need it.

In early morning there is a stillness on the river that can be felt sharply in the chest. I know there are whitetail deer along this stretch. I've seen them. And wild turkeys and squirrels, too. They are there now along the banks, and although not in view, their eyes are penetrating. They watch me glide. And they see me as a log floating on the water and they drink. Smooth, soft and silent, boat and boatman do not scare them. It feels good to be once again a part of things natural.

This is the time of the mallard and the honker. A hen hidden on a back slough sounds a series of low, gutteral quacks. And a drake responds with an excited, high-pitched voice. After I have drifted past, the two will come together on the river.

A chorus starts somewhere off in the distance and grows in intensity at each stroke of the paddle. Soon the sounds in unison are near the river in a staggered V formation. The Canada geese are treetop high coming on fast and sure with slow, powerful wing beats and bugling notes of fall migration. As they fly over the river, their chests and necks dip and rise gracefully with each wing beat. Despite the fact that I ceased paddling and sat quietly mesmerized at their appearance, the honkers flare at my presence and angle off sharply to the east. Their nasal cries take on a panicked squeal, and they quickly put distance between us.

The sun climbing steadily through the trees sets a misty glow to the "riverscape." The breeze picks up, and the russet leaves flutter and crackle from spindly limbs. The day is blossoming bright. Gone is the filtered veil of intimate dawn. My thoughts turn to camp.

The cedar logs have burned low, and the wind that stirs the coals bellows them crackling orange. My wife Kathy and daughter Brittany are huddled close to the embers as I beach the canoe. It is the aroma of bacon and eggs now that dominates the morning air. Our tent, nestled in the oaks, drips with autumn dew, and the beagle Radar greets me with long ears and a wagging tail. The dawn float had filled my spirit, and only the return to camp could cap off a greater sense of natural living. We were together, sharing what the woods and the river had to offer. There would be times for fishing, hiking, photography and just plain talking, and for a family what more could there be together?

The Complete Canoe Camp

Rivers and streams in almost every part of the country are avenues to the finest camping and outdoor adventure available to us today. The combination of swift, silent canoes and modern lightweight camping equipment results in comfortable, mobile outdoor living that has few equals. Depending on the size of the canoe, the number of passengers, and packing ability, the canoe camper has a choice of conventional gear or lightweight, compactable backpack gear. With the addition of ultralight fishing gear, miniature cameras, and lightweight but warm clothing, the canoe camp can be a complete and wonderful outdoor experience.

Conventional Canoe Camp Equipment

In a 17-foot canoe, a camper can carry nearly every bit of essential camp gear. Equipment includes a modern exterior framed 8-foot × 10-foot tent, down or Dacron Fiberfill II sleeping bags with their own stuff sacks and waterproof plastic covers, and foam sleeping pads. For the outdoor kitchen, pack a gas stove, ice coolers of appropriate size to handle individual or family needs, gas lantern, and food bag with nonperishables (dehy-

Left—All is well at camp and the boats are beached for the afternoon. Below—There is good talk to be shared around the fire.

drated and freeze-dried foods and snacks), plates and utensils. The clothing bag should be stuffed with extra socks, underwear, slacks, shirts, rain gear and jackets. Everything that is essential for a comfortable, efficient camp a boater can pack. Also important is the manner in which the gear and food is packed, stowed and secured.

Individual canvas or heavy nylon stuff sacks are best for dividing up gear into stowable sizes. Everything should be bagged to keep it organized. As a further precaution against rain or spills, heavy-duty plastic garbage bags are used as outside coverings and tightly secured to make them virtually waterproof. The most common mistake canoe campers make is believing gear does not have to be tied down for flat water trips. Lash all gear to center thwarts so in case of a spill none of it will be lost. Lashing only takes a few extra minutes and is worth the extra effort.

Keep loads low and amidships unless traveling alone where some of it can be used for trim. Long items such as tent bags and poles along with fishing rods can be packed on either side of the keel line so they are out of the way. Some tents have poles that break down into numerous sections and don't take up much room. Tents should be folded into carrying bags so they fit amidships. Multi-section, break-down pack rods are much easier to stow and keep from breaking, than one or two piece rods. The heaviest items should be packed on a plastic floor cloth first and lighter gear packed on top of them. Try to keep most of the load below the gunwales. There will be times when that is impossible. When the load exceeds gunwale height, a canvas or nylon pack cover should be placed over the individual packs, tied as one large bundle, and secured to the thwarts. This keeps the lighter, top-of-the-load items from falling off and gives protection in case of bad weather or heavy water.

Good food and plenty of it is a welcome part of the canoe camping adventure.

Just a few of the choices a canoe camper has in the way of tents.

Camp Food

Don't skimp on food. Dehydrated and canned foods are fine. A mixture of fresh and canned meats and vegetables offers pleasing variety. I feel the success and morale of many camps is based on the quality of food and how it is prepared. Your canoe offers enough room for a generous selection of good, nutritional foods. For packing food, items like flour, instant soups, milk, salt, and sugar can be removed from rigid, hard-to-pack boxes and double-sacked with plastic. Identify the sack since many powdered or granulated foods look alike. Cooking instructions or recipes can be cut from the box and placed in the plastic sack. A day's menu at a canoe camp might go like this:

Breakfast

Eggs and blueberry pancakes. An omelet made with powdered eggs hits the spot when served with bacon or sausage. A baking mix, like Bisquick, really proves its worth for drop biscuits or easy light pancakes. A real treat on the river is to add a cupful of berries (frozen blueberries work great if there are none available for picking) to a cup of baking mix. Combine milk, egg and oil with batter and pour out the cakes on a hot griddle. Serve with syrup or honey, butter and hot coffee.

That's canoe camping!

Lunch

Our family likes camp lunches light because they usually come at odd times after fishing or swimming. Smoked or dried sausage or salami, cheese, crackers, soup and fruit provide simple but satisfying lunches. Plenty of cold drinks or in early spring and fall hot chocolate, bouillon or coffee tops off the meal. Sweets may not be recommended nutritionally, but they can be satisfying desserts for river lunches.

Supper

Our favorite is fresh caught bass, trout, walleye or panfish fillets coated in a batter of egg, salt, pepper, Bisquick and beer—mixed to the consistency of pancake batter. Fillets are fried fast in hot bacon grease or oil in a skillet. They are done (flaky and light) when golden brown on each side. Top off with hush puppies (2 cups cornmeal, 1 cup flour, salt, 2 tsp. baking powder, 3 tbsp. bacon grease and chopped onion. Add enough water to make stiff dough. Roll into thumb-size pieces and fry with fish in deep fat), wow! A salad made with fresh watercress tops off the dinner. Camp meals like this are just as unforgettable, as the river camps themselves.

Portaging

TO PORTAGE, according to Webster, is the act of carrying. Boats or goods are carried overland between navigable waters along a specific route.

Portaging has been associated mainly with canoeing because special techniques and equipment have been devised for the portaging of canoes. However, portaging kayaks and inflatable boats around river obstacles is just as practical and may be a bit easier. Small rafts can be deflated and backpacked for long portages. Kayaks can be side carried without much problem since most of them weigh under 40 pounds.

Many of the methods that apply to canoe portaging also apply to other river craft as well.

Why Portage?

There are a variety of reasons that can make portaging necessary. In order to get from one lake or pond to another, a short overland portage may be necessary if there is no water channel connecting the two bodies of

Good balance, a good carrying yoke, and strong shoulders and legs are keys to successful portaging.

Opposite page—One man portages while the other hauls gear. Canoe is up in front for good visibility.

Left—Young girl displays sidearm thwart portage with lightweight canoe. Below—Two-man portage for short distances to and from landings works well.

water. Sometimes a stream or channel connects two or more lakes, but the water might be impassable due to swiftness of the current, rocks, bridges, gradient, or water depth. Rather than fighting water or water obstacles, it is often deemed safer and more practical to beach the boat, stow gear on board or in backpacks and walk from one body of water to another. The distance between bodies of water, the number of portage miles, may vary from only a few yards to several miles. Some areas, like the lakes and river district of the north central United States and the Canadian provinces, are characteristically portage lakes and rivers. Portaging can be considered a very natural part of any canoe trip.

When planning a canoe trip, a paddler should realize that portaging can only be described as *work*. Long portages may be impractical. Short portages over or through extremely rough terrain may not really be worth the effort. But portages under 3 miles over relatively mild terrain can add a change of pace to an extended cruise and can be somewhat enjoyable. Portaging is basically a means to an end, offering degrees of satisfaction and adventure. Short, flat portages under a mile should not present any problems even for novices.

Aside from portaging from one lake or stream to another, portages are sometimes required to reach paddle water at the start of a trip or get to the road or pickup vehicle after the trip. In relatively unknown areas, it's a good idea to consult topographic maps to gauge the distances of portages ahead of time. Some trips have

actually been ruined before they began by sore shoulders, backs and hands—paddlers who tried to bite off more than they could chew.

Portaging is also used to bypass obstacles, danger areas or difficult stretches that canoeists feel are not worth the risk or beyond their paddling abilities. Low bridges, fences, blind bends or drops, characterized by heavy current, are spots for novice and veteran alike to consider portaging. These decisions often come upon the paddler very quickly. On a new stretch of river and if in doubt, the best rule is to portage. That decision may require some extra work and loss of float time, but smart boaters will stay dry and enjoy the rest of the float. Nearly every canoeist who has progressed to the advance stage of paddling has wished, at some time or another, that he or she would have chosen portaging over ''blind luck.'' Staying on a time schedule, keeping up with the other boats, and fear of being too cautious are flimsy reasons for not portaging. Good canoeists are good portagers.

Portaging Techniques

Most persons, and some boaters, think of portaging as a one-man struggle with a canoe balanced on top of the shoulders. That is but one technique of portaging and, if done correctly, should not be a struggle. However, there are many ways of carrying a canoe over land. The first and most simple for very short distances is the *side carry* by one person with hands on the gun-

wale at amidship and the canoe carried snugly against the hips. Frequent rest breaks will be needed, but this technique is all right for portages under 200 yards for a single person.

There are also two-, three- and four-person carries, using handholds near bow and stern with canoe righted or (with four men) in the inverted position. Two men, with their gear stowed on board and carrying light day packs, can carry a canoe a long way by taking slow, short steps and using bow and stern handholds.

Over snow and ice, a canoe or kayak can be towed like a sled. In some northern climes, lake and river water opens before all the snow has melted from the ground. Gear and paddles can be stowed in the boat and pulled by one or two persons with a bow rope of 10 or 15 feet in length. Sledding the canoe over deep, soft snow is much more practical than trying to carry it. Snowshoes help, but even then breaking through the crust is hard on legs and shoulders when carrying a boat.

A single person portage is common and when using some type of carrying yoke that evenly distributes the weight of the boat, this method works reasonably well.

An on-the-spot yoke can be made by taking two paddles and lashing them across the center thwarts. The shaft knobs can be tied on opposite sides of each other against the gunwales while the blades can be lashed to the other thwart so they overlap. The blades, with rolled up jacket or life vest as shoulder pads, ride on the portager's shoulders like a yoke while the for-

Cartopping can be a form of portaging from one lake or stream to another. Strong tie-downs are a must.

ward portion of the canoe is supported with hands on the gunwales. If a lot of portaging is predicted, commercially manufactured carrying yokes, available from most canoe manufacturers as optional equipment, are handy. Yokes, with cushioned pads angled to fit the shoulders, mount on the center thwart and can be left there, ready anytime for portaging. Paddles can be tied to the thwarts when not used as carrying yokes.

Getting the canoe onto one's back can be accomplished by positioning the canoe on its side, with the bottom of the hull facing you. Lift the boat onto your knee and then with the other hand grab the center thwart and in one continuous motion, using your knee to help lift, roll the canoe over and onto your back. By starting off with a good center of balance, at the yoke thwart, you will have little difficulty placing the cushioned pads on your shoulders. Legs should be spread to about the width of the shoulders for good balance. The front end of the canoe will be tilted upward so the boat is resting on the shoulders and supported by the arms. The portager, of course, will not be able to see overhead or to the sides, but should have a good view directly ahead when the boat is tilted. Walk with smooth, steady steps.

Coming out from under the canoe can be accomplished in a variety of ways, depending on the strength of the portager. Some paddlers bring arms in to the shoulders, slide boat forward off the carrying pads and yoke. Then, in one continuous motion, lift the boat off the shoulders, roll it over, grab the closest part of the center thwart or gunwale, and slide the canoe down off the hips and onto the ground.

Another way is to drop the downward end to the ground, bring arms in to the shoulders, lift off the pads, and rotate head and body. By pressing the canoe upward and using the arms for support, walk out from under the boat, being careful not to let it roll over and fall.

A third method of getting out from under a portaged canoe is to set the front of the boat on a limb, fence or wall and duck walk out from under the boat.

Portage Packs

Small to medium size day packs or soft, internally framed packs make ideal portage packs. Conventional backpacks ride high enough to interfere with yoke portaging. However, they are fine for other portaging techniques. Remember that portaging is work. Gear should be limited as much as possible.

L. L. Bean of Freeport, Maine, makes a wonderful woven ash pack basket, rigid enough to carry breakable items but flexible and low-riding enough for comfort.

Portaging Tips

Sometimes the easiest looking portage routes are not the best. Dense timber and brush can make portaging frustrating. Consult local canoeists, rangers and topographic maps for best routes. Sacrificing straight portages through dense or hilly terrain for longer routes through flatter, clearer lands is usually best.

Avoid abrupt turns or stops when portaging alone with a yoke. Hitting trees and brush with the boat can be frustrating and lead to painful wear and tear on shoulders, neck and legs. Portage slowly at your own pace.

More than one canoeist, comfortable in the boat with a pair of tennis shoes or boating moccasins, has forgotten to pack along a pair of hiking boots for portaging. Feet and ankles suffer strain when carrying a boat. A good pair of hiking boots, able to protect the feet and ankles against strain, abrasions, wet ground or snow, are as important as a good carrying yoke.

Portaging is laborious, no doubt about it. But the right equipment and know-how, along with good planning, makes it a satisfying part of the paddling experience.

Lining

This is the standard lining technique going upstream—longer bow line than stern line.

WHEN UPSTREAM or downstream paddle control of canoe, kayak or inflatable boat becomes impossible because of shallow, rocky water or swift current, the boater may elect to *line* the craft and prevent injury. It is just one of many techniques a paddler has available as an alternative to negotiating impractical or dangerous waters or those beyond the abilities of the floater. Good boaters make frequent use of lining methods because they work. Uninformed beginners may not be aware of the technique or may believe that getting out of the boat and avoiding difficult stretches is not an acceptable practice. Employing the lining method often shows good judgment. Lining can be a fun alternative to portaging and a good chance to stretch the legs.

What is Lining?

Lining is a technique most effectively used by two persons on shore by which bow and stern lines are used to "line" or guide a boat through a difficult or impassable stretch of water. One-person lining is possible with one or two ropes (manipulating each at the same time). However, two-person lining, one person slightly ahead of the bow and the other at the stern, can be the most efficient method of maneuvering a boat through a nasty stretch.

Lining can be employed either upstream or downstream. Bow and stern ropes should each be about 50 feet long and made of ¼-inch nylon or dacron rope. Be sure, before lining, that ropes are well secured to bow hooks, rings, cleats, bars or grab loops. A weak knot could lead to a damaged or lost boat. For upstream lining, the bow line is kept longer than the stern line in order to angle the boat into the current. The stern line is used for checking the angle. The distance from the liners to the boat depends primarily on the nature of the shoreline and the water. The boat can be lined when going upstream in the calmest water possible, so that it can be easily pulled and guided. Lining distance will vary as ropes are lengthened and drawn to maneuver the boat through and around obstacles.

Downstream lining requires that the bow line be kept shorter than the stern line. The short line keeps the stern headed away from the bank because of the force of the current. And the distance from liners to boat can

Another technique of lining or walking a canoe through an unfloatable passage.

Extremely steep or rocky banks can make it too tough for safe lining.

be varied by lengthening or drawing line as needed. The downstream current in combination with the ropes works the boat in or out.

Is Lining Easier Than Portaging?

Lining can be either easier or more difficult than portaging, depending on the nature of the shoreline and the obstacles in the stream. For short stretches where gear can be kept on board, lining is usually the preferred method. If the land along the river is impractical for portaging—no clear trails and steep terrain, it is usually better to line. Where portaging routes would take the boaters away from the stream, lining might be the best technique.

On the other hand, some streams can be so full of rocks, logs or debris that lining is frustrating and next to impossible. An extremely swift current could discourage lining. Jagged, boggy, slippery, steep or meandering shorelines are often so tough to line (without falling or getting wet) that it is far better to portage. Upstream lining can be hard work pulling against the current. The longer the distance that needs to be covered, the more favorable portaging becomes.

The Hazards of Lining

Lining a canoe along a rocky, moss-covered shore where it is difficult to stand much less tow an 85-pound boat demonstrates one of the hazards of lining. Going upstream, the bow liner although doing his share of the pulling often has the better deal. He can work further inshore, away from the slippery rocks, while the stern liner is snubbed close to the boat and nearly in the water The importance of a pair of sturdy non-slip wading shoes or hip waders can't be emphasized enough here. Barefooting is dangerous. And shoes with little support can lead to sprains and bruises.

In regard to techniques, the main mistake that should be avoided by liners is lack of rope control (resulting ordinarily from a mix-up of signals from bow and stern men), which leads to the boat turning broadside in a heavy current and flipping. Keep the bow angled into the current and make sure it does not get too far broadside.

When some boaters give up and head home, those who use lining to get through the obstacles may be in for special treats.

Poling—A Tradition

CANOE POLING is a tradition that is not widely known or used even among canoeists. The American Canoe Association sponsors national poling competition, and good polers are a pleasure to watch. The most satisfying poling, though, comes from doing rather than observing. It is a technique that can be self-taught if a few rules of the pole are followed.

The setting pole is a low water tool used to navigate shallow rocky streams, ponds or lakes where a paddle can't really get a good bite on the water. Al Beletz, American Canoe Association Poling Chairman, in his article, "Canoe Poling Evaluation" (*Canoe* Magazine) estimates most small streams generally have an average poling depth of 4 to 12 inches. "Ideal for probing from the standing position."

Standing in a canoe? Yes. The pole is used to snub, check and alter downstream travel. For upstream maneuvering, the pole bites against the bottom to drive the canoe forward against the water.

It takes a special stream or a special stretch for poling. The stream should be uniformly shallow if a pole is to be used exclusively. However, it's also a good

Fishermen often use poling methods for working the shallows.

idea to always have a paddle along to rectify poling mistakes or in case you encounter deep water.

Poling can be used to navigate streams considered too narrow or too shallow for standard paddling techniques. A simple 10- or 20-foot-long pole, made of straight grained spruce or aluminum, opens up a new and different world of stream running.

Small stream navigation can be a pleasurable, slow-paced, intimate relationship with the often secretive world of meandering water courses. A poler gets close to stream life in and along the water. There is time to get involved. Birds, animals, and fish take on a special meaning, and the poler becomes *part* of the environment rather than an observer. It is a floating world in miniature. But best of all, both downstream and upstream, poling is possible.

It is the constant snubbing action of the pole on a downhill run that keeps the canoe on course. This is a skill acquired mostly by feel. An open canoe, 15 to 17 feet in length, is fine for poling. Regardless of the size, the downstream end of the canoe should be trimmed so it will stay in alignment with the current. A single poler can stand behind the center thwart when going upstream and just in front of the center thwart when running downstream. Without trimming, either by body positioning or cargo, canoes will turn broadside.

Whether going upstream or downstream, the pole is snubbed or pushed on the side of the boat that opposes the current. So the side of the canoe opposite the pole is angled very slightly toward the current. This angle and the working of the pole keeps the boat in control and is the basic guiding principle behind poling. Quick and constant snubs and smooth, timely pushes can keep a canoe exactly on course and enable the poler to maneuver around rocks and other obstacles. The pole can also be used to brake the canoe to a complete stop while going upstream. On slow downstream runs, medium pressure can be put on the pole for sure stops. Swifter runs require a series of braking snubs, similar in many ways to pumping the brakes of a car.

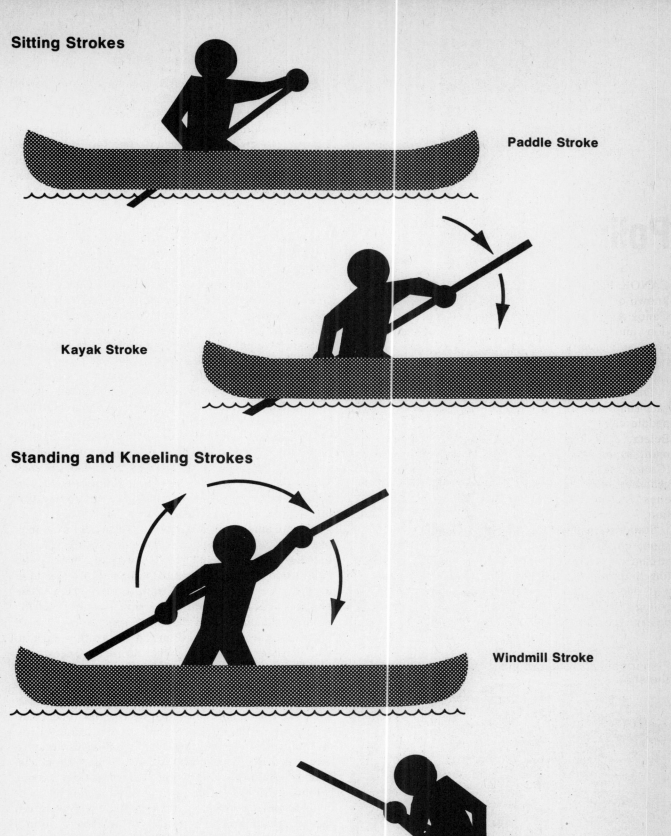

Sitting Strokes

Paddle Stroke

Kayak Stroke

Standing and Kneeling Strokes

Windmill Stroke

Kneeling Stroke

Poling techniques can be used on shallow streams for quick, sure control.

Standing or Sitting

Poling seems to violate the commandment, "never stand up in a canoe." And it does. The pole however, is not only used as a snubber and pusher, but also as crutch and balancing stick. Foot and body balance is especially important. The foot on the poling side should be slightly forward of the other foot—and with the feet at least 12 inches apart for good balance. A pair of deck shoes or boating moccasins with non-skid soles aids surefootedness. Barefoot poling can be slippery.

Standing is the traditional method of poling and the trickiest to master. However, a poler in the standing position has good pole angle for quick, strong snubbing downstream and upstream pushing. Standing in a canoe requires good balance, quite similar to downhill skiing in that flex at the knees (to absorb the jolts) and a looseness at the hips with responsive weight shifting right and left, are the ingredients for good balance.

The standing poler has the advantage of being able to better see the course downstream or upstream. When poling from a standing position, a canoeist feels like he is walking on water. The entire body and all the senses are alert to the boat and the current underfoot.

Sitting kayak-type of strokes can also be used when poling downstream, using a lightweight aluminum pole. Upstream pushing from the sitting position can be used in slow currents. Moderate to swift currents, however, require standing or kneeling, again with the boat trimmed downstream. Finding the course of least resistance is a constant and entertaining challenge in upstream poling. The middle of the river most commonly displays the strongest current, so the poler seeks the edge of the current and side eddies closest to shore.

A rather wide grip is required to insure good arm and shoulder movement, which in turn assures solid snubbing and pushing strokes. Choose the grip and leverage that feels best to you. But remember not to use the pole in front of your body, but rather to the side when shoulders and hips are rotated. The snubbing end of the pole if hooked or caught only momentarily on the bottom could be enough to throw you off balance and into the water. Work the pole to one side or the other and don't get caught behind it.

One does not have to be a purist poler to enjoy this delightful change of pace. In fact, the combination of pole and paddle serves nicely on many small and medium float streams. And the combination of the two techniques adds immensely to the pleasure of the total canoeing experience. Used as a fishing tool, the poler-fisherman combination is a sure, silent way of working quiet, clear streams.

The American Canoe Association

"**DO YOU LOVE** nature—hate noise? Do you prefer to spend leisure time enjoying what's left of our natural environment—in the mountains, forests and deserts, the lakes, rivers and streams? Do you like to camp, hike, swim and ski? Do you love the spirit of competition? The American Canoe Association is in a pretty good position to know what makes a canoe or kayak paddler tick. One nice opportunity you have in store is that the 'not too many' friends you choose share your views about the outdoors. So the canoeist you meet 20 miles up the river is getting away from it, maybe daydreaming a little, like you. A canoeist is often a fast friend, even before you learn his last name. You don't have to own a canoe or kayak to belong to the ACA. All that is necessary is an interest in one or more of the

campaigns on issues that affect the waterways and access to them. As with most environmentally concerned groups, there is strength in numbers. It is through the Association that individuals can make their feelings known as well as take active roles in public hearings concerning river use and development.

The Association is a member of the International Canoe Federation and represents American canoeists in all international canoeing matters. As "Class A" members of the U.S. Olympic Committee, the ACA serves as the sport's governing body for all American canoeists in national and international competition.

One benefit of the ACA that proves helpful to many canoeists is information on river trails, canoe cruises and touring. Members of the ACA can obtain this in-

Organized in 1880

American Canoe Association

National Headquarters: 4260 EAST EVANS AVENUE, DENVER, COLORADO 80222
Telephone (303) 758-8257

many different recreational or competitive activities of canoe sport."—from *Canoe with the ACA* (The American Canoe Association, organized in 1880.)

Because the sports of canoeing and kayaking are learned better from qualified instructors and enjoyed more by groups of people, the American Canoe Association provides a strong voice for organized canoeists across the country. Whether solitary paddlers or canoe club members, everyone concerned about the two sports and the preservation and protection of fine canoeing and kayaking waterways benefits from the ACA.

Because the foundation of good canoeing is good water, one of the primary concerns of the ACA is conservation and preservation of canoeable waterways and the natural environment. The Association actively

formation on an advisory service type basis. Educational and training services with emphasis on sharpening canoeing skills and increasing water safety and enjoyment are also available from the Association or from cooperative programs with the American National Red Cross, Boy Scouts, Girl Scouts, YMCA, YWCA and other national and local groups. The ACA organizes competitive canoeing such as Flatwater Paddling; Slalom and Wildwater Racing; Long Distance Racing; Canoe Poling; Sailing and Rafting. Racing rule books are provided by the Association.

Canoe Magazine

One of the real bonuses of belonging to the ACA is the fine magazine they publish six times a year. After reviewing several issues of *Canoe*, complete with

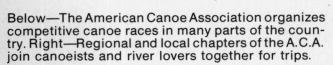

Below—The American Canoe Association organizes competitive canoe races in many parts of the country. Right—Regional and local chapters of the A.C.A. join canoeists and river lovers together for trips.

four-color covers and inside features, I found them hard to put down. Photos were good, story topics and writing were better. The novice paddler, as well as the veteran, can enjoy the magazine. The editors balance how-to's, equipment evaluation, and true canoe and kayak adventure stories. Written and edited in a professional manner, the magazine definitely incites the canoeing heart to pump faster.

An ACA membership is based on the calendar year. And all those who join after September 15th are accredited for the following year. All classes of membership—Sustaining ($14), Governing Member ($10), and Junior, those who have not reached their 18th birthday ($6)—entitle persons to participate in all local, divisional and national activities as well as to receive subscriptions to all official publications. The ACA is divided into 13 geographic divisions, and activities in the individual, self-governing divisions are determined by the interests of the members and the available canoeing waters.

Membership applications can be obtained by writing: American Canoe Association National Office, 4260 East Evans Avenue, Denver, Colorado 80222 or by telephone: (303) 758-8257.

In addition to the ACA, the American Whitewater

Affiliation (AWA) is a volunteer organization of paddlers and clubs interested in white water sport. The AWA publishes the bi-monthly *American Whitewater Journal*, which offers entertaining float features along with up-to-date information on techniques, equipment, safety, conservation, racing and river access develop-

ments as well as a complete listing of affiliated clubs and how to contact them.

The AWA publishes an excellent pocket *Safety Code* for river boating in canoe, kayak or raft. Individual membership is $5 per year and club affiliation is $10 per year. For applications write: American Whitewater Affiliation, P.O. Box 1584, San Bruno, CA 94066.

PART 3
INFLATABLE BOATS

Is the Inflatable for You?

IF YOU BRIDLED a giant caterpillar and climbed upon its saddled, fuzzy back, you could liken the ride to that of an inflatable boat in a swift current.

The caterpillar ride of an inflatable—that rolling, liquidy rhythm of bouncing water—is probably the safest and most stable of river float craft. For streams with average to swift currents, and riffles and rapids of significant size and power, inflatable boats (sometimes called "rafts") are the best overall choice. Keep in mind, though, that not all inflatable boats sold today are capable of safely negotiating such powerhouses as the Colorado River's Cataract Canyon or the Green River's Gates of Ladore. Far from it.

It takes special skill and equipment to tackle white water stretches with extremely high pucker factors. Compared to the stability of canoes and johnboats, inflatables allow a greater margin of error. Mistakes made in a canoe or johnboat can result in instantaneous dunking. Those made in rubber or nylon boats can be wet lessons learned without the harshness of capsizing. Where others might swamp, the inflatable will bounce off rocks, logs and banks or caterpillar a way through rough water and whirlpools that may not have been the intended route. While by no means infallible, rafts in moderate currents demand less precise attention to techniques. Some floaters enjoy a greater sense of re-

An inflatable river boat with rowing frame and oars. Note extra oar.

laxation while floating and fishing. As a float boat, inflatables have many advantages.

Family Inflatables

Unlike canoes, trim or balance, (fore and aft, starboard and port) is *less* critical because of the inflatable raft's air chamber design, flat bottom and wider beam. With excellent stability even in swift stream currents or rough lake water, the single inflatable, 10 to 13 feet in length and weight capacity up to 2,000 pounds, is a superior family float craft.

What the canoe lacks in stability and roominess, it makes up for in tradition, swiftness and maneuverability on river or lake. While being a stable craft with a good deal of load space, the hand-propelled inflatable is downright sluggish on lakes and slow streams. Maneuverability is poor. Where there is constant, exciting challenge involved with canoe operation even in the laziest of currents, there may be little or no contest in an inflatable. Boredom and hard work sometimes result. Swift water, of course, is the great equalizer. Challenge and physical exertion stimulate canoeist and rafter alike.

Inflatables are easier to row rather than paddle. Even though boats up to 16 feet can be effectively paddled, rowing affords the floater greater comfort and power. Many inflatables come with oarlocks fastened to the top of the side chambers. The boatman straddles an inflat-

able or canvas seat or kneels on the bottom of the boat to use these integral oarlocks. Far better, particularly for larger inflatables, is the rowing platform which accepts rigid oarlocks and provides the rower with a seat.

The rowing platform, constructed of wood or metal with simple design, elevates the rower and passengers off of the boat floor. As a result, all passengers, includ-

There is a vast difference between boats made for white water and those designed for ponds.

113

ing children and fishermen, enjoy a comfortable ride with freedom of movement. Alternating boatman-passenger roles adds excitement to the float. With a minimum of instruction, children too can handle the inflatable in moderate currents without difficulty. As a family float craft, inflatables certainly rank high for fishing, camping, and river exploration.

The Lone Boatman

A boat from 6 to 10 feet in length is ideal for the lone floater. A longer inflatable without passengers may require some type of ballast in the bow of the boat to hold the nose down in choppy current or head winds. However, in mild to moderate current the solitary floater need not be overly concerned with trim. Ride and maneuverability will not be substantially improved in such situations with more weight. On the contrary, without passenger weight, drag is decreased, and the single floater will notice a marked improvement in handling and maneuverability. The boat becomes wonderfully responsive when rowing from an amidship platform with a set of proper length oars. One of the real pleasures of solitary rafting is that most of the drag weight and resultant work are eliminated.

Safety is always of prime importance. Even though the solitary floater has stability in his or her favor, the lone boater should be aware of pitfalls. Being sucked into a beaver sharpened branch, swept into brush, rocks or bridge abutments, or being swallowed up by a hole at the bottom of a chute are predicaments usually caused by careless downstream observation and failure to plan maneuvers ahead of time. A canoeist might be able to avoid a rock with one good stroke. But missing the same rock in an inflatable involves a greater number of strokes executed far upstream from the menacing boulder. A solitary floater's biggest problem on moderate current might be complacency. When this is overcome, the raft is an ideal boat for the person who likes to seek adventure alone.

Advantages of the Inflatable

An inflatable 10 to 13 feet long with a beam of 5 to 6 feet may only have a hull weight of 70-110 pounds. Yet that boat has a carrying capacity of 700 to 2,000 pounds. The basic principle of inflatables—floating on air—makes these incredible statistics possible. That's why inflatables have extremely *shallow draft* and can caterpillar over the shallowest of riffles.

Because inflatables are relatively *lightweight*, portaging can be accomplished with ease. Over short distances where vegetation is sparse, two men can carry the boat loaded with paddles, fishing rods and camping gear; or one man can carry the craft, the other carrying the gear. Portaging long distances may require the crew to deflate the boat, pack it in a canvas or nylon sack, and strap the load onto a pack frame. One- or two-man pack boats, ideal for mountain lakes, weigh 15 to 50 pounds and are more than worth their weight when fish are hitting far from shore casting range. Larger boats weighing over 100 pounds are impractical to portage long distances. Portaging weight should enter into a decision on what size boat to purchase.

Aside from being lightweight, another important advantage of the inflatable is deflatable *compactability*. A boat of 10 to 13 feet in length can be deflated, rolled and stuffed into a carrying sack approximately 2 feet wide by 4 feet long. It can be transported in a camper or the trunk of a car. Stored in the basement, closet or garage, inflatables take up a minimum of room and may be the most practical boats for apartment dwellers or compact car owners. Over short distances, inflated boats can be secured and carried on the roof of the car without a cartop carrier.

Safety and durability are the results of modern inflatables being constructed of heavy-duty nylon, coated and impregnated with polyvinyl or Dupont Hypalon. These materials can last as long as boats made of aluminum, fiberglass or wood with a *minimum of upkeep*. Inflatables should be stored in cool, dry places. Boats exposed to the sun and elements for days at a time will, no doubt, wear out by cracking and peeling faster than those stored under cover. Water should be drained from boats and talc sprinkled liberally on surfaces before storage. Punctures and pinholes can be mended with special boat repair kits that accompany each new boat and should be carried on board at all times.

Inflatables are available in a wide range of qualities and prices. Avon, Camp-Ways and Zodiac are of higher quality with larger price tags than the bright yellow Taiwan imported boats. The inexpensive craft are built for quiet paddling along lake shores or running streams of mild to moderate currents. Their life span is shorter and upkeep more demanding than costlier models. Expect to pay double the price for a better boat, which may be in the $400 to $1,300 range. The added cost is reflected in top-notch materials and construction and will pay off for those interested in a sturdy, long-wearing, reliable inflatable boat.

Accessories needed for a floating inflatable rig are a set of top quality oars, a rowing platform, life preservers, an inflation pump and an extra oar or two for long trips.

For the serious fisherman floating streams with moderate to swift currents, the inflatable boat has the edge over the canoe or johnboat because of stability and fishing pace caused by boat drag. Besides, the inflatable is a fine overall choice for any kind of stream recreation. There's nothing like the feeling of riding an inflatable caterpillar. It's got a spirit all its own.

Above—For family running, an inflatable boat is a good, stable choice. Below—Here's one way of running the "rapids" in an inflatable.

Choose the Right Inflatable

THERE WAS A time not long ago when rubber rafts (originating from inflatable "Liferafts" used for water emergencies) were lumped into one big category. For many people, the rubber raft was the black military surplus boat with double- or triple-tiered air chambers. They were not much to look at but in great demand by pioneer river runners in all parts of the country. About 15 years ago, before modern companies began manufacturing "rubber boats," the old surplus rafts were in heavy demand. And even today a good number of surplus boats can be found in use.

About 10 years ago, the yellow rubber rafts imported from Taiwan began increasing in popularity. These boats, newcomers to the float scene, joined the surplus boats as choices for prospective river runners. While the surplus boats, gallantly decorated with waterproof patches, were fading from the scene, the yellow import boats were floating strong.

Within the last 5 years pleasure rafting has boomed to the point where new breeds of boats are being manufactured to help meet the demand. Generally speaking, the new boats fall into two distinct classes: 1) double-walled river running boats made of heavy-duty nylon and coated with a Neoprene or Hypalon-based material; and 2) fun or pack boats (most of which are not suitable for river running) constructed of polyvinyl, plastic, or synthetic rubber. The latter class of boats can be enjoyed on flat streams and quiet lakes.

Consumers, in the meantime, have been deluged with the new crop of boats, some of which find their way into discount stores and sporting goods shops. Inflatables of all kinds have received tremendous exposure not only in river resort areas, but in large cities as well.

Exposure for any sport is generally good as many new and better products result. However, there is a vast quality and price difference between inflatable boats used as dingies, or for pond fishing and backpacking and those used to float streams and rivers.

One manufacturer of polyvinyl and synthetic rubber boats states that his boat can be used on the ocean, a river or a lake, but it is compact and light enough to be carried by a child or packed on a bicycle. The boat quite possibly could be used on a quiet pool in a small stretch of river. But, as a safe, adequate river boat that particular model falls dangerously short. Today's consumer must sift through advertising puff.

The most important consideration in choosing the right inflatable is separating fact from fiction when shopping around for boats. There are boats especially designed for stream and white water river use and those better suited for lakes and ponds. Generally speaking, an adequate marina or fishing float boat 10 or 11 feet in length will cost around $200 with oars and options extra. Better boats of the same length without oars but with many "options" included as standard items will cost $400 to $800.

An inadequate river boat usually sells for under $400. An inflatable designed for ponds and packing into mountain lakes sometimes costs less than $60. It is important for the prospective river runner to separate the various classes of inflatables. A boat suitable for strong currents will cost more because of better materials and construction. I have tried both the "cheap" boats and the "expensive" ones in rivers of all classes and find the expensive boats perform far better in all sorts of currents than the cheaper ones.

The Difference Construction Makes

A good river boat is firm and taut due to the air pressure it can hold. A poor one, on the other hand, is "soggy" to the touch despite maximum inflation. This sight and touch test makes a difference on the river. All inflatables have built-in water drag which makes them somewhat difficult to maneuver. But firm boats are far superior to soft boats in handling and ride, and they are safer too! The importance of this attribute is magnified in moderate to heavy currents that require strong, full strokes. The firmer boats respond. The softer boats drag. This can mean

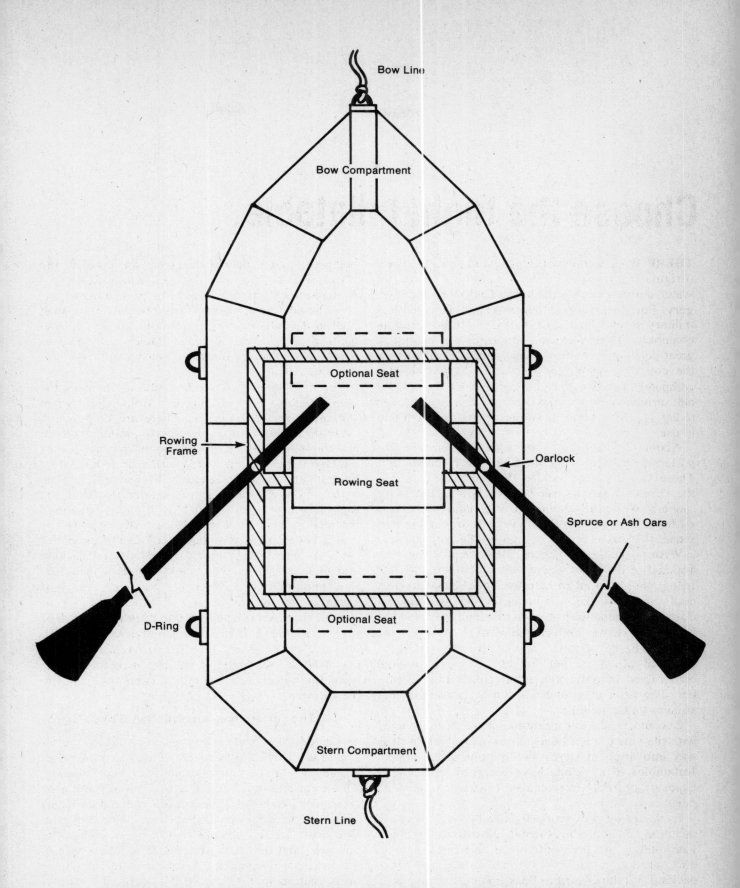

Bow Line

Bow Compartment

Optional Seat

Rowing Frame

Oarlock

Rowing Seat

Spruce or Ash Oars

D-Ring

Optional Seat

Stern Compartment

Stern Line

Basically, this is what the well-equipped river boat should have for safety and comfort.

Above, left—Construction of this boat suits it for lakes and mild rivers. Above—Some boats are suited for marina or tender use. Left—Size is an important factor in choosing a boat. Below—Life raft for emergency use is designed solely for that purpose.

More and more plastic boats are finding their way to a variety of stores. Some of them can be used for gentle currents on some sections of streams. They are far better for small lake use.

Above—Some high performance inflatables can even be used for salt water fishing. Below—This canoe shaped craft is fine for mild currents and small lakes. Right—A boat able to withstand rough use and heavy currents looks something like this.

Medium priced inflatable fitted with rowing frame makes good fishing boat for moderate rivers. Well-equipped fishermen wisely are wearing life preservers.

sideslipping a log rather than running into it, or moderate oar work compared to back breaking labor. You can make the feel test for yourself when considering various brands. Inferior boats have a tendency to bend or fold in the middle when picked up at the bow and stern by two people. This same folding occurs under choppy current and affects maneuverability considerably. The better boats have flow-through flex rather than concentrated flex at the beam. Boat design and hull material account for flex variations.

Basically, manufacturers of good, modern float boats use the latest double- (sometimes called triple-) wall construction. The core of the wall is heavy woven nylon cloth. Both sides of the cloth are coated and impregnated with PVC (polyvinyl chloride) or Dupont Hypalon for toughness and longevity. The manner in which the coating is applied, how the fabric panels are bonded together, and how the seams are adhered produce significant differences among various inflatable brands in regard to construction. Variances in quality are also determined by density and gauge of the nylon threads used in weaving the inner core, the type of weave, and whether or not a weave or single nylon shell is used as the core.

Dropping down a notch in quality are the boats constructed of Neoprene rubberized nylon (or canvas in older boats). They lack the firmness and strength of the double-wall boats due to the thinner coating and poorer nylon material. They are typically yellow in color and imported. However, these boats have produced many enjoyable floats and are quite adequate on streams with mild to moderate current flow up to Class III. They cost considerably less than the woven nylon cloth inflatables.

How Many Air Chambers?

A river boat should have two or more separate air chambers or compartments. Heavy water boats can have as many as six. Some boats have built-in inflatable thwarts as opposed to separate inflatable seats.

The Right Size for You.

If I were to choose the best all-around boat for two to four persons, it would be 12 to 13 feet in length with a beam of 60 to 80 inches. That's a good size to handle—small enough for narrow streams and large enough for broader waters. A boat of that size

weighs 50 to 70 pounds which is relatively easy to handle. The stowed dimensions of such a boat might be around 24 X 48 inches, making transportation possible even in a convertible sports car. Storing such a boat in the house or apartment would be no problem at all.

Inflatables for pleasure cruising come in sizes ranging from 6 to 18 feet. The usual number of expected passengers determines the right size for you. Choose a boat that you can handle and that affords ample room for camping, fishing or photography gear. If your choice is narrowed down to two boats of different lengths, choose the longer, broader model.

Standard Features Versus Options

Generally speaking, the better boats offer more standard features. Some manufacturers offer marine plywood floorboards, bow canopies, hand pumps, foot bellows, maintenance kit, duffel bags or carrying cases, and owner's manual. Dollar for dollar, the cost of these features, offered as options by some suppliers, does not make up the discrepancy in cost between first- and second-class river boats. But they do make a difference.

Beware of Bargain Boats

Discount and military surplus supply houses sometimes advertise "bargain boats" for lake or river use. Prospective floaters should remember there is no such thing as a bargain when it comes to good river running equipment. Perhaps the most common error of novices is falling for money saving come-ons. The best word of advice is to buy your boat from a reputable boat dealer or supplier that backs his product with solid facts, a good reputation and a fair warranty. Some store clerks, not familiar with river running and river craft, categorize most inflatables as white water boats. Search and research on your own. Ask the advice of knowledgeable floaters, professional guides, state and federal fish and game agency personnel, and water management officials.

Good brands to consider are Avon, Bonair, Zodiac and Camp-Ways. Sears-Roebuck and Montgomery Ward also offer a selection of float boats. For the names and addresses of the various manufacturers, see the list of manufacturers and suppliers at the back of this book.

Inflatable Boat Equipment

Unfortunately, some people buy good boats, good platforms and then skimp on oars. Proper length is important, and they should be made of spruce (good power and flex) or ash (tough on rocks) for heavy or moderate waters. Oars not only control boats . . . they master the current.

A GOOD, SOLID foundation to enjoyable, safe river running is built by combining a strong, well-designed inflatable with a sturdy rowing platform, oarlocks and oars. Skimping in one or more areas could interfere with proper rowing strokes. Strokes in mild to strong currents should be positive and strong. A weak link in the system is sure to cause problems because strong currents are relentless testers. And as amazing as it seems, some manufacturers and suppliers of inflatables, while offering optional comfort accessories with their basic boats, have sometimes forgotten to make available to floaters what could be the most important piece of river floating equipment.

The Rowing Platform

In the next section, Inflatable Boat Strokes, strong emphasis is placed on oar angle in relation to boatman and water bite. Good oar angle is vital to controlling the maneuverability of inflatables. Combine inherent sluggishness from water drag with the force of the current, and control without proper oar angle and bite becomes exceedingly difficult. Yet most novice floaters, accepting without question the standard rowing features that some manufacturers have given them, find their inflatables unyielding in a current and more work than fun. The basic problem lies in the fact that oarlocks are mounted on side air chambers. Instead of a rigid, oarlock base that encourages strong strokes, those mounted on air chambers have too much give. This, combined with low seat positioning, makes the blade angle more horizontal than diagonal.

To further weaken the rowing position, undersize, understrength oars made of aluminum or plastic with poor blade design are often recommended. Oars 4 or 5 feet in length that break down into several pieces might be adequate for small pack rafts for lake or pond use, but they are useless in moderate to heavy currents. They are not long enough, have too much flex, and will sometimes fold completely in two under the force of the current. Built-in "slide through" oarlocks permit the oar shafts to slip which results in wasted effort, poor blade angle and inconsistent blade bites. The best function the standard oarlocks perform are as seconds in case of emergency or rowing platform failure.

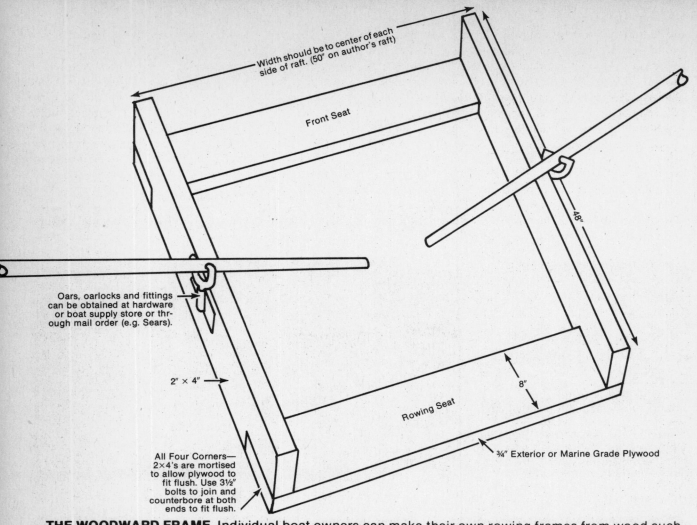

Width should be to center of each side of raft. (50" on author's raft)

Front Seat

48"

Oars, oarlocks and fittings can be obtained at hardware or boat supply store or through mail order (e.g. Sears).

2" × 4"

8"

Rowing Seat

¾" Exterior or Marine Grade Plywood

All Four Corners— 2×4's are mortised to allow plywood to fit flush. Use 3½" bolts to join and counterbore at both ends to fit flush.

THE WOODWARD FRAME. Individual boat owners can make their own rowing frames from wood such as this Woodward Frame, designed and built by Daniel F. (Woody) Woodward of Jackson Hole, Wyo. This design is sturdy, provides good support and can be simply and economically built.

Because of excellent stability, a boatman need not be overly concerned with low center of gravity. A rowing platform of wood or metal construction, mounted on the side chambers, gets the rower up off the floor and automatically yields better oar angle. Clamp-type oarlocks that do not slide and are not weakened by a through-shaft pin hold oars firmly without weakening them. Mounted slightly forward of the rower's sitting position, oar shafts can slide through the untightened clamp locks for good personal rowing fit. Proper extension from the oarlocks puts the entire blade of the oar into the water. The distance between handles for most comfortable rowing is approximately the width of the chest of the rower. Oar length is determined by boat width at the oarlocks. This width will vary from oarlocks fitted on rowing platform mounts and those that come standard with the boat. Generally speaking, 10-12-foot boats need 9-foot oars, while boats over 13 feet should be equipped with 10-foot oars. Just as important as proper length however, oars should be cut of hardwood, with spruce, ash or maple being the preferable

and most durable. An extra oar (rather than a canoe paddle) should be carried on board at all times and two are recommended for long trips or very rocky rivers.

Platform Construction

A do-it-yourself carpenter or handyman of modest skill can design and build a sturdy rowing platform to custom fit any inflatable. Basically the platform should be sturdy enough to support boatman and passengers and at the same time provide a solid base for oarlocks (see illustration). Marine plywood 3/4- to 1-inch thick is a good all-around choice for seats. The platform should be neither too light, with a chance of cracking under passenger weight or oar strain, nor too heavy, where its weight could possibly damage side air chambers. Side chamber oarlock supports, up to 3 inches thick, can be used edgeways with top and bottom seat sections (for greater support and less give than single board seats) recessed and screwed or bolted to the side supports. This type of design, cut to fit any size boat, can be built with two or three seats, spaced strategically throughout the length of the boat. Support blocks can be fitted inside the top and bottom seat panels for strength.

Many novices begin with a single board placed across the air chambers used as a rowing seat and oarlock platform. Structurally unsound, the single board has a tendency to 'give' too much, and the weight of the rower and the action of rowing concentrates a good deal of stress on side air chambers. The platform, on the other hand, is engineered to distribute weight throughout the entire length of the air chambers.

To hold the platform in place, holes can be drilled in the platform's oarlock supports. Short lengths of nylon rope can secure the platform to built-on oarlocks, carrying handles, D-rings, side ropes or grommets.

Standard oar horn sockets can be mounted flush against the wooden oarlock supports for good strength. Some type of oarlock fastening device is often advisable in deep heavy water to keep oars from bouncing out of oar horn sockets. However, oarlocks can be kept "floating" under most normal conditions and definitely where shallow water could hook a blade and break it.

The wooden platform can be painted or given two coats of varnish to protect the wood. It should be stored to prevent warping.

Metal Platforms

Commercial floaters and some recreational rafters order custom-made tubular steel or aluminum plat-

Right—Cargo bags come in all shapes and sizes. All should be waterproof and, particularly in heavy water, lashed to D-rings. Below—A well-equipped boat for river use that is stable and safe. This one has commercially manufactured rowing frame, heavy duty oars, D-rings and life lines.

Left—Some boats are simple and basic. Wood panel, with foam taped on, is used for seat. Boat like this is adequate for mild or moderate currents. Above—Plastic bailing bucket is essential in white water and in case of emergency.

forms, designed so that rounded air chamber supports are contoured to fit inflatable pontoons. Wood, aluminum or ice chest seats are built right into the frame. Oarlock platforms and oar horn sockets are also built-in for maximum strength and efficiency. There is little chance of the professionally made metal platform ever failing. That's why commercial floaters, who place such importance on good platforms or frames, pay $150 to $300 for a good frame. For some floaters that would equal the cost of the inflatable. Check with your local welder or metal-working shop to see what the cost would be for a steel or aluminum frame. For heavy water floating, it is certainly worth the cost.

Wooden or metal platforms should be cushioned by rubber abrasion or wear pads on all spots where platform meets air chamber. Old rubber inner tubes, cut into sections and cemented to the pontoons or secured to the frame itself, serve nicely as cushions and prevent boat wear. It is important also that all rough spots, splinters, cracks or metal burrs be sanded, filed or trimmed from platforms before use to prevent abrasion and punctures.

Inflation Pumps

There are three different types of inflatable pumps sold on the market today—foot bellows, hand pumps and electric air pumps. Best overall performance at streamside is usually displayed by a good foot bellows. They range in price from $20 to $40. Multiple fittings at the end of the bellows hose adapt the pump to most inflatable valves. Strap and carrying case protect the pump and render it packable.

Single and dual cycle (inflates on up and down stroke) hand pumps are adequate for boats up to 10 feet in length, however, they usually only are used as topping off pumps on larger rafts. A good foot bellows usually performs the task of inflation faster with less labor than does the hand pump.

Small, electric pumps around 5 inches long which plug into a car cigarette lighter are next to useless—they never quite get the job done. They are fairly adequate for rafts under 6 feet, but even then a foot bellows or 2-cycle hand pump is faster and easier in the long run.

The gas station air pump is the main cause of "blown" boats, it's best to dismiss this as an inflation source.

Carrying and Storage Cases

Canvas, duck or nylon carrying and storage cases come as standard equipment with the better inflatables. Others are offered as options. Army duffel bags from surplus stores are fine for some boats. Carrying and storage bags are important in that they protect boats and make them compactable for transportation.

Motors

For lake use, flat water stretches, and upstream travel, inflatables with built-in transoms or attachable motor mounts for outboards or electric trolling motors are practical.

Inflatable Boat Strokes

FOR LAKE FLOATING, the inflatable boat differs only slightly in maneuverability from the ordinary rowboat. In fact, because of increased water drag, the inflatable requires a bit more muscle than rowboats. Except for use in small ponds and lakes, inflatables are not the best oar or paddle powered craft. That's why many of them are equipped with motor mounts and outboards or electric trolling motors for lake use.

Used in river currents ranging from moderate to swift, though, inflatable rafts really shine. The drag that makes them frustratingly difficult on flat water also yields exceptional control in fast water. However, rafting, any way you cut it, relies on sheer stroking or paddling power. Sure, a feel for the current, alert downstream observation, course preplanning, and some finesse are part of it, but arm, leg, and back strength and conditioning are important too. Whether for mild flat water or white water (controlled back rowing strokes) conditions, rafting boils down to rowing or paddling. And both are rigorous exercise. Rowing particularly requires a strong back and arms, good equipment and a basic knowledge of strokes and current.

Position Strokes

For all practical purposes a boatman will sit on the rowing platform with his seat positioned at or near amidships and with the bow of the boat and himself facing downstream. There are exceptions to this positioning, of course, when jockeying for fishing or photography angles. But the downstream facing position and the strokes that control it are the basics for boat maneuvering in a moving current.

By facing downstream, the boatman has full vantage of the water course and obstacles. Maneuvers can be planned ahead of time. A boatman can back row away from obstacles or a sucking current. He can sideslip the boat to move laterally across the stream with one oar and a minimum of effort. From this position, the oarsman has visual control and strongest stroke power.

Position strokes—short choppy slices into the water, alternating left and right oar, in an almost up and down hand motion *against* the current—maintains bow-first direction. The alternating left-right strokes are quick and rhythmic and slow the boat enough in the current to

Boatman facing downstream uses position stroke for course.

establish a steady downstream track. Minor changes in lateral movement can be made by ceasing the positioning strokes and allowing for current adjustment or by making the strokes predominantly left or right. From this vantage, using the position strokes, the boatman is ready in an instant to begin back row power strokes when the need arises.

Back Row Power Stroke

On a downstream course, extended deep back rowing against the current can stop the boat's downstream progress, move the boat upstream, or sideslip the boat in either direction depending on current force and dominant left or right oar. Back rowing requires more brute strength and deep, solid stroking than any other technique. And it is this stroke, done as casually or as rapidly as the situation demands, that can stop the boat at a good fishing hole, sideslip the boat away from a log or rock, or keep it away from a dangerous hole or chute. This is the stroke that puts equipment to the test. A weak, cracked, rotted or softwood oar can snap like a toothpick. Poor blade angle, due to improper oarlock positioning, or oars that are too short may contribute to the failure of a boatman being able to negotiate a narrow course with sucking left or right currents. An inferior oarlock pin or oar-oarlock fastener system can pop out under pressure. The aluminum or steel rowing platform not riveted, bolted or welded securely may come apart. A wooden platform of ill-design, inferior wood or weak supports may splinter and fail.

Back row power strokes should be made neither too shallow nor too deep. Proper oarlock height and positioning set the entire blade of the oar in the water so no broad surface is wasted. Too much of the oar shaft in the water indicates too deep of a stroke. As a result, when a blade hits bottom or an obstacle, tremendous

Current is pulling boat into rock and back rowing is needed to sideslip away from it.

pressure is exerted on oarlock fasteners, pins and braces. Breakage is possible. Medium depth strokes have broad, sweeping power and the blades can be recovered quickly and smoothly upon completion of the stroke. By exercising more pull on one oar, the boatman can sideslip away from the paddle with the strongest sweep depending on the direction and force of the current.

It is advisable in back row stroking to keep as steady a downstream bow as possible. Too much one-oar sideslipping and a boatman will find he has lost downstream control of the boat. Once control is lost and the boat spins out, regaining control in heavy current is often difficult and in the narrow stretches sometimes impossible. While rotating uncontrollably downstream, collisions, missed courses, punctures and even flipping are more likely to occur. Try always to "keep ahead" of inflatable maneuvering in back row power strokes. Because the boats are not acutely responsive, once they go beyond the control limit, recovery to a stable position is difficult. After a day's float with several hours of back row strokes, you will discover muscles you never knew you had.

Broadside or Perpendicular Power Stroke

It was my turn to negotiate an "L" bend in the white water of the Green River's Desolation Canyon in Utah. I discovered quickly that back row power strokes were sucking me into the current and a jagged, ominous cliff. The guide instructed me to back row with the right oar, turning the raft to a broadside, downstream position. I was facing the cliff, perpendicular to the current. With a couple of strong backstrokes at right angles to the current, I moved the boat quickly away from the dangerous obstacle. More broadside strokes with alternating left-right oars kept us in a safe position as we completed the "L" bend. The broadside power stroke is a finesse technique in which the boatman does

not fight or row against the main force of the current. The important thing to remember in broadside floating is to face the obstacle or main currents so the boat can be back rowed away from it. Resume normal downstream facing position and positioning strokes after the "L" bends or similar currents are negotiated since they present the best downstream observation.

Forward Stroke

The forward stroke with oars and blades swept forward and used with the current are weak directional strokes used for minor course changes in swift water or landing bow first in flat water. They can be used as mild positioning strokes when a change of pace, more than any other reason, is desired. Novices will sometimes try to overpower a swift current with forward strokes by rowing away from obstacles. It's awkward and ineffective and requires extra effort.

Steering or Rudder Stroke

In some moderate currents, one oar can be used as a stern rudder. Some of the larger commercial rafts have stern rudder control. The rudder can be used for fishing long, quiet stretches or for a nice change of pace. A back and forth sculling stroke can also be accomplished from the stern for a snail's pace fishing speed through deep, still stretches.

Shallow Water Strokes

During low water periods or when passing over shoals and gravel bars it may be necessary to use shallow water stroking for control. This can be difficult maneuvering since no solid bit of water can be taken. Shallow water strokes should be made well in advance of obstacles. Sometimes only half the blade can be used. Long, fast oar sweeps, taking care not to hang up the blade, are most effective, usually from a broadside boat position.

Above—As shown by slow shutter speed, there is too much flex in rubber oarlock for good control and bite. Right—Passenger helps keep bow from being sucked under the heavy current.

Inflatable Boat Safety

COMMON SENSE safety precautions and standards apply to all types of boating—rafting, canoeing, kayaking and john floating. Some degree of swimming or floating ability is advisable and a healthy respect for water and float streams should be cultivated. Persons displaying a fear of water and an unwillingness to overcome the fear may be better suited for other sports. However, in most float running adventures a certain level of excitement or apprehension is quite normal—that's part of the thrill of river running. Other factors, such as the effect of water temperature, the difficulty rating of the stream, the floaters' level of skill, and the selection and maintenance of good equipment are important safety factors to consider.

Inflatable rafts have built-in stability and are rather difficult to overturn. With better stability, inflatables can generally be described as safer boats. The inflatable allows for mistakes. And because the inflatable is made of a pliable material, bruises and cuts—possibilities when tipping or hitting obstacles with canoes—are not as likely with inflatables.

The Most Common Safety Violation

As simple as it sounds, the most common violation of safety in inflatable boating is complacency or overconfidence. Inflatables can be used as toys, diving platforms, rowboats and suntan mattresses on lakes and ponds, however these uses are not the subject of this book. In still water, inflatables can be handled by persons with little or no previous boating experience. On streams with moving currents, however, skill, strength and a knowledge of what is dangerous or unrunnable water are prerequisites to safe floating. The very reasons that make inflatables safe, extraordinary stability and "forgiving" construction, have a tendency to give the novice the false confidence that "anyone can handle the boat." That is not true on streams of moderate to swift currents, and it is particularly not true on

A good feeling for water, respect, not fear is the best attitude.

This raft is crowded. The man in front stands a good chance of being bucked out in heavy water.

A hand pump is a necessary emergency tool.

dangerous rapids and unrunnable streams.

Because of the water hugging drag, due to wide beam and soft design, inflatables require rowing or paddling maneuvers made well in advance of obstacles. In terms of maneuverability, an inflatable is sluggish. This sluggishness and the power, skill, and knowledge needed to overcome it in a current can lead many novices into early trouble.

Swimming Ability

Rarely do non-swimmers balk at the chance of "riding in a rubber boat." The number and popularity of commercial pleasure float trips across the country attest to that fact. Again, inherent stability can be the great deceiver. The likelihood of commercial boat runners flipping over in moderate or moderately swift currents are slim. But inflatables are subject to errors in judgment, like any other craft. They can be vulnerable to punctures, obstacles, currents, entrapment, whirlpools and chutes. Therefore you should learn to swim or stay afloat if you ride or operate an inflatable.

Inflatable Instruction

The foundation strokes of inflatable stream running are rather easily learned and quite similar, in theory, to conventional rowboating. The addition of current, though, brings a new dimension to the subject. (See the section on Inflatable Boat Strokes). Strength and stamina, proportional to the strength and character of the current, are needed for consistent control. It is wise to receive a degree of instruction first before negotiating any river of moderate or fast current. There are a number of white water rafting schools that offer instruction. And heavy white water rivers should be attempted *only* by qualified rafters.

Rivers of moderate current may be of special challenge not only because of the current, but also because of bends in the river, numerous braided channels, downstream obstacles and water temperature. One approach is to float any new stretch of stream either with a fishing guide or commercial pleasure floater first. Make mental notes and support them with rough maps or with written notes. Remember, stream channels may be constantly changing. A "River Chart" or "Guide" published a year before may not necessarily be reliable. Some guides will let passengers pilot the boats through various stretches of water. This is excellent practical experience and an effective way of learning boating skills. Ask plenty of questions. When not actually handling the boat, observe how the boatman handles various water conditions. A lot of inflatable handling may look like sheer muscle power—and granted, there is a substantial blend of that—but firsthand onstream observation is a great teacher.

As in preparation for any rigorous sport, pre-float conditioning, especially where inflatables are concerned, is important and recommended. At home you can do push-ups and sit-ups for basic toning of rowing muscles. Rowing your inflatable on lake or pond will give you practical exercise, and a definite feel for the oars, and assurance in your equipment. Start slow. Mild currents and wide stretches may not be your idea

Repairing a puncture in the bottom of a river boat.

of why you purchased an inflatable, but you will be surprised how much you learn. Start with 1- to 2-hour floats and work up to half-day cruises.

Inflatable owners who find themselves in trouble do so because they begin trips with a, "What do we have to lose?" attitude.

What About Flipping Over?

Your chances of flipping over in streams of moderate or moderately swift currents are really quite slim. Mistakes in judgment and poor downstream maneuver planning are commonly responsible for capsizing.

Beware of sucking holes at the bottom of chutes or rapids. Heavy whirlpools (although they may look harmless) have the power to pull bow or stern down so forcefully that the boat is flipped or water pours in. The weight of passengers sitting on bow or stern chambers can in some instances aid the whirlpool. Strong powerful strokes are needed to row out of a whirlpool.

Holes, chutes and haystacks can grab inflatables —especially if they are out of control—and broach them. This can cause sideways flipping, because the controlling, stabilizing effects of oar blades have been negated and the boatman is at the mercy of the current. It is at this time that rocks, boulders, logs and snags positioned in a strong current can also flip the boat.

Since inflatables are light, have an air space under them when overturned and are made of soft materials, getting away from an overturned boat is not difficult. Neither is staying with the overturned boat difficult when conditions warrant that. There are a couple of things to avoid though. Never let yourself get pinned between the boat and a stationary object such as a log, bridge abutment or a rock. Rope entanglement, either with bow or stern lines or boat line (some inflatables have nylon hold ropes around the exterior air chambers), usually results from sloppy lines inside the boat or lines that are too long (all lines should be stowed properly). Ordinarily there is enough time to jump away from sucking currents or snags when all signs point to a boat being sucked into an obstruction. The best policy is to avoid those situations by careful stream observations and course planning.

Inflatable White Water Myth

Perhaps the most dangerous detriment to safety and one widely promoted is that all inflatables are white water craft. Nothing can be further from the truth. Some boats due to their light duty construction with an insufficient number of air chambers are dangerously susceptible to puncture and sinking. Because inflatables are now sold in a variety of stores throughout the country, unknowing sales clerks and uninformed buyers are sometimes swayed by the white water myth. Remember, relatively few boats and even fewer boatmen are qualified for white water.

Puncture Protection

Good safety practices call for a hand pump, a repair kit, a bailing bucket, and first aid kit to be on board (and in good working order) at all times.

131

Camping With Inflatables

THERE IS A stimulating adventure in riding an inflatable boat down the twisting course of a free spirited river. My only regret after such a ride is the sad realization that the time sped swiftly by. Soon it's time to get off the river, pack the boat and head back to the city lights. Where did the hours go?

Several years of one-day floats convinced me that with a bit more preparation, I could extend day trips into overnighters. And only then did I realize full enjoyment of the total river experience. For getting to know the water is only half the joy. Living with the land along the river in a manner reminiscent of trappers and explorers completed the cycle. At the end of a day's float, I knew the best was yet ahead—pitching a late afternoon camp; trying to fool a few fish to supplement the evening meal; cooking over an open fire; sharing camp talk and stories with a good friend; peaceful sleep spiced with cricket, frog and horned owl music; and

knowing that in the morning I would again meet a new, morning-fresh river. After 2 days on the river, my appetite was satisfied. I could pull off the stream knowing I received a full share, and what a good feeling that is.

Sound Pre-Planning the Key

There is no mystique surrounding inflatable boat camping. Being a stable craft able to handle relatively large loads, there are few problems with packing and little concern about taking in water or tipping over. Simple, common sense procedures make the inflatable simple to pack.

Aside from having a reliable boat of 8 to 13 feet in good repair, rigged with the best oars and rowing platform available, sound pre-planning is the most important consideration of the float camper.

You can do most of your pre-planning before the rafting season begins. First of all, decide what streams

Plan camping spots along the river according to public access points.

are within your boating skill range. Flat, lazy streams could be a chore with a boat loaded with passengers and camp gear. White water rivers may be out of the question after seriously and honestly evaluating your ability level. Moderate to swift streams, neither dangerous nor boring, usually is the logical choice.

Remember, it does not take a glamorous stretch of water in far-off places to make a float-camp memorable. On the contrary, some of my finest experiences have been on familiar streams within 100 miles of home. You may choose to take an extensive float camping vacation in the Northwest, the Rockies, Smokies or Canada, and that's fine. Consider, though, that the less familiar an area, the more planning and research should go into the float. Be sure of two things: (1) Have confidence (supported by knowledge) that you can handle the river you want to float and (2) be certain you have a place to camp. There are detailed sections in Part I/General Floating on reliable contacts, float timetables, difficulty ratings, river maps and charts and landings. Those sections will help you determine who to contact and what questions to ask when planning a trip.

Agencies that will assist you in planning are the National Park Service, National Forest Service, Bureau of Outdoor Recreation, Fish and Game Departments, State Park Offices, and State Travel Departments. On a local scale, boat landings, marinas, sporting goods and tackle stores can supply valuable information. District ranger and warden stations are good sources. Chambers of Commerce in many towns, although supplying a lot of information, sometimes confuse publicity fluff with good solid facts. Make it your business to get the facts from people who know.

Float Camping Logistics

Before putting in the water, designated pickup points, with rides or vehicle waiting, should be determined. There is nothing more frustrating than to take out after 2 days of floating and find out that your ride back upstream has failed to show due to a misunderstanding or a failure in communications. Avoid this confusion by pinpointing on identical maps the area where the vehicle will be waiting. One map accompanies the floaters; the other, the pickup person.

When two vehicles are available, the best method is to leave one of them at the final take-out point so

Left—Inflatables can be big enough and stable enough to carry all equipment for a conventional camp setup like this. Below—Water is the key to good camping, so choose a spot with good water, and even though it may look pure, it's best to purify it.

floaters, gear and boat can be transported back to the starting point. It's always a good idea to make sure beforehand that a vehicle can be parked overnight at put-in and take-out points. A note left taped inside the windshield can explain why the vehicle is parked there.

Some floats are planned to rendezvous with a pre-set camp after the first day or with a vehicle that will have food and camp supplies. This technique is all right on well-known stretches where camping is limited and a floater does not have much choice. However, being self-sufficient with all necessary gear aboard gives campers a nice sense of freedom. With a good choice of camping locations, the floater can get off the river to set-up camp when and/or where the need arises. Weather, float times and current speed often make this the most practical method.

Campsites

Fortunately, men and agencies with foresight have set aside some fine camping areas along many float streams. Because of increased river use and more people camping, designated campgrounds are the rule rather than the exception. In other words, there are relatively few places where floaters can take-out at will and set up camp. Even along federal and state lands, camping may be restricted to designated areas only. This is just some of the information that can be uncovered when planning a trip. It is important therefore to make sure camping areas are well within range for overnight trips. It's best to take-out a little early and set camp. Floating a river in darkness is lonely and frightening and can be dangerous.

Despite the remoteness of lands along certain rivers, check on whether the land is private or public. This can be done by reading maps supplied by parks, forest, state or county. While planning the trip, if you see that most of the lands bordering the stream are private, you may have to seek permission in advance if you want to set up an overnight camp. Another alternative is to float a stretch with more public access areas.

It's a good idea to choose a campsite above the river. In case of water fluctuation, you won't have to move camp. Higher elevation usually affords a better breeze and in turn keeps away mosquitoes and flies. Unless

Pack along plenty of food on river trips. Appetites soar and good food does wonders.

otherwise stipulated on campground regulations, burn what is burnable and pack out trash that will not burn.

Camp Gear

Depending on the size of your boat and the number of passengers, you will probably have the option of packing a standard size camp outfit or a lighter, more compact "backpack" camp. Either way, tent, tarp, sleeping bags (stowed in heavy-duty waterproof bags even if they have their own stuff sacks), stove, lantern, cook gear and food can be stowed around the air chambers, leaving the middle of the boat free for passengers. It's a good idea though to keep all items in heavy canvas bags with plastic sacks over the bags tightly locked for extra protection and to lash the bags down. This keeps small items, sharp edges, and breakables from rolling around on the floor of the boat.

Food and Drink

"Soft-pack" insulated bags are effective coolers for perishables and drinks in inflatable boats. Bags can be protected from the sun and ice melt by wrapping in a blanket or tarp. Where rigid coolers have a tendency to bounce and tip over in small inflatables, the soft-packs more or less take the shape of the boat bottom. However, a properly tied-down rigid cooler does offer greater insulation. Some manufacturers now offer rowing frames that incorporate a rigid cooler as a rowing seat.

Nylon food bags should be protected by a plastic sack, well secured. Also, cook gear, plates, cups and utensils should be kept together in their own bag. Whether food be fresh or canned, dehydrated or freeze-dried, pack along plenty of it. Healthy snacks, like fruit and nuts, can be refreshing. A floater cannot depend on river water as being suitable for drinking. Purification by boiling, halazone tablets or chlorine is standard procedure. A 5-gallon water container, filled at home, will take care of most drinking-cooking needs on an overnighter. In addition to all the camping essentials, always pack along a hand pump or bellows to keep your boat firm. Rubber or nylon repair kits are a must and should always be kept on board. Inflatable boat camping—adventure supreme—is a product of your imagination and skill.

Good rain jacket, rain pants, cowboy hat and plenty of warm clothing are helpful items.

The Commercial Float Trip

Good outfitters are not afraid to advertise their company.

136

THE KENNEDY family may have gotten the ball rolling. Various members of that famous clan were photographed quite frequently riding the white water of some angry western river in pursuit of thrills and solitude that wiped minds free of political complexities. A host of other senators, congressmen, governors and celebrities followed suit. White water running was in style. And the chic thing to say at Washington parties was, "Oh yes, I ran Cataract Canyon last week. What a thrill."

The celebrities ordinarily did not have the skill nor the time to run major western rivers on their own. They hired commercial floaters who did the work for them. They simply sat back and held on. Being good sports most of the time, they pitched in with chores, took their turns at paddling and rowing and generally had a good time of it.

Signing on for a river running expedition down a white water river is by no means limited to famous or rich people. A sample of 1976 rates for oar-powered trips down the Colorado River show average cost to be between $245 and $320 per person for 5- to 6-day trips and $325 to $440 for trips of 8 or 9 days—which is really plenty of river and floating for the average person. These rates include all food, sleeping bags, cargo bags and in some cases, transportation to and from the river. Some operators offer reduced rates for families, children and groups. And private charter trips are offered in addition to regularly scheduled trips for those who wish their own private float.

A 3- or 4-day motorized raft trip, offering the same services, runs from $175 to $230; $350 to $550 for a 9- to 10-day trip.

Float tripping is by no means cheap and not everybody can afford it. Those who can and who sign up with a good commercial outfit, usually get their money's worth. Here's what to look for.

How to Find a Good Outfitter

Word-of-mouth is often the best advertising for river running outfitters. Good evaluations and reports seem to snowball in the outfitting business. Repeat customers are enthusiastic salespersons and often invite friends along on future trips or recommend certain outfitters. The bad outfitter rarely gets repeat business and depends on new blood each trip to stay in business. Most bad outfitters don't last very long in this highly competitive business. But there seem to be a few that crop up each year. Finding a good outfitter—one that will give you your money's worth—requires diligent research if one is not recommended by friends or relatives.

Usually the best outfitters are also the best businessmen. After all, they are making a living at river running. Some of the good ones advertise in outdoor magazines and general consumer publications. They advertise in specialty magazines such as *Canoe, Down River,* and *Camping* and *Backpacking Journal.* There are, of course, sound business reasons for advertising. Good outfitters, in addition, are proud of their services and are not afraid of calling attention to their skills. Some outfitters will also advertise in the local newspapers of resort towns, close to rivers that will be floated.

Look at an outfitter's brochure. If it answers most of your questions, the outfitter probably runs a good business and knows how to deal with people. Personal letters with questions should be written well in advance of the start of boating season (April or May in some areas). And you should receive replies to your letters either from the outfitter himself (or herself) or an outfitter's representative. A phone call can also do the job even though it's best to have the exact rates in writing. If an outfitter does not reply to your letters or cannot be reached by phone, look for another outfitter.

The Good Outfitters

Good management and knowledgeable guides are vital to the success of a top-notch outfitting business. Some outfits start small and offer great personal service. Some outgrow themselves and fail to cope with expansion. River runners who have been in business for some time and have established good reputations have done so because they did not let expansion and demand stand in the way of quality.

Regardless of the type and size of the *boats* used, they should be clean and orderly. Rowing frames should be painted or stained and be sturdily built. Oars should be in good condition. Boats will usually have the outfitter's company name printed on a side air chamber if they are worthy of being advertised.

Whether a trip is thoroughly enjoyed or just tolerated is often dependent on the *quality of camp food.* Camp meals should be of good to excellent quality and menus should be varied. You can and should expect, for example, bacon (ham or sausage) and eggs or pancakes for breakfast every morning. Sandwiches, fruit and cookies for lunch. And for the evening meal, the menu should range from chicken to steak, complete with potatoes, dessert and coffee. Some outfitters supply wine for supper. Most suggest that customers bring their own alcoholic beverages if they want them.

Food can be prepared Dutch oven style or over gas stoves. Foil cooking is also popular. Either way, food should be fresh, hot and served in an appetizing manner. Outfitters supply the cooks and dishwashers, customers are expected to serve themselves.

Most management agencies or major rivers require that acceptable portable *sanitary facilities* are set up at each camp. This is the outfitter's job, and the "library" should be set up shortly after boats are beached for the night. Portable toilets, privacy curtains and toilet paper are supplied. Ample warm water for washing hands should be available nearby.

Some outfitters supply and pitch *tents* each night, especially during the rainy spring period. Modern, easy-to-set, well ventilated tents have replaced the old "guide tent" of heavy white canvas. During the dry seasons, tents may still be used and requested, but floaters are encouraged to sleep under the stars. *Sleeping bags* with removable washable liners are supplied by most outfitters at the request of the client. If you can, bring your own warm sleeping bag. Nights can be chilly despite the 90-degree daytime temperatures.

The outfitter or owner of the float business may be a terrific guy who comes highly recommended. However, some businesses have grown to the point where the head man does not or *cannot* accompany every trip. The success of your trip then may be up to the party or *trip leader* and the other guides. There are a lot of fine guides. By nature, they are usually independent, rugged characters who are excellent outdoor instructors by their very examples. Some play their guide role to the hilt. They too can be enjoyable. On the other hand, there are a few who treat all paying customers like dudes, greenhorns or tenderfeet and rarely communicate with the floaters. You can never really judge a guide until the trip is underway. The good ones blossom while the bad ones wilt. The best ones are not only excellent boatmen, but also fine story tellers, joke

Right and below—The river running experience can range from a wild white water ride on a bucking raft to a beautiful, serene float, communing with the best that nature has to offer.

makers, poker players, historians, and naturalists —sensitive to the river and the people.

As a paying customer you will have most of the difficult chores done for you. Some outfitters encourage participation with some chores that are more or less enjoyable and may be some worth to you later on. This feeling of being of some use or value on an extended float trip is important. A good outfitter and a good expedition share a common respect for each other. Not every outfitter/client association reaches that balance point. But it is amazing how many do on the river. Some outfitters are now turning to paddle floats instead of a single boatman on the oars doing all the work. Paying customers help run the boat. They get plenty of exercise, learn something about river running, and usually fall asleep quicker at night. The number of paddle floats are increasing each year.

There is a double bonus in river floating. All day long you can enjoy the river and streamside scenery. At night there is a good quiet camp to look forward to—one steeped in campfire philosophy, a soft guitar, gentle voices, and the sounds of owls, crickets and frogs.

Finally, a good outfitter provides a practical list of suggested clothing and gear to the customer in advance of the float. Then, the novice floaters, as well as the guides, can be comfortable, warm, dry and happy.

Left and below—Most people do not have the skills nor the equipment to run rivers such as these. Only qualified outfitters can do the job the right and safest way.

Inflatable Powerboat Techniques

THERE IS LITTLE doubt that outboard motors can play a significant role in running some white water rivers. Burks Smith, Vice President of Bonair Boats, Inc., Lenexa, Kansas, says that using a powered boat requires no less skill, only less muscle power. And he is right. A mistake made with a motor powered inflatable can not only ruin a motor, but swamp a boat as well. In addition the use of an outboard engine on some streams may be illegal.

Smith, an ardent river runner, has developed a basic guide for inflatable powerboat techniques: "High performance inflatable boats are specially designed craft that have the ability to accept outboard motors that are quite powerful for the size of the boat. Although they maintain their shape and rigidity through inflated chambers, they are quite unlike inflated rafts. High performance inflatables have solid transoms for mounting an outboard motor and rigid floorboards which run the entire length of the boat and are necessary for the boat's proper operation. They also have V-shaped bottoms to provide stable tracking and stability on turns.

"Because of their design, high performance inflatables are extremely difficult to capsize, and almost all will support their full rated capacity even when filled with water. Multiple air chambers are always provided as a safety factor in the event one chamber is damaged. Like all inflatables, they are very forgiving and are difficult to damage in a collision because the shock is absorbed by deforming the boat's structure rather than failure of the hull. These features make high performance inflatables ideal for white water use.

"When choosing a high performance inflatable to run white water, pick a boat that is large enough to be stable in the kind of water you expect to encounter. The larger the better, but 12 feet is about the minimum size. Shop around and choose a quality boat made by a company with a good reputation for inflatables. Avoid 'bargain' inflatables as they are almost always of inferior quality. The boat should be equipped with an outboard motor capable of propelling it at between 20 and 30 miles per hour on calm water and should be loaded to no more than half its rated capacity for white water use.

According to powerboat experts, it takes just as much river skill and almost as much muscle to run an inflatable with a motor as it takes to operate one with oars.

Left—High performance inflatable boats have rigid sectional floors and heavy duty motor mounts. Below—Bow cover or dodger on this boat is necessary for heavy water running.

Inflatables can take high horsepower motors for plenty of drive.

"Only certain rivers are suitable for running with a powered boat. Of course, the water must be deep enough to accommodate the draft of the outboard motor, and there must not be any rapids that cannot be crossed while going upstream if a round trip is to be made. For round trips, always go upstream first since there is a smaller chance of damaging your motor going up rapids, and you can always drift back to the launching point in the event of trouble. Minimum equipment is a life vest to be worn at all times, a repair kit for the boat, a first aid kit, a set of basic tools, a spare propeller, and a pair of oars or paddles. In remote areas, survival gear is recommended.

"Inflatable powerboats are usually much smaller than the rafts that are commonly used for white water, and therefore there is a greater likelihood that the boat can be upset by a sufficiently large wave. The whole secret is to use your power as an 'equalizer' to avoid dangerous waves rather than total reliance on the boat to get you through anything you may encounter. Guiding the boat through rapids that are potentially dangerous requires considerable skill at both reading the river and boat handling."

Upstream Techniques

"If sufficient power is available to overcome the current, crossing rapids upstream is actually easier than crossing them downstream. You have a good view of the rapids, and because considerable power must be applied to overcome the current, the boat will be very responsive, and you can maintain a stationary position in relation to the shore to consider the best plan of attack.

"When approaching rapids from below, steer the boat clear of the largest standing waves downstream of the rapids by getting as close to shore as possible without running aground. The boat will be traveling slowly in relation to the river bottom, so the probability of serious motor damage is diminished while traveling upstream. Most rapids have a tongue of relatively less turbulent water that denotes the deepest water, and the best route to cross will be rather obvious. If there is no well-defined tongue of water, choose the spot that appears deepest and least turbulent. Make sure there are no boats approaching from above the rapids before continuing.

"The largest standing waves are usually directly downstream of the deepest part of the rapids so it is necessary to guide the boat from the calmer water near the shore into the tongue directly upstream of the roughest water. This is the most dangerous part of the maneuver because a loss of power at this point will sweep the boat backwards into the most dangerous part of the rapids. Once ahead of the standing waves, give the boat full power and climb up the tongue to the calm water above the rapids. The biggest danger here is loss of propeller thrust because of the larger quantities of air bubbles in the water preventing the propeller from getting a good bite. If the engine loses thrust and begins to race, immediately reduce power to an idle to release the trapped air around the propeller and apply power again before the boat loses its forward momentum. In some cases, it is necessary to get a flying start so the boat will cross the most turbulent areas on its own momentum. Each set of rapids is different and takes a slightly different technique. Learn on easy rapids and don't attempt anything that you feel is beyond your skill

"Upstream traffic is not allowed on the Grand Canyon portion of the Colorado River and perhaps a couple of other popular rivers because of the very heavy traffic downstream. On any river it is wise to check for downstream traffic before attempting to cross rapids upstream."

Downstream Techniques

"Floating rapids downstream with power is exactly the same as with a raft, except that you use your motor instead of oars for guidance, and as mentioned earlier, an inflatable powerboat is usually smaller than a raft. Because the current is generally quite swift, it is not practical to use any power except for steering as this would add to the speed at which you approach obstacles and greatly increase the danger. As with running rapids upstream, the idea is to avoid rocks and dangerous waves.

"It is difficult to see rapids from upstream, so as you approach them, turn the boat into the current and hover above the rapids by matching the speed of the current in order to determine the best route. If necessary, tie the boat up on shore and walk around to get a better view. If you have crossed the rapids upstream, use the same route downstream.

"Once the best route has been determined, steer the boat into position to enter the rapids at the best point and approach the rapids with the motor in gear and at an idle so power will be available if needed. Halfway down the steepest part of the rapids, apply enough power to move the boat out of the path of the largest waves and toward the calmer water near the shore. Keep a sharp eye out for rocks and shallow areas, as the motor is most likely to sustain damage at at this point. It is best to keep the motor tilt unlocked to reduce a possible impact to the minimum. If you cannot avoid a large wave, steer directly toward it to present the bow of the boat to the wave. Never approach a wave sideways.

"The secret to successful white water boating is careful planning and skillful operation of your boat. Become familiar with each set of rapids before you tackle them. Even if you have run the same rapids before and feel you know them by heart, look first anyway. Even slight changes in the flow of a river can significantly change the character of a set of rapids. If at all possible, take two boats for extra safety."

PART 4
KAYAKING

Is the Kayak for You?

Two-seat kayaks may be fine for small families.

If you feel at ease with water and have a desire to get *into* it, the kayak is for you.

THE GLORY OF kayaking has been heralded with the thrills of white water running. And the kayak, under the control of a skilled boatman, is surely in beautiful form slicing the froth of a turbulent river.

For the average person, though, in the process of selecting a craft for all-around general floating, white water photos and slalom races frighten rather than excite. There will always be a small select group of adventurers who thrill to the prospects of kayaking in heavy water. They are willing to take the necessary instruction and devote hours of practice to the Eskimo Roll. Someday they will be the models in breathtaking white water photos. This fraternity of white water kayakers should be admired. They share a common bond with sky divers, mountain climbers, freestyle skiers, and surfers. They are dedicated disciples to sports requiring more than average willpower and training.

The majority of prospective river runners do not choose kayaking as an alternative to canoeing and rafting largely due to the technical white water image associated with the kayak, and the fact that the calmer, less spectacular side of kayaking receives little publicity. Dieter Stiller, 20 years with the Hans Klepper Corporation which produces Klepper kayaks and folding boats, says, "River *cruising* kayakers are not spoken to." Nor are they talked about. There is a peaceful side to kayaking—one that average people can truly enjoy. Actually, kayaking is two sports in one. White water thrills and competition on one side and relaxing cruising on the other. The latter sport has barely been tapped.

Family Kayaking

There are two-seat kayaks. I have seen photos of two-seat kayaks with small children stuffed in between the paddlers and in the bow section of the cockpit. For obvious reasons, a cramped kayak is a potential trap. Two persons are the limit and single place kayaks are more fun for everybody.

Family kayaking is not only practical, it offers rewards that are extremely satisfying. Oft quoted naturalist, Aldo Leopold, said it simply, "Recreation is valuable in proportion to the intensity of its experiences." Well, kayaking is intense. That does not mean it can't be relaxing. But it *does* take instruction, and it *does* take a fair amount of skill. With a minimum of instruction, sometimes absorbed from books or magazine articles, family members can enjoy canoeing and rafting on streams with slow to moderate currents.

A minimum amount of kayak instruction ordinarily will not produce an enjoyable first ride. In fact, a prospective kayaker may not even be able to get into a kayak without practicing some basic techniques first. A kayak has to be balanced almost like a bike. It has a natural tendency to roll over. You and your paddle are the stabilizers. What happens if you roll over when sitting in a semi-enclosed cockpit? How do you get out of the boat? How do you get back in? These questions are answered by instruction and practice.

If you and your family want to feel like part of the current and you want to feel the thrill of the most responsive boat known to man, then the kayak is worthy of consideration. Whether you choose lake or stream cruising or white water running is a matter of individual or family desire.

The Lone Kayaker

The single place kayak, a mere 30 to 40 pounds in weight and 13 feet long, puts the kayaker at near perfect union with the water. The boat becomes part of the body, and because of the sitting-cockpit position a kayaker must assume, the center of gravity is naturally the lowest of any hand-propelled craft. A kayaker does not overpower the current, he *is* the current.

For the lone kayaker, there can be no finer intimate relationship with water. The lone kayaker, though, is never really alone. He should be part of a group of individual kayakers. Solitary floating is not advised although there are some kayakers who are aware of the risks involved and float alone. Cockiness can be a side product of numerous hours of instruction and practice. For a kayaker this is an unfortunate hazard. Confidence and cockiness, raised the same way, are easily confused as kayak proficiency increases.

With their low center of gravity, kayaks have amazing stability, but stability is based on *balance*.

The lightness and design of the kayak make it easy to handle, portage, cartop and store for the single floater.

Advantages of the Kayak

Weighing less than any other float craft of its length, the kayak's *shallow draft* and absence of a keel enables it to float in water only a foot deep. For low water floating in late summer or fall, there are few stretches that the kayak cannot skim over. However, if dragging or portaging are necessary, the task is simply done with *light kayaks* weighing around 25 pounds or heavier touring models in the neighborhood of 35 pounds. Three or four kayaks can be carried on the top of a standard size passenger car fitted with a rack. Compacts can even handle one or two boats.

Today's kayaks are made of fiberglass, plastic or a combination of fiberglass fabric and multi-laminate resins for strength. Any of the materials are super strong, virtually dent proof and resist abrasions and cracking. Occasional waxing enhances the exterior finish of the boat. Boats should be kept covered and stored on racks. There is little *upkeep* when it comes to kayaks.

The average price range of a single-place kayak is $300 to $400 for well-known commercially manufactured models and from $200 to $300 for those made locally. In popular floating and white water resort areas, there is a growing number of local kayak manufacturers, most of whom produce good to excellent boats for a lower price than nationwide manufacturers. The lower price is often the result of the absence of middle men in manufacturer-consumer sales and the absence of boat shipping costs. What the locally-made boats lack in exterior finish, they usually make up for in design and quality matched to the conditions of a particular local stream. Double kayaks, not usually produced locally, cost anywhere from $400 to $500.

Spoon blade, double kayak paddles, made of fiberglass, cost from $30 to $50 and with the exception of heavy white water use will usually last for the life of the boat. Because the kayaker is sitting inside his boat, using all parts of the body for paddling, a comfortable, trim fitting, and top quality flotation vest is standard equipment. Usually called "competition vests," they cost more than the standard life preserver, averaging about $20 to $30.

Depending on the degree of proficiency, water temperature, length of float, and nature of the stream, other accessories are important. Spray covers keep water from entering the cockpit. A helmet is a must for white water or riffles where rolls or exits in swift, rock filled streams are common. Flotation bags for kayak bow and stern compartments may be necessary. Some bags double as watertight cargo carriers, handy on extended cruises for keeping extra clothes and cameras safe and dry. In cold mountain waters a complete wet suit outfit is advisable in the event white water or a capsize are encountered. Since much kayaking is done during high water in the spring, water temperatures can be extremely cold. Wet suit pants, tunic, boots, and gloves can make the difference. In less harsh climates, windshirts and rain suits are adequate. Warm weather,

warm water kayaking, often the most fun, can be enjoyed in a swimsuit.

The shape and lightness of a kayak make it a swift, responsive performer. Downstream runs are most common, and the glide is an exhilarating one. However, practical upstream maneuvering is possible in a kayak when negotiating mild or moderate currents. One thing for sure, you'll save money on gas. You'll be amazed what arm power can do for the Eskimo boat.

An area seldom mentioned when talking about kayaks is the fishing, camping and hunting opportunities the boat can open up. When a kayak is "packed" like a backpack with lightweight, compact fishing and camping gear, floaters can reach remote areas swiftly and silently. While fishing is impractical from the kayak itself, the boat provides enjoyable access into good holes. Likewise, hunting and wildlife photography, when guns and cameras are protected in waterproof cargo bags, are well within reach of the kayaker. Extra care, extra skills, yes. But there's also a lot of satisfaction in being a *complete* kayaker.

Not everyone will want to use a kayak in surf like this.

Kayak Equipment

A life preserver or vest is standard equipment. It should fit perfectly.

DICK HELD, kayak and canoe maker from Cedar City, Utah, told me recently, "I wouldn't kayak in a bathtub without a helmet." Held's words come from years of kayaking experience in white water rivers across the country. "I was kayaking last year in Utah, when I just started a roll and hit my head. The rock was about a foot underwater, and I never saw it. Even with my helmet on, I was knocked unconscious momentarily, but I was able to recover, complete the roll and paddle to safety. It took me a while to get over the shock. Without that helmet on, I doubt if I would have made it out of the river."

Most good kayakers will agree that the helmet should be considered the most important piece of equipment. While life vests deservedly receive a great deal of emphasis because of their widespread use, helmets, on the other hand, often go unnoticed. They are for some, unattractive and somewhat restrictive. To others, helmets violate a "devil may care" attitude that infringes on the wildness and freedom of the sport. For experienced kayakers, a helmet is as important as a paddle.

"Some kayakers have a tendency to shun helmets in what appears to be deep, unobstructed rivers," Held says. "Amazingly enough, this is where most of them run into trouble. Most white water rivers, regardless of their depth, have submerged rocks and boulders. In rolling or exiting from a boat in moderate to swift current, a head-on collision can be disastrous. It doesn't take churning white water in a rock garden to prove the worth of kayak helmets."

Held's remarks, along with a good number of other experts interviewed, support the general kayaking rule that all kayakers, from novices to experts, in any type of moving current should wear some kind of helmet.

Types of Helmets

Kayakers have used baseball batting helmets, construction hard hats, rock climbing helmets, hockey helmets and downhill ski racing helmets. They all work, provided they fit well enough to protect most of the head and have a chin strap to keep the helmet secure.

A good kayak and canoe helmet should fully cover

The most important piece of equipment in swift water is a helmet; note, also, the spray skirt.

the back and side of the head. It should be fairly lightweight, ventilated and floatable. Some helmets are adjustable to fit all sizes with a snap-on chin strap. High impact plastic seems to be the most popular protection material. Various styles and colors of helmets, available from white water specialty shops, have influenced kayakers to accept and wear helmets more readily.

Life Vests

It is important to use a U.S. Coast Guard approved life vest for kayaking. Most vests sold in stores today are Coast Guard approved and are quite acceptable for a variety of water sports. However, the choice and fitting of a kayaking vest are extremely important. A kayaking vest should be trim and snug fitting yet with plenty of freedom of movement—proper fit is important—a vest that is too large or one that is not zipped or snapped can be ripped off the paddler in strong current. Ill-fitting ones are bulky and have a tendency to hang up in the cockpit, exposing the kayaker to the perils of entrapment.

Few kayakers will argue the fact that it is easier to perform the Eskimo Roll without wearing a life vest. And the roll is initially learned without a vest until the paddler gets the feel of it. Mastery of the Eskimo Roll, though, is not complete until it can be performed with a life vest. No excuse should prevent the kayaker from wearing a vest at all times.

Author wears wet suit tunic and diver's mask. Wet suits (tops and bottoms) should be considered standard equipment for most kayaking.

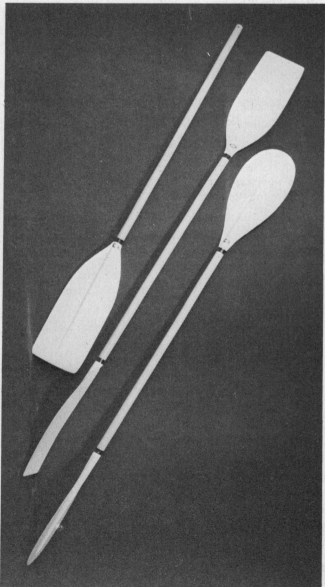

From left: single blade paddle; double flat paddles; and feathered spoon paddles.

The Wet Suit

There are several reasons why wet suits are commonly described as standard equipment. Kayakers are part of the water. They sit in the stream. Spray skirts do not alter the fact that the water can be, and usually is, cold. Many kayaking activities are in full swing in the spring, when high cold water dictates the finest challenges and spectacular white water events. But aside from this prime time, cold, mountain-fed kayak streams are usually cold year-around. Wet suits, then, are sources of protection and warmth. They can extend the kayak season. They protect the body against abrasions, are formfitting and comfortable. Most important of all, wet suits can and do save kayakers' lives. They act as a shield against the numbing water that can render even the best of swimmers helpless. They can prevent hypothermia. In short, the wet suit can increase enjoyment and comfort immeasurably.

Wet suits are made of neoprene or a combination of neoprene and nylon which adds durability. Pants and tunic (either long or short sleeve) should fit snugly. Heavy-duty, large rustproof zippers are standard for tunics and pant legs.

In addition to pants and tunics, boots, gloves and hoods made from the same neoprene-nylon material are needed at times for comfort and safety. They retain body heat significantly and are worthwhile additions.

Windshirts, rain gear and warm-up suits are adequate for warm water streams during mild or warm weather. None of these items, however, are substitutes for wet suits. The novice, or intermediate, or veteran is better off employing the extra margin of safety and protection of a wet suit.

Kayak Paddles

Most kayak paddles today are constructed of either fiberglass, Kevlar or ABS plastic. Some are made of wood and aluminum or a combination of both. Fiberglass and Kevlar are generally considered the best overall choices.

Nearly all double-bladed kayak paddles used today have blades that are feathered at 90 degrees to each other on the shaft. There are two types of blade designs —spoon, for experienced paddlers, and flat blade for novices. Unlike blades of old, today's so-called flat-bladed paddles are feathered and do have a slight degree of curve for more power. There are right- or left-control paddles, based primarily on which hand grip is more favorable to the paddler. With the double paddle held horizontally by the paddler and the left spoon facing him; a left-control paddle has the right spoon facing up. A right-control paddle has the right spoon facing down.

Proper length of paddles is determined by the size of the paddler, size of the craft, and use. Shaft grip should be about 6 inches from the blades. This leaves a com-

Above—Author, Charles Farmer, blows up a combination cargo-flotation bag that keeps equipment dry and keeps the boat from swamping. Below—Kathy Farmer pushes flotation bag in place in stern section of kayak. Bags fit into bow and stern sections of the boat.

fortable, well-balanced paddling position with elbows angled at about 90 degrees. Generally, longer paddles are used for white water cruising, wide kayaks and two-man boats. In contrast, shorter paddles are used for slalom kayaking. Robert Jay Evans, a U.S. Olympic kayaking coach, and author of *Fundamentals of Kayaking* (a bible of the sport), has prepared the following paddles length chart.

Paddler's Height	Slalom	Wild Water or Cruising
5'4"	80"	83"
5'6"	81"	84"
5'8"	82"	85"
5'10"	83"	86"
6"	84"	87"
6'2"	85"	88"

Spray Skirts

A spray skirt is a rubberized nylon or Hypalon skirt that the kayaker wears around the waist and snugs with a drawstring. A shock cord sewn into the bottom opening of the skirt fits around the cockpit coaming (lip) and is secured by the paddler in the seated position. The skirt keeps spray and water from entering the cockpit. In the event of a hasty exit from the boat, the shock cord attachment pulls free from the coaming and does not entrap the paddler. The skirt weighs around 10 ounces or less. Although it stays attached to the paddler in event of exit, its design and weight are scarcely noticeable.

Learning Equipment

Face mask or goggles, nose clips and ear plugs are invaluable pieces of equipment when learning to exit from a kayak or practicing the roll. The face mask allows the novice to watch proper blade sweep and angle for recovery strokes. Since a good deal of time may be spent upside down in attempts to master rolling, nose clips and ear plugs block out water. In difficult stretches of white water, where rolling or exiting is the rule rather than the exception, paddlers also have the option of wearing nose clips and ear plugs.

Standard Equipment

Most kayaks come with molded cockpit seats, foam knee braces and adjustable, multi-positon foot braces. Knee and foot braces are items that enable paddlers to stay in kayaks for recoveries or rolls. The initial tendency for the novice is to exit the boat when flipping. Soon that urge is squelched and braces are used for a voluntary locked position. Boats are equipped with grab loops of nylon line, threaded through 3/8-inch holes drilled through solid plugs in bow and stern.

Flotation Bags

Bags that can be inflated and deflated for fitting in stern and bow compartments of the kayak displace water and prevent swamping. They also serve as additional flotation for kayaks. Combination flotation-cargo bags can be inflated and provide safe, dry watertight storage for gear.

Two kayaks can be easily loaded and hauled on top of vehicle.

Kayak Strokes

Number one frustration—trying to track a straight course on flat water. Don't expect much at first. However, this is the basic foundation to good stroking later.

WAIT UNTIL you experience the dramatic maneuverability of the kayak. You are operating from a comfortable seated cockpit position which puts you low in the boat and the water. Your craft will probably weigh under 38 pounds, a mere wisp of a boat. Like a wild, unbroken pony, the kayak is fast to fly and extremely sensitive to the touch. With the feathered double-bladed paddle, stroking the kayak is a completely different experience.

Control or Fixed Hand

The control or fixed hand of a paddler retains a constant, palms down grip on the shaft which regulates the blade for various strokes. The unfixed hand is loosely gripped and relaxed to the point where the shaft can rotate smoothly within the grasp. Because of dexterity and strength, the control hand for a right-handed person is usually the right hand and is the left hand for southpaws.

Simple forward stroking then, on the fixed side, is performed with the wrist arched slightly up for full follow through. After the first forward paddle stroke, the control hand or wrist is dropped so the paddle is rotated 90 degrees through the unfixed hand and wrist.

Follow through to the original position at the end of the stroke and continue rhythmic paddling, keeping shoulders and arms swinging smoothly and with slight rotation at the hips.

Don't Get Discouraged

If you are like most novice kayakers, your first introduction to basic forward and backward stroking will be on a pond or lake where you have the chance to develop good blade control without the initial worry of currents and obstacles.

While lake paddling, you will discover almost immediately why the kayak is best suited to current rather than still water. Sure, you can fly over the surface with deep, powerful forward strokes, but straight course tracking will not come easy. The kayak because of its rocker*-bottom keel-less design has a tendency to turn "into" itself on flat surfaces with no currents. The pointed, dagger-like bow (and stern) is extremely sensitive to even mild strokes. You'll experience the need for several one-sided recovery strokes if one stroking side is initially stronger than the other. Lake practice

*Rocker—The longitudinal curvature of the bottom of the kayak at the center line of the hull.

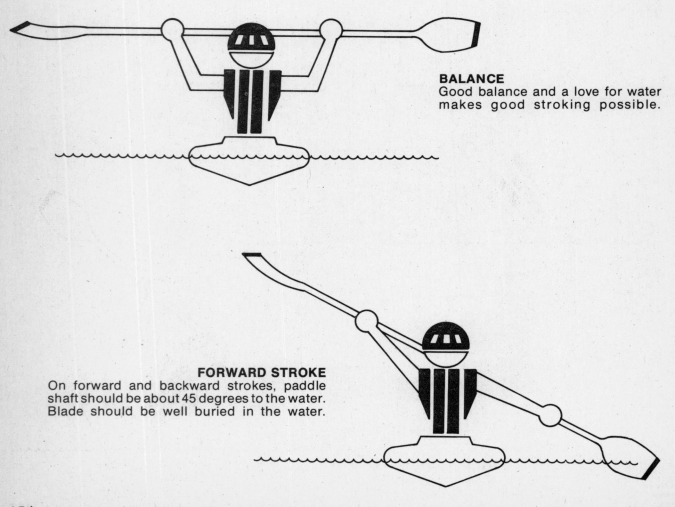

BALANCE
Good balance and a love for water makes good stroking possible.

FORWARD STROKE
On forward and backward strokes, paddle shaft should be about 45 degrees to the water. Blade should be well buried in the water.

does accomplish a feel for equal power stroking and rhythm. Eventually it becomes apparent that delicate matched pairs work a lot better than strenuous efforts on either side of the boat. Straight tracking becomes second nature, and blade balance is quite evident.

Lake cruising can be good sport in itself. There comes a special feeling as a result of skimming over a smooth currentless surface. Perhaps the real value for prospective river runners is the realization that the arms, shoulders, wrists and hands are undergoing quite a bit of strain when balancing and paddling the boat. The first few times out a paddler can become quite weary after 30 minutes or so of sitting in a kayak. The importance of good physical condition and proper muscle tone is strikingly emphasized. The double paddle itself, which can weigh 3 or 4 pounds, can become heavy and burdensome. For river cruises and white-water treks, arms, wrists and hands should be well toned and geared to the stress of current sweeps, draws, forward and backward strokes.

Forward Stroking

For strong forward strokes, bury the entire blade in the water rather than slicing or splashing it across the surface. The stroking paddle, then, will angle from the hand into the water at about 45 degrees. Sweep the forward stroke in a straight line along the gunwale, rather than following the exact gunwale curve which could provide too much off-steering. Match the stroke in intensity and design on the other side, remembering foremost to retain fixed and unfixed blade control. Soon a good rhythm is developed with the forward stroke.

Backward Stroking

Only the stroke not the blades is reversed for back stroking, and for most novices this move will be a bit awkward at first. It is easy to skim or splash the back stroke blade, causing a weak, rocking, off-course surge to the rear. It is a bit more difficult to retain good blade angle on back strokes than forward strokes, probably because forward blade angle can be more easily checked and corrected. A misangled back stroke can lead to an abrupt wet exit.

The Sweep

The sweep is a strong turning stroke, used for full or partial turns to the right or left. It is easily made by

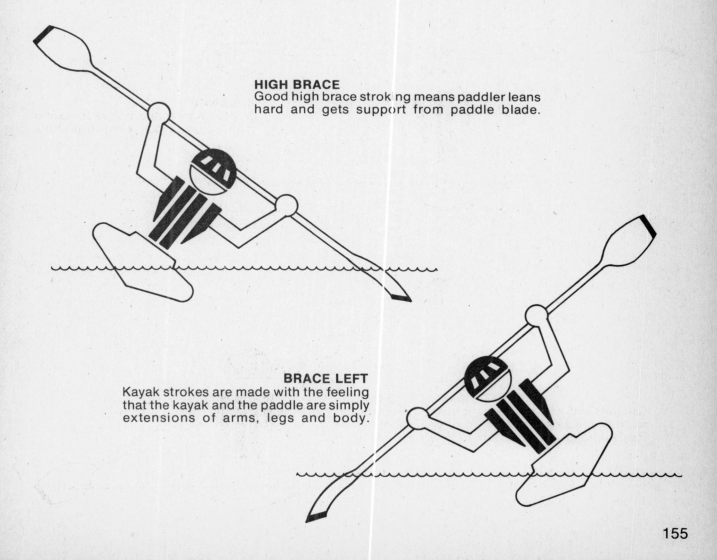

HIGH BRACE
Good high brace stroking means paddler leans hard and gets support from paddle blade.

BRACE LEFT
Kayak strokes are made with the feeling that the kayak and the paddle are simply extensions of arms, legs and body.

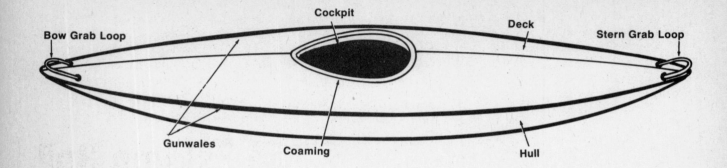

Bow Grab Loop · Cockpit · Deck · Stern Grab Loop · Gunwales · Coaming · Hull

stroking a wide arc beginning at the bow and ending close to the stern. A short, delicate sweep, when combined with a forward stroke on the opposite side can be used for directional control, as an alternative to turning.

The Inverted Sweep

This stroke begins with a draw to the bow, continues as a power stroke to the stern and finishes strong with an outward movement of the paddle. The stroke turns the boat swiftly to the paddle side and is fine for positioning the kayak for runs between obstacles or good positioning in chutes.

The Draw

This is a basic canoe stroke that is equally effective when applied to the kayak. Reach out high and far (paddle bracing technique and practice will help in this move) and slice paddle into the water. Pull yourself and the boat to where the paddle was inserted. The stroke is completed neatly by slicing the blade up toward the stern at the finish. Initial draw practice may result in capsizing, but it is vital to the effectiveness of the draw to lean far and hard.

Steering Stroke

As with a canoe paddle, the kayak paddles can be held at stern and used as a rudder for slight course changes and corrections. Since the rudder is placed at the stern, it does not give much horizontal stability. Do not depend on it too much and in no way should it be substituted for Duffek or back brace strokes (see below).

Sculling Strokes

It is the forward and backward sculling pull that keeps the boat from capsizing when recovering to the normal paddling position. Begin as a draw stroke and work the blade to the gunwales, alternating the angle as you pull yourself to the blade. The sculling stroke is fine for moderate course position changes while continuing on a set downstream course.

The Back Brace

The back brace is a good technique for retaining stability in rough water. However, it is more than just a balance stroke. It can be used for turns up to 180 degrees and sharp angle course changes out of eddies. The shaft is held in front of the body at chest level with the vertical face (as opposed to the flat, power face) at an angle to the water. A lean in that direction is needed for the back brace to be effective. From that position, it is easy to go into a quick forward stroke for rapid propulsion on the paddle side.

The Duffek Stroke or High Brace

This stroke was named after a Czech kayaker named Duffek who first used the high brace in the 1953 slalom championships. The value of this stroke is that it can be used to change boat direction sharply without much loss in speed. It can also be used for amidship bracing in heavy water, sometimes called a Side Brace.

The paddle is held high with the upper blade over the paddler's head and the working blade inserted forward and out at high climbing angle. The success of the high brace, as the name itself describes, is strong lean into the working blade. The paddle acts as a pivot point, similar in theory to when a pole is planted on the turn in downhill skiing. Good speed, whether from strong paddling or swift current, produces the sharper, more positive turn and enables the paddler to brace high and lean hard. The Duffek turn can be completed with a short, solid draw stroke to regain balance and then a forward power stroke to recover any lost speed.

Many of the strokes described here often come quite naturally when a paddler has had canoe or rafting experience and knows how to read current. Natural skills, of course, are welcome assets for novice kayakers. However, the sharpening of those skills, using precise blade angle consistently and aggressively leaning into braces, are the honing devices that separate good kayakers from mediocre ones. Kayak stroking is a robust wet sport in which aggressiveness is usually rewarded and timidity most commonly regretted.

The Eskimo Roll

THERE WAS A time when the Eskimo Roll was considered a showy maneuver performed only by the experts. Now, kayak instructors teach the roll to beginners and consider the mastery of it essential to the safety and enjoyment of a prospective river runner. There are some rather good river men who shun the roll. They claim, "I'll make it down the river without a roll." It is not really worth arguing with the non-rollers because most of them *can* make it down the river without a roll. Needless to say, those that continually substitute a wet exit for the Eskimo Roll never really make the grade as competitive kayakers. But then again, that may not be their ambition.

Refusing to learn the Eskimo Roll, failing to include the technique in the list of basic fundamentals, is a self-inflicted handicap that can seriously dampen enthusiasm, confidence and enjoyment of the sport.

When rolling is learned, the fear of capsizing is diminished significantly. This means strokes and maneuvers can be carried out with full sweep and vigor. But perhaps the most satisfying reward of the time and effort needed to master the stroke is the feeling a paddler gets knowing he has a good chance to recover from an upset without disrupting the ride and having to start all over. Not all rolls will be successful in tricky water, but those that are mean rich satisfaction for the paddler. Mastery of the roll keeps a kayaker in control even after capsizing. The technique can save your boat and possibly save you. A prospective kayaker is foolish not to take advantage of this self-righting maneuver that makes the kayak and kayaking something special.

How to Learn the Roll

My wife and I, intent as novice kayakers some years back, read several instructional booklets on the Eskimo Roll in preparation for our practical exercises. Equipped with wet suits and face masks, we found an ideal warm springs pool just outside the town of Jackson Hole, Wyoming, where we lived. We were bound and determined to learn the roll on our own. After about 2 hours of rolling over and hanging upside down from our boats like the pendulums of clocks, we came close to performing successful rolls. But we never quite made the grade. On paper the roll looks fairly easy to master.

"For a right-handed roll, hold the paddle along the left gunwale with the active blade almost at the bow. The plane of this blade is parallel to the surface of the water. The left hand holds the inactive blade at the end of the lower edge, just behind the hip at the side of the boat. The right hand, with wrist cocked up vertically, grasps the shaft as far forward as is comfortable. Lean forward. Capsize to the left. Now slice the active blade horizontally out from the hull, as far to the left as you can, turning your body from the waist toward that side. The recovery stroke begins from this point. It should be a continuous smooth action in which the action blade follows an arc which traces a diagonal path from the left front quadrant, then overhead, then to the right rear quadrant. When seen by an observer, the active blade sculls close to the surface in a rearward arc while the kayaker levers himself up at the other end of the paddle."—from *A White Water Handbook for Canoe and Kayak* by John T. Urban.

Diagrams accompanied the text explaining the Eskimo Roll step-by-step, and all seemed in order until actual performance. What my wife and I lacked, and which we soon received, was expert guidance. A friend of ours, an avid white water advocate and veteran of many kayak, canoe and raft trips on the Snake River in Wyoming, was quick to point out a couple of mistakes that had held us back. We completed our first successful roll after about 15 minutes of instruction. Once learned correctly the technique has a definite unforgettable feel, and the paddler, from then on, can judge for himself a good roll (strong and smooth enough to right paddler and boat in heavy water).

Learning and mastering the Eskimo Roll are two completely different propositions. The roll has to be instinctive. Good timing and "follow through" are musts. But there are so many variables involved with actual application of the roll: the degree of surprise as a result of capsizing; whether to make a left- or right-hand roll, depending on current and proximity to obstacles. Mastering the roll requires regular and almost religious

HOW TO DO THE ESKIMO ROLL

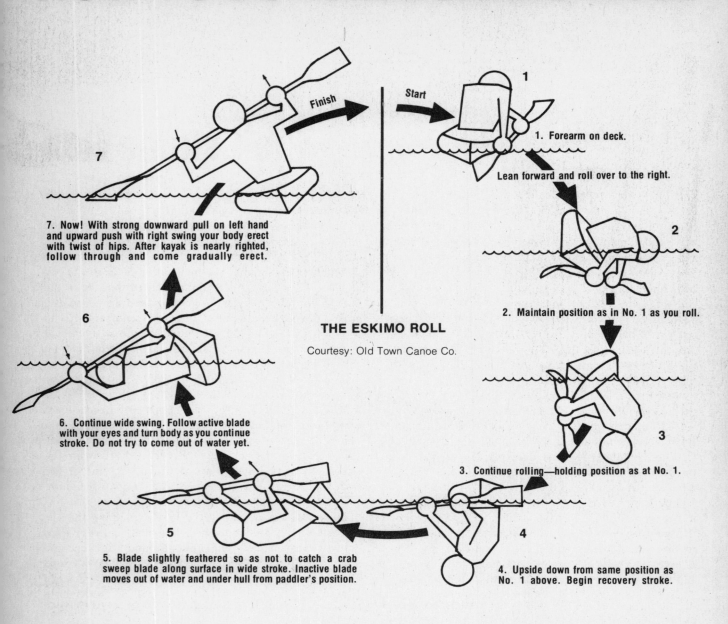

Finish **Start**

1. Forearm on deck.

Lean forward and roll over to the right.

2. Maintain position as in No. 1 as you roll.

THE ESKIMO ROLL

Courtesy: Old Town Canoe Co.

7. Now! With strong downward pull on left hand and upward push with right swing your body erect with twist of hips. After kayak is nearly righted, follow through and come gradually erect.

6. Continue wide swing. Follow active blade with your eyes and turn body as you continue stroke. Do not try to come out of water yet.

3. Continue rolling—holding position as at No. 1.

5. Blade slightly feathered so as not to catch a crab sweep blade along surface in wide stroke. Inactive blade moves out of water and under hull from paddler's position.

4. Upside down from same position as No. 1 above. Begin recovery stroke.

practice in all types of water situations. As a result, kayakers can perform the maneuver so smoothly and naturally that shoreline observers in downstream races sometimes do not realize that a roll has been executed.

The most important foundation to mastering the roll is to seek guidance of an expert, and if not, a friend then from kayak classes.

Where to Learn the Eskimo Roll

The water temperature of the practice pool should be warm enough to be conducive to learning. Then you can concentrate on techniques rather than staying warm. A swimming pool, warm water pond or lake is ideal. Remember, for a brief moment (although it seems at first, you hang forever), you will hang suspended under the kayak. Water should be at least waist deep and free from obstructions. Your teacher or buddy should stand just outside paddle distance. He or she will stand by to help you in case you need it and watch for torso position, strong sweep and recovery. However, the first step in learning the Eskimo Roll is simply called the roll.

At one time, the Eskimo Roll was considered to be a fancy trick. Now it should be mastered by anyone who enjoys white water kayaking.

The Eskimo Roll

With face mask or nose clips on, roll over with your kayak. This is the easiest part of the Eskimo Roll. You will be making a conscious effort to stay inside the kayak by pressing against the knee braces. Even this maneuver may take two or three tries because it is unnatural to stay in the boat, especially upside down. Hang there for a few seconds suspended. If you have a face mask on, look at your body position and your boat. Relax. Then release your knee-hold and push away

from the boat. Exit first without your paddle and then practice exiting while holding on to it. Eventually, you will gain confidence. You *can* exit from the kayak in an Eskimo Roll position if you need to. Rolling and exiting are important basic steps toward gaining assurance in yourself and your boat.

In making the actual roll and recovery (coming up on the other side in a complete roll), it is good to remember that the momentum of the initial roll should be continued throughout the process until recovery is achieved. As a beginner you will experience a pause,

Above—When you learn the Roll, you will spend a good deal of time in the water. Choose a warm, flat spot and have patience. Left—An instructor, with face mask and snorkel, can help a novice learn the Eskimo in a relatively short time.

hesitation or suspension (with your boat on top of you) that often negates the smooth, continuous fluid roll. Instructors often say this is the phase of learning that separates the learners from the doers. The basic roll is to acquaint the paddler with staying in the boat and the upside down position. The kayaker uses his knee braces but harnesses the momentum of the roll (the very act of capsizing) to help complete the cycle. It is this momentum, plus timely stroke sweeps, that enables completion of the roll. Some kayakers can roll using only their hands—not a paddle—to recover, showing the importance of follow-through.

Lean forward and to your right with the paddle and blade over the right side of the boat. The paddle should be held firmly, with knuckles out and the left hand ahead of the body and right hand slightly behind your side.

Roll smartly and smoothly to the right. Go with the momentum, twisting at the waist toward the roll direction. A smooth, continuous movement is initiated where the forward blade begins a sweep from its starting point near the bow. This sweep is directly out from your left side. As a result the active paddle blade ends up skimming near the water surface.

With your body nearly parallel to the surface, three-quarters of the roll is complete. A strong, smooth downward sweep with the left hand, and a push upward with the right, will lever your body and boat erect. It is important to regain your stroking balance immediately at recovery even during pond or pool practice. While completing the roll, you have temporarily lost sight of your course and recovery strokes are necessary to put you on the desired path.

An unparalleled feeling rises within you after completing the first Eskimo Roll during an actual run.

The difference in learning and mastering the Eskimo Roll in the pool and using it effectively on the river is similar to batting practice before a ball game and the true performance during the game. Practice perfects the technique. And until it is used with confident regularity, a kayaker has a tendency to tuck the maneuver too deep in the bag of reserve maneuvers. In fact, actually using the Eskimo the first few times in capsize situations may be just as tough as the initial mastering of the maneuver. But, with use, the maneuver itself becomes fun and instills a great deal of pride in the kayaker. Mastery of the Eskimo Roll, both from right- and left-hand position, separates the complete kayaker from the mediocre one.

Kayak Techniques

Getting in and out of a kayak is not as easy as it sounds. This is the proper bridge-paddle method for left side entry as demonstrated by the author.

THERE ARE FEW boats that demand as much careful attention as a kayak. The very act of entry into the cockpit of the slim, rocker-bottomed craft can be a frustrating affair without some simple but basic instruction. Exiting from the kayak, likewise can faintly resemble one's crude attempts at walking on a tightrope—again without any instruction. Give a man a canoe or a raft, and chances are that entry and exit won't be much of a problem. The kayak is a boat that must be harnessed and controlled from the very beginning. She is, by her nature, a fickle, nervous lady. Before dreams of riding her into the froth get the best of you, slip into the "saddle" for an introduction to how temperamental and tricky she can be.

Getting Into a Kayak

The kayak paddle, used as a brace or bridge from the bank (or the deck of a pool) to the aft deck of the boat,

Above—The beginning of a wet exit as author is ready to eject. Right—All novice and veteran kayakers alike get wet. Try to retain boat contact to keep it from floating downstream.

steadies the kayak for safe, sure entry. For right side entry, squat next to the cockpit on bank or deck, face the bow, and hold the paddle behind you with both hands. The left hand and left paddle shaft should be gripped securely and placed just to the rear of the coaming behind the seat. The flat side of the right paddle blade is bridged snugly on shore or deck. With the brace in place, slip the left foot into the boat slightly port (left) of center and in front of the seat. Be careful not to hook your heel on the front edge of the seat as this can throw you off balance. At this point, you will be putting quite a bit of weight on the paddle and your arms, so without too much hesitation and with a firm brace, slide your right foot over the coaming and into the cockpit. When your feet are in place, the next move, shifting the buttocks over and into the sitting position, comes quite naturally. All moves should be made smoothly and carefully since more than one kayaker has gotten off to a quick, wet start when the bridge slipped or the feet got tangled. On rocky shorelines, choose a rock or piece of shore that provides the best possible grip for the paddle bridge.

Strokes will be rough at first and the kayak will be "goosey."

Getting Out of a Kayak

The Dry Exit—Getting out of a kayak, or dry-exiting, is the same procedure as the entrance, only done in reverse. The most important consideration in dry exiting is to find a good "parking spot" with a solid enough bank so that the paddle bridge holds firm while the legs and the body are lifted and swung out of the boat. Remember to keep a paddle or hand grip on the boat after exiting.

The Wet Exit—This technique is best learned and practiced in comfortable, waist deep water in a pool or lake. A face mask or nose clip is a good practice accessory. The wet exit means that after capsizing, the kayaker swiftly and smoothly exits from the boat. Try it first without your spray skirt attached to the coaming. Since it is a natural reflex to exit from a boat in the process of rolling over, remember to stay in the cockpit by exerting pressure on the knee braces until the boat has completely flipped over. The exit from the boat will be done in somewhat of a vertical line, rather than a diagonal one. The exit will be smoother and more natural, when after a full roll, you release the knees slowly from the knee braces and let your body, staying in more or less the same type of sitting position, slip out of the cockpit.

Most novices are surprised how easy this move is. Practice exiting away from the boat and at the same time holding on to the cockpit rim.

Practice the maneuver without a spray cover or paddle and with a coach or partner standing nearby until it is down pat. The same moves are made with the spray cover attached except that in the process of rolling use one hand to release the shock cord around the coaming. Then slip out of the cockpit. Because the spray cover is designed with a shock cord attachment, the very act of exiting can release the skirt from the coaming in an emergency.

Under floating conditions, a one-handed release is required. While gripping the paddle with one hand, use the other hand to release the skirt and to hold on to the boat. Otherwise, the kayak will be swept downstream. Keep the shaft and blade of the paddle away from your face. The trickiest part of the wet exit in a current is to retain contact with both paddle and kayak while guarding against being hit by them.

The Paddle Brace Recovery

The paddle brace recovery teaches paddlers how far they can lean to one side or the other. It gives the kayaker a definite feel for the inherent stability of the

Good grip on paddle and good balance will help develop techniques and strokes.

boat—and because there are different hull styles, various boats have different critical points. This drill is the basis for the kayak brace strokes, so fundamental to good paddling. Knowing the critical point of your boat encourages full, strong paddling.

In 1 to 3 feet of water, bend at the waist and lean from the boat almost to the critical point. You may go beyond the critical point and be forced into a wet exit. After reaching out as far as you can, slap the water near the bow with a flat blade, which swiftly recovers the kayak to an upright position. Because of an extremely low center of gravity, a kayak responds to strokes quickly.

After the bow brace has been successfully performed, extend the paddle a full 90 degrees from the boat. Slap the water and recover to a full upright position. Lean out farther until you know you are well beyond the critical capsizing point. Now you know that it is your paddle that is keeping you from rolling underwater.

You can recover with the slap stroke and steady "up and down" sculling (drawing the blade to the boat) from a nearly impossible position with shoulder and head immersed in the water. Again, the power of the blade and the righting capabilities of the round hulled kayak come through positively. What the kayak lacks in stability is compensated for by responsiveness.

Paddle Recovery

This technique gives the kayaker a feel for recovery rolls, such as the Eskimo Roll, and serves to introduce the paddler to the upside-down, mixed up feeling that often occurs when you are under the boat. In waist deep water, roll left or right with a coach or partner on the opposite side. Your helper will firmly grip the paddle,

holding it parallel to your boat on the water surface about 6 inches away from the cockpit. After completing the roll, reach up, grab the paddle shaft, and right yourself with the coach keeping a firm grip on the paddle.

Half Roll Right and Left

The previous section of this book was on the much touted Eskimo Roll and that technique is important to learn. However, half rolls to the right and left, certainly pave the way for a better and faster grasp of the Eskimo Roll.

Sitting in your boat with a coach nearby, place the paddle parallel to the left gunwale for a half roll right. The front blade should be parallel to the water with the right hand palm down along the middle of the shaft. Lean forward and capsize to the right. With the paddle reach for the surface of the water with wrists actually breaking the surface. The forward blade should be about 2 feet away from the bow and swept to the right in an arc of 100 degrees. You may need help, at first, from a coach to keep the forward blade in the nearly 100 degree arc and close to the surface of the water throughout the sweep.

In a half roll to the left, the paddle should be parallel to the right gunwale with the front paddle blade parallel to the water and the left hand palm down along the middle of the shaft. Lean forward. Capsize to the left. Sweep the paddle to the left in a 100 degree arc.

The kayak is you, and you are the kayak. Both the boat and the double-bladed paddle are mere extensions of your ability to balance, stroke, think and judge currents. Everything is interrelated. And although kayak techniques seem complicated on paper, they are better understood and appreciated in the water.

Kayak Safety

A HIGH DEGREE of risk is built into the sport of kayaking. Kayakers are adventurers. Many non-kayakers describe the sport as "dangerous," "too risky for my blood," and "why die sooner than you have to?" All of which, no doubt, cause the prospective kayaker to ask, "Is the sport worth the risk?"

For many, it is not. For a relatively few, it is. Although the number of kayakers has grown in recent years, the increase cannot be described as booming or even strong. Steady, maybe. But slow and, fortunately, selective. Not everyone wants to sit in a cramped, "goosey" boat and be subjected to the roaring, overpowering froth of angry spring currents. Besides, a kayak can unsaddle a rider quicker than a rodeo bronc.

Experienced kayakers will tell you that downriver cruising is *nearly* as safe as walking the suburban streets. But then again, good kayakers have fewer accidents than novices. Kayaking is not a sport for the meek but neither is it a sport to be dreadfully feared. It is the violation of primary safety rules, rather than the sport itself, that gets most people into trouble.

You Need Qualified Instruction

You can learn some basics from a book. But the key to a safe kayaking foundation is qualified instruction. Beware of anyone who tells you, "I can have you rolling down the river in a day." Kayaking is a learned skill. It helps to have good balance, a strong swimming stroke, a love of rivers, and muscle power. Kayaking is a unique combination of all these ingredients plus the skill of instant stroking and bracing to every type of water and situation.

Instructors can make learning fun, however, expect to pay from $30 to $100 for competent instruction. Choose a course that offers physical preparation and toning in combination with basic water techniques.

A "Safe" Kayak

When choosing a kayak, most of them will look basically the same. Closer investigation often turns up significant safety differences that could prove one boat safer than another.

Feeling at ease in the water is important to kayak safety.

Above—Always kayak in groups and learn techniques from qualified instructors, starting out in flat water. Below—Smooth stretches of water can be just as much fun—if not more—than white water rivers. Choose waters to match skill level and ability.

Good fitting life vest is vital. Learn all techniques and strokes with your vest on.

A large man or woman, for instance, should not buy a custom or manufactured boat with a cockpit and hull so tiny and snug that it fits like a glove. Emergency ejecting from such a boat with the added bulk of a life vest plus the added interference of current could prove difficult, if not impossible.

Avoid buying kayaks with rough or unfinished edges along the coaming, seat and inside of the cockpit. Those rough spots could hang up wet suits, wind jackets or life vests and prevent quick, smooth exiting, as well as cause exit cuts.

Modern kayak hull materials were developed to replace fiberglass that cracks under stress. In strong current, they could be deformed, but unlike fiberglass, not broken. However, unbreakable hulls, unless supported by foam pillars or tough vinyl flotation bags, can trap paddlers inside. Manufacturers are now considering "breakaway" decks that give under heavy stress or a reunion with fiberglass alone or fiberglass in combination with one of the new plastics.

Footbrace bars have been responsible for trapping paddlers inside boats. They are being replaced with single "pedal-type" foot braces that are less likely to trap.

Even closer inspection reveals that some racing and white water bows, called low-volume bows (slimmer, lower and more projectile-like than even the conventional bullet-shaped bows), are susceptible to being pinned under rocks, ledges or trees. Hulls or decks of that design should be made of fiberglass or material that will break away under heavy stress.

New spray skirts should always be tested. Shock cord attachments should be fitted to the coaming lip secure enough to keep the skirt in place when the kayaker is seated and stroking. It should have enough give, though, to expand off the lip on hasty exits. Sometimes cords are made to fit a bit too snugly. In wet exit practice sessions, novice kayakers should learn to automatically pull the spray skirt free with one hand.

In any type of exiting or rolling, special care should be taken not to let paddle or boat hit the kayaker.

A helmet, with chin strap fastened, should always be worn when kayaking streams of moderate to heavy current or slow shallow streams with numerous obstacles.

Kayak Entrapment

The kayak with its deck and cockpit design is more likely to become trapped by rocks or snags than either the canoe or raft. For this reason, kayakers should take special precautions against entrapment.

Kayakers should avoid steep ledges and undercut rocks and trees. Due to the design and flexibility of the kayak bow, forward pinning in these water traps, further complicated by the force of downstream current, is nearly always fatal unless help with ropes is immediately at hand. Even then, the problem of getting

Wet suit, flotation bag and grab loops, at bow and stern, mean safer kayaking.

to the pinned kayaker often makes rescue impossible.

White water kayaking is a sport of many varied and split second decisions. When to try a roll, as opposed to wet exiting, is just one of those decisions. A kayaker should remember that a boat can be repaired or replaced, but limb and life is worth much more. That last "one more try" is often a critical decision. With heavy sucking currents moving the boat and paddler into trapping obstacles like rocks, trees and shoreline brush, it might be best to forget that last attempt at rolling and exit away from the boat.

The trouble may not be completely over even after exiting from a pinned boat. Kayakers, as well as canoers, swimmers, and wading fishermen have been foot trapped when they have attempted to walk in a strong current instead of floating and swimming to slower, safer calmer waters. With foot and ankle wedged in between rocks, logs or bottom debris, the force of the current can quickly sweep the person into a horizontal position with feet further locked into place. Rescue is nearly impossible with the time element and force of current providing insurmountable odds.

In slow or moderate currents, a kayaker, aided by a life vest, has a good chance of swimming or dog paddling to shore. In heavy water, float facing downstream, with feet and legs out in front and held high off the bottom to prevent entrapment. Legs can be used to fend off obstacles and protect the head and face.

Exposure

Getting wet is part of kayaking—but precautions against exposure, hypothermia and immobility due to the cold water and outside temperature should be taken. With the exception of kayaking in warm water or hot weather, a wet suit with boots, gloves and hood should be considered standard equipment. High water periods, often best for kayakers, can provide the coldest water of the year. A complete wet suit is the best insurance against exposure and immobility. Generally, water temperature from 36 to 40 degrees Fahrenheit renders boaters immobile in 10 to 13 minutes. In the process of complete immobilization however, varying degrees of numbness and pain that seriously obstruct thinking ability and swimming skills occur. A wet suit is cheap insurance.

Kayak Camping

KAYAK CAMPING! Impossible you say? No. Tricky? Yes!

There have always been a few persons, who because of stamina, willpower and perseverance, have been able to camp with a minimum of gear. A kayak camper is one. Once a highly Spartan and little heard-of endeavor, camping by kayak is now practical and comfortable.

Lightweight, super-compact backpacking equipment has been refined to the point that kayakers can fit a very complete and satisfying camp in the bow and stern sections of most touring kayaks. The secret to enjoyable kayak camping is to keep the weight limit under 20 pounds, stow everything in waterproof cargo-flotation bags, and avoid waters which are most likely to cause repeated attempts at Eskimo Rolling. Kayaking with camp gear on board can be teamed with unhurried cruising to obtain the ultimate in paddling solitude. The camping kayaker is an ultra-light backpacker or boat-packer, who does not burden himself with gadgets.

After you have mastered kayaking strokes and techniques the real fun begins. Now you are ready to use your boat to explore waterways in a quiet, efficient manner. Like the Eskimos, Indians and trappers, you

An important part of all camping considerations is planning the trip during stable weather periods. This photo shows storm build-up.

Lightweight, compactable dehydrated foods, when taken out of their rigid cardboard packing containers, are excellent for kayak camping.

have eliminated the frills and can concentrate on the basics—the peace and the satisfaction that comes with being self-propelled and self-contained.

Equipment

Before packing in cargo bags, some items like single-burner stoves, fuel canisters, sleeping bags, dehydrated food, fishing tackle, camera and film should be packed first in their own protective containers. Soft packs or containers made of nylon or plastic are easier to stow. By "double packing" some items, they are not only further protected against accidental dunking but are easier to organize and find in the cargo bag.

A good, down pack sleeping bag is the foundation to enjoyable kayak-camping. For all-around camping I would choose one with a comfort range that goes down to at least 10 degrees. There are some good Fiberfill II pack bags on the market, but they do not compact as well as down, and for this reason alone (at least for kayaking), the northern goose wins out over synthetic insulation.

A three-quarter length foam pad of ½- or ¾-inch thickness can be easily stowed in the hull of the boat as it conforms nicely to the shape of bow or stern. Sleep will come easy with a good sleeping bag and foam mattress. And the cargo-flotation bag makes a handy pillow.

You can pack a lightweight, 4- to 7-pound nylon tent or fashion a shelter from a lighter and more compactable tarp. This decision depends on the amount of rainfall typical of your camping area and whether or not flies and mosquitoes pose a serious threat to your peace of mind.

Since many areas do not allow open fires, consider a single-burner pack stove as standard equipment. Some pack stoves can be temperamental and hard to light. I've used the Gerry Mini-stove on backpack and boat-camp treks for about 3 years now and find that brand reliable and convenient.

Choose cook gear as you would for backpacking. A medium-sized fry pan, 2-quart kettle and 1-quart coffee and soup pot serve most needs adequately. A backpack grill also comes in handy.

You might allow yourself the first-night luxury of steaks and a beer or two, but after that dehydrated meals are more practical. Add some zip to meals by

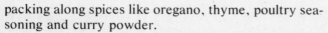
The beauty of nature along the river is one of the many bonuses of kayak camping.

packing along spices like oregano, thyme, poultry seasoning and curry powder.

The river you travel will probably not have water pure enough to drink straight. Since it is impractical to pack water in a kayak, purify what's available by boiling or by using water purification techniques. Powdered fruit drinks, hot chocolate, coffee and tea can be enjoyed from the purified water.

Fishing rods should be of the backpack variety, sectioned so they can be broken down and packed in an aluminum or plastic container not more than 3 feet long. Daiwa, Fenwick, Berkley, Garcia and Orvis all make pack rods (for spinning, fly-fishing or a combination of both) that are ideal for kayak-camping. Ultra-light fly and spinning reels can be packed in the cargo bag along with the rod. In the event of swamping, the rod won't be lost. The cargo bag, when inflated, fits snugly in the bow and stern compartments and will remain there even if the boat is trapped underwater.

Lures and flies can be packed in small plastic boxes or canisters (film cassette cans are handy for storing flies) and then kept together in a plastic or nylon ditty bag.

Clothing

Kayaking demands a lot of exercise. Keep clothing loose and light in the summertime when traveling warm waters. In colder climates and where water temperatures dip below 50 degrees, a wet suit, including frogman's gloves and boots should be worn. Extra or dry clothing can be packed in a nylon sack. You might want to wear a pair of tennis shoes for kayaking, but don't forget a pair of boots for camp use. Lightweight rain gear takes up relatively little space in the clothing bag. Keep it on top so it can be reached easily.

Extra Gear

Spray skirts, wet suits, nylon windbreakers, gloves and helmets can be considered standard equipment for some waters. Life vests, of course, are a must.

Look out over the shimmering river. The kayaks are beached for the night. They glow in the setting sun. The river has taken you to a quiet spot. Bask in the delights of a simple camp. Pride overwhelms you. There was a learning period. Long, by today's standards. You got through it. And now, alone, tired, happy, you reap the tremendous rewards of total kayaking.

Kayak Surfing

ABOUT 24 years ago. Don Golden's wife brought a newspaper article about white water boating to his attention. Not long after, he purchased a used Klepper double kayak, tried it, and liked it. A couple of years later, it occurred to him that a person in a kayak could ride the ocean surf much like the surfboarders do. He and his son tried it time after time and found they were spending a lot of time upside down in the water.

Gradually, by trial and error, they made equipment modifications and developed techniques that worked. They eventually sold the double kayaks and bought two, single foldboat kayaks. Others became interested in the kayak surfing techniques not only in the United States but in other countries as well. The foldboats were sold and replaced with fiberglass kayaks of various designs.

Don Golden, kayak surfer from Oakland, California, says he dislikes flat water. "I'm mediocre in the river and have never been on a float trip. *Good* surf is pure ecstasy though," Golden adds with enthusiasm.

Kayak surfing, as the name implies, is based on the same principles as surfboarding, only the kayak surfer sits in his boat and uses a double paddle to catch the waves and get good rides. "In general," Golden says, "I prefer the largest waves I can find providing they can be picked up and ridden without serious wipeout at

Kayak surfer catches a good wave in snub-nosed surf kayak.

Above—Nose of kayak caught in the surf and sucked down by current. Below—Kayaker caught in the force of a breaking wave—wet exit might be best here.

least 50 percent of the time. Although hard to find, a swell in the 10-foot range is delightful and one in the 15- to 20-foot range is pure ecstasy.''

Golden's longest ride was about 1/2 to 3/4 of a mile from the center peak at Steamer Lane to the beach at Cowell's in Santa Cruz. ''That was a very rare occurrence, but rides of an 1/8 to a 1/4 of a mile at Steamer Lane in the big winter surf are fairly common. The best surf is usually between October and late April.''

Surfing kayaks are shovel-nosed boats that resemble conventional kayaks in profile but lack the extremely pointed bows and sterns of the river boats. Snub-nosed kayaks are designed for speed and quick maneuverability. They are less likely to purl or move in circles on the break of a wave with that type of design.

According to Golden a spare set of paddles, attached to the forward deck of the boat, should be considered standard equipment for all kayak surfing. ''You can easily break a paddle when you get rolled over, and you *will* get rolled over. If you get dumped and don't grab either the bow or stern lines, the boat can blow away or get carried off by a wave. You probably will have to let go of your paddle in order to swim fast enough to catch the boat. So a spare paddle is a must.''

Unlike some types of boat use—where floating ability might suffice in case of swamping—a kayak surfer should be a strong swimmer. Golden offers these tips to beginners. ''Learn the basic paddling techniques in calm water—the same basic techniques learned for white water kayaking. Learn how to capsize a kayak with the spray sheet attached and get out of the boat quickly and smoothly while the boat is upside down. You should practice this until the exit becomes second nature so you don't panic when you unexpectedly capsize.

''Learn a good Eskimo Roll and be able to do it either

The ride in a surfing kayak is fast and thrilling.

Surfing kayakers work in groups for safety. Small waves are good for beginning practice.

right- or left-handed until it is instinctive and can be performed under the most unfavorable conditions. The reason more people don't take to surfing is they get discouraged from getting wiped out so often. It's pretty fatiguing when a lot of spills are taken and a person can't roll. It's a lot easier to roll after a capsize than to get out of the boat, empty it, and get back in.

"The most common problems for the novice are fear and lack of confidence. Being proficient with techniques and surfing helps alleviate the fear and gradually builds confidence. Some kayak surfers go to the other extreme when they advance above the beginner stage and are overconfident and foolhardy. Either way, kayakers can get in trouble in the surf."

Special Safety Precautions

A kayak surfer should always grab a bow or stern line before exiting a boat so that the boat won't be lost due to wind, current or wave action.

Wear a wet suit and crash helmet. The surf can be cold, and the suit helps retain body heat. But even more important than that, the suit protects the skin against cuts and abrasions. A good crash helmet similar to the ones worn by competitive white water kayakers is vital. It protects against injury in accidental collisions with boat, paddle or bottom.

Carry readily accessible spare paddles—Don Golden suggests that two extra paddles be carried.

Surf kayaks should have watertight compartments fore and aft and should be equipped with secondary flotation, such as foam in the compartments in case they are broken or punctured.

Learn to handle the various situations that you may run into before you actually encounter them. If you get wiped out and are not prepared, figure out how to best handle that situation the next time it happens.

Always use the buddy system when kayak surfing.

What Can You and Your Boat Survive?

Golden says, "If you are after big waves, periodically you are going to be in the wrong spot at the wrong time and really get chewed up. Gradually you learn that you and your boat can survive almost anything. Once you realize this and learn the best ways to handle potentially bad situations, much of the initial fear will vanish. Actually, if a wave isn't big enough to scare you, it may be fun, but it's not really exciting. Even after years of experience, you will probably still get into situations where you'll wonder if you can survive. I don't believe you ever overcome the fear such a situation creates. This is just one of the *prices* you pay for exposure to some fantastic waves and rides. I wouldn't have it otherwise."

Kayak Surfers—What Are They Made Of?

"Good muscular coordination, a certain amount of physical strength, good swimming ability and a certain amount of derring-do are all traits that help make a good boater.

"However, I think anyone can learn to be a good boater if he or she wants to badly enough. But not everyone can learn to *like* it. Enjoyment of boating, particularly the more exciting and potentially dangerous forms of it, is a highly personal thing. Perhaps it takes an adventurous personality. I think skiers, ice boaters and kayakers are all out of the same mold. Perhaps it's an affinity for speed, exposure to potential danger. Maybe it's pitting yourself against the elements or concerting with the forces of nature to your own personal pleasure. I don't really know. I just hope I can continue to enjoy it for many years to come."

Folding Kayaks

Double place folding kayak holds family of three.

THERE'S A NICE alternative for people who desire a kayak or canoe but don't have the storage space or the capability of cartopping or trailering a conventional boat.

Johann Klepper started making folding kayaks in Germany in 1907, and his company's kayaks and boats have been popular ever since. "Klepper," according to Dieter Stiller, manager of the Hans Klepper Corporation, "is the oldest, and the original maker of kayaks (commercially) in the world."

Klepper's folding kayaks are clever examples of unique boat engineering. An internal frame of ash and birch hull and deck members and cross ribs resemble (without the skin) the frame of early Indian skin covered canoes and kayaks. Over the frame a decking of hemp and cotton, impregnated, waterproofed yet breathable, is stretched. The hull cover is made by vulcanizing five layers of Hypalon rubber and long hemp. According to the Klepper Company, hulls often last 15 years under average use and care before a new hull replacement is needed.

The boat is assembled or taken apart in about 15 to 30 minutes by one person. Snaplock fittings are responsible for fairly simple assembly and take down, eliminating the need for screws and bolts. The Klepper boats have gunwales formed from I-beam girder construction. They have built-in sponsons, long tubes in the chambers along the gunwales. These are most commonly inflated by mouth and make the boat virtually unsinkable and quite stable.

The Klepper "Aerius II" is a double-place kayak with an overall length of 17 feet, 1 inch, a beam of 34 inches, and weighs 64 pounds. An optional sailing rig is available for it. Three small bags, compact enough to fit inside a VW, carry the entire boat. A fourth bag, (4 feet 9 inches x 9 inches) carries optional sailing equipment if desired.

The "Aerius I," a single seater, fits in two small bags. The boat has an overall length of 15 feet, is 29 inches at the beam, and weighs 55 pounds.

Accessories for Klepper foldaway boats include doublebladed touring paddles, rudder assemblies for lake use where winds are common, motor mount crossbars, handtiller for sailing, and spray cover that closes cockpit against spray and rain.

This folding kayak was packed in to a high mountain lake in Wyoming.

PART 5
APPENDIXES

Ask the Experts

Dick Ludewig

From Cody, Wyoming, Dick Ludewig is an experienced outdoorsman, who is an avid canoeist. Proprietor of Western Travel Merchants, a Rocky Mountain-based travel agency that specializes in outdoor adventure trips, Ludewig can be described as the *complete* canoe camper. He has a sound working knowledge of canoeing and the wilderness and how to live with it. In addition, Ludewig is an accomplished outdoor chef and a master of sourdough pancakes, light, fluffy fortifiers of mind and body—just right for the start of a day's float trip.

How did Dick Ludewig first become interested in canoeing?

"I was born and reared in the Hawaiian Islands and, early on, learned to manage an outrigger canoe proficiently, both competitively and for recreation. It was natural that when I left the Islands to live in Wyoming, my interest in canoeing would be transferred to the "Indian-style" canoe. My interest has continued, and my love for the sport has grown. Now instead of the warm waters of the Pacific, I rejuvenate my body and spirit on the Snake River of Wyoming."

What advice can you offer beginners?

"Learn canoeing early and learn from a knowledgeable and experienced canoeist. Accept that person's advice and do what he or she may say until one has had an opportunity to learn from one's own experience. It would seem to me the most common problem for the novice is to find an experienced canoeist who is willing to share his or her time or talent. A novice should learn his or her boat, its reactions to various paddling strokes, and how 'to make the boat go.' I cannot help but re-emphasize the importance of learning these things in concert with one who has 'done it before'."

How does a person gain enough courage to float white water?

"By doing it! First in the company of an experienced canoeist and then finally alone (in one's own canoe). Begin with relatively calm water and work up to streams with higher difficulty ratings. Difficult white water does cause me significant apprehension, although I don't think I can really call that *fear*. It is especially distressful if my paddling partner appears more afraid or more concerned than I do. That's why it's good to learn with a good, confident canoeist,

"While I don't think I really overcome my apprehension, so to speak, I do learn to float with it. If confronted with difficult situations, I know that I have top equipment (boat, paddles, preservers) and I know my limitations. This enables me to make several different decisions. I can go ahead, confident in my equipment and ability. Or I acknowledge my limitations and *I don't go*."

What makes a good canoeist or kayaker?

"I think one who insists on good equipment, has good judgment, and knows his or her limitations, will make a good recreational canoeist. With extra work and dedication, the same prerequisites are needed by good competitive boaters also.

"I feel almost anyone can learn to be a good canoeist, but it does take a special kind of person to want to be a good paddler in the first place. The ultimate benefit, the exhilaration, the involvement, the freedom offered the paddler is different from that offered the person more comfortable in the seat of an easy chair. Some people would rather stay home and watch canoeists on television. So the sport isn't for everybody. The person who enjoys the outdoors recognizes its discomforts as well as its comforts. Usually that person finds that chilly hands or chilly feet or both are worth the experience."

Peter A. Sonderegger

Peter Sonderegger is the editor and publisher of *Canoe*, the magazine of the American Canoe Association. Not only does Sonderegger produce a fine magazine, good reading for novice and veteran paddler alike, he himself is an avid canoeist who thoroughly enjoys what he and his magazine preach.

How did Peter Sonderegger first get interested in canoeing?
"As a youngster in Wisconsin, I was introduced to a grand lady—an Old Town wood-canvas canoe. The thrill has been there ever since."

What was the first lesson you learned that no one could have taught you?
"Never stand up in a canoe."

How does a person gain enough courage to float white water?
"Understand how to handle the body when going through white water. Feet should be first and out of the water. Depending on the severity of the rapids, this body float can be an exhilarating experience and does much to bolster confidence in running white water. I have a respect for white water. If you don't have a respect for it, you will have problems."

What advice can you offer beginners?
"Take lessons from competent instructors. A careless attitude toward the sport and improper equipment are the most common problems for the novice."

What makes a good canoeist or kayaker?
"A good canoeist evolves from hard work and experience. They are made, not born, and anyone willing to take the time and effort can learn."

Sheila Link

Sheila Link is an eager canoeist and canoeing instructor from Bradley Beach, New Jersey. Also an enthusiastic camper and angler, she combines her backcountry skills with wilderness camping and canoeing throughout the United States and Canada. Sheila is a qualified survival instructor and has experienced a variety of difficult field tests which have given her the credentials to teach and give survival demonstrations. She has been a member of the Board of Directors of the Outdoor Writers Association of America and was one of the directors of *Outdoor Women*, an organization she helped found for learning and sharing outdoor sports and activities for women.

How did Sheila Link first get interested in canoeing and kayaking?
"I was looking for another way to travel through the wilderness and felt that canoe trails would provide a wonderful method. Later I sought more excitement and a great challenge, so I learned kayaking in order to run white water streams."

What was the first lesson you learned that no one could have taught you?
"Caution!"

What advice can you offer beginners?
"Spend lots of time paddling solo in order to learn how to really control your canoe. And learn to 'read' water by observing current direction, how the water breaks on the surface of the stream and over rocks, logs and ledges. Learning how to read water is often the biggest problem a novice faces."

Do you still experience fear while floating?
"You'll gain courage as you gain experience and competence. And your courage will be in direct proportion to your developed ability. Sure I still experience fear in white water, but since that adds to the fun and excitement, I don't expect or even want to completely overcome that sense of potential danger. In fact, a person can be in trouble if he or she fails to recognize a hazardous situation."

What makes a good canoeist or kayaker?
"Good paddlers, in my opinion, combine intelligence, courage, strength and stamina with competence. Anyone can learn to be a competent paddler if he or she wants to work at it. But only a few become truly expert because of the unique combination of characteristics and physical capability required. Not many people, relatively speaking, are willing to give up the time and effort necessary to become expert."

Peter Sonderegger

Sheila Link

Rip Collins

Rip Collins, from Boone, North Carolina, in the heart of New River country, is a canoeing gentleman. To accompany him, his wife Margaret, or the Collins children on a New River float trip is a peaceful, educational adventure. Rip not only knows canoes and the art of making them respond with gentle, smooth strokes, he knows the country, the animals, birds and fish in and along the river. He is what one might call the complete canoeist because he savors every river trip he makes.

Rip Collins fought successfully against the power dams on the New River. But another kind of progress recently set he and his family back a stroke or two. His house and canoe store overlooking the river were taken away from him because they blocked a proposed four-lane highway between the towns of Boone and Blowing Rock. You can't keep a good man down. Rip and his family have relocated and will operate a canoe trip and rental concession on the New River called "Adventure Outfitters."

The Collins family, no doubt, will continue to provide quality canoeing experiences down the river they love so much. Rip has recently written a book about the New River and surrounding area, tentatively called *Blue Ridges and White Water*, now at the publishers.

How did Rip Collins first get interested in canoeing?

"My first experiences with a canoe were at Boy Scout Camp on a small lake. But it has been a love affair ever since. I have drifted streams since my own boys were Boy Scout age and younger."

What was the first lesson you learned that no one could have taught you?

"When it comes to rivers, the difficulty has been (until recently) to get good information as to where to go; where to put in; and where to take out. Also how difficult a stream might be. At least for our area, we now have guide books which cover most streams including stream classification and a discussion of difficulties which may be encountered."

What advice can you offer beginners?

"It is important for a beginner to learn the stream classifications and follow the guide books. The novice on our streams is most likely to be too ambitious and seems to prefer to start with the rougher rivers. In reality, the novice should start with easy drifting until he or she can well manage the boat. Another problem I see frequently is people trying to travel great distances by canoe. They sometimes get overcome by darkness before reaching their destination, and this can lead to trouble."

How does a person gain enough courage to float white water?

"I am at the age and experience in life that I devote my time and energy to the easy Class I and II streams. The more I canoe, the greater is my respect for the dangers of white water and the need for extreme safety precautions. For white water thrills, there must be some element of danger—that's what makes it exciting."

What makes a good canoeist or rafter?

"I divide canoe people into two categories. Those who like to drift the easy streams for the quiet peace and to enjoy nature. This is what I like. The other group seeks the thrill of white water. These decisions are made by the individuals according to personal psychological make-up. But, I think that it is important to point out to the more timid personalities that there is good sport in safe, quiet drifting and a person need not be a daredevil to experience this phase of canoeing. It is like comparing backpacking to mountain climbing."

Eric Evans

Eric Evans is a seven-time national kayak champion (6 years slalom and 1 year wild water) and was a member of the 1972 U.S. Olympic Team. He has been involved in the sport for over 12 years and has been a top ranked kayak slalomist since 1967. He has been on every U.S. World Championship team since then. Evans is the only American K-1* paddler to ever win an international event in Europe.

Aside from active competition, he has run clinics for paddlers in just about every area of the country. Eric has taught at various kayak schools and has helped make instructional white water movies. He served on the American Canoe Association National Slalom Committee for 2 years. Evans is currently the editor of *Down River* Magazine, published by World Publications in Mountain View, California.

Evans himself had an excellent teacher, his father Robert Jay Evans, former U.S. Olympic Coach and author of the book, *Kayaking* (Stephen Greene Press, Brattleboro, Vermont) which is considered the bible of the sport.

How did Eric Evans first get interested in canoeing and kayaking?

"In 1964 I became interested because of my father Robert Jay Evans. He was an avid open canoeist in the late 1950s but switched to a kayak in the early 1960s and has been an enthusiastic kayaker ever since. It was his enthusiasm for the sport that got me started. Living in Hanover, New Hampshire, my Dad and I were prime

*One-person racing kayak utilizing double-bladed paddle.

movers of the Ledyard Canoe Club of Dartmouth College. This really got me going.''

What was the first lesson you learned that no one could have taught you?

"The first lesson that cannot be taught and I feel is true for nearly every person is how to keep your kayak going in a straight line while paddling on flat water. *Everyone* is frustrated at first.''

What advice can you offer beginners?

"Learn the fundamentals and get them down cold on flat water before going in white water. Learn the roll. Wear proper clothing. And do not fear capsizing. Only by pushing your limits will you be able to learn.''

Do you, as an expert kayaker, still experience fear?

"No. Fear is not a problem. Only on a *very* difficult river does fear enter into the picture for me.''

Can everyone learn kayaking?

"Not everyone can learn. A person must be able to swim and should be at home in the water. A kayaker must put up with cold—both in and out of the boat. Some persons dislike this part of it. Physical discomfort, at least for kayaking, is a natural part of this type of boating.''

Eric Evans (r.) with his father Jay Evans.

Burks Smith

Burks A. Smith

Burks A. Smith is Vice-President of Bonair Boats Inc., Lenexa, Kansas, one of the largest and most respected manufacturers of inflatable boats in the country. Burks himself is a dedicated floater and an expert in running white water in motor-powered inflatables. Smith says, "Contrary to what many oar-power purists may like to believe, using a powered boat requires no less skill in 'reading' the river, only less muscle power.''

How did Burks Smith first get interested in canoeing and rafting?

"I first became interested in white water boating when a friend invited me along to run one of southern Missouri's toughest white water streams, the St. Francis River. Even though neither of us had much fast water experience with canoes, and the trip was punctuated with capsizings, it was such a unique experience that I decided to pursue it further at every opportunity.''

What was the first lesson you learned that no one could have taught you?

"An experienced white water boat handler can *tell* you everything you need to know, but you don't actually learn it until you are on the water in a real situation. There is no substitute for experience.''

What advice can you offer beginners?

"In a canoe, most beginners tend to lean toward the upstream side when approaching a hazard, a maneuver that almost always results in capsizing. In a raft, most beginners fail to maneuver the raft to the most advantageous position and put themselves at the mercy of the current.''

How does a person gain enough courage to float white water?

"Gaining enough courage to float white water is a personal thing that each individual must deal with on his own. Having confidence in your ability and your equipment plays a significant role. Floating white water is thrilling, and fear and thrills are so closely related that it is hard to distinguish between the two. Every white water boater experiences some fear if the river is challenging. That's why they are running white water in the first place. The key is maintaining composure and good judgment. Never let fear turn to terror.''

What makes a good canoeist or rafter?

"A good boater is knowledgeable about techniques and knows the limitations of this equipment and his own ability. Anyone can be a good boater if he takes the sport seriously. I can think of no limitations imposed on the sport, except that the requirement of *sincere interest* MUST be present. Everything else seems to fall into place with that foundation.''

Al Button

Cliff Jacobson, of Hastings, Minnesota, a fine canoeist in his own right, recommended that I contact Al Button. Jacobson described Button as probably the best C-1* canoeist in the United States. He won several medals at the world games and is an American Olympic Team hopeful. Button also designs and builds canoes and kayaks.

How did you first get interested in canoeing and kayaking?

"I first became interested in canoeing at Boy Scout Camp, near my home on Lake Geneva, Wisconsin. When I moved to St. Paul, Minnesota, about 10 years ago, I joined the Minnesota Canoe Association and they introduced me to kayaking."

What was the first lesson you learned that no one could have taught you?

"I found out that nature can be serious, even deadly. I had a brush with death from hypothermia before I had ever heard of the term. Through that experience, I learned a great respect for white water because several swims and cold water nearly killed me. I capsized several times in heavy rapids and made two serious mistakes. I did not have protective clothing (wet suit) on, and I had been paddling alone. I will never make those mistakes again."

What advice can you offer beginners?

"Beginners should find a club and ask plenty of questions. You will save money by getting the right boat and gear that matches the area you will be paddling. By joining a club, you can often get equipment at reduced prices. It's a good idea also, to learn through classes

---

*One-person racing canoe utilizing a single paddle.

and clinics. Self-taught techniques can be fun at first, but you can save time by learning through competent instructors. It is easy to get discouraged with canoeing or kayaking by starting out with the wrong equipment or wrong style. A canoe club is a good way to meet friends that share your interests and are willing to help you. Trial and error methods are slow and can be dangerous."

How does a person gain enough courage to float white water?

"A person should have the desire to float white water. If the desire is there, then he or she should seek qualified instruction to learn the proper techniques for enjoying white water. Start with easy goals and work up. Realize that courage will come with experience. I myself experience fear on rapids that are near the limit of my ability. But this feeling, this type of fear, is similar to the nervousness a speaker or performer feels before a performance. It alerts the senses. Most of this fear can be overcome through experience—knowing a particular run will be fun instead of scary."

What makes a good canoeist or kayaker?

"Anyone can learn, but people are different so there are different rates of learning and different levels that can be reached. A good kayaker, for instance, must have a good sense of balance; must be aggressive; and not too fearful of anything. Good reflexes have to be developed and also a feel for what the water is doing so it can be read correctly. 'Natural talent' helps, but I have seen some *zero* talent beginners turn into really good boaters through persistence, desire and practice. Usually they developed through the help of experienced teachers. Since white water varies from easy to horrendous, there are river stretches and sport for everyone."

Al Button

Cliff Jacobson

Cliff Jacobson

Cliff Jacobson does not really consider himself an expert canoeist (although he comes highly recommended), at least not in white water. He calls himself a very competent canoeist in white water, but mostly he says, "I'm a wilderness tripper, so my comments are basically for wilderness open canoe paddlers." Modest as he is, Jacobson authored his first book, *Wilderness Canoeing and Camping* (Dutton).

How did Cliff Jacobson first get interested in canoeing and kayaking?

"My first canoe experience was at a Boy Scout summer camp. I think it was the silence and beauty of the canoes that attracted me. As I became more proficient with a paddle, I liked to go alone—at sunset and early in the morning especially.''

What was the first lesson you learned that no one could have taught you?

''The importance of really waterproofing your gear for a canoe trip. A friend and I inadvertently shot a 5-foot falls once with a heavily loaded open canoe. When we came up, our canoe was nearly swamped, and there was a good rapid below and another falls. Rocks were well submerged, but the water was very heavy and foamy. Our tightly secured waterproof packs gave the canoe enough buoyancy to bring us through the rapids and safely to shore. Without the added buoyancy I think we would have lost both our outfits and canoe —possibly our lives.''

What advice can you offer beginners?

''First, read all the canoe books you can find. Although we learn from experience, there is a wealth of information in good books. Both your wilderness tripping education and your white water techniques will be enhanced by this knowledge. Secondly, join a club. Even if you are a solitary person—one who likes to cruise wilderness rivers alone—you need to develop your paddle skills, and you really can't do this alone. You need the presence of a rescue party in the event of a capsize, and you need to study the techniques of others. Only a club can provide these things.

The most common problem for novices is being underprepared. New paddlers don't understand the value of a wet suit in cold water, a good paddle, or a good vest-type life preserver. Most don't realize the importance of additional flotation in open canoes. These are things that can be learned from books. There is no excuse for being unprepared, equipment wise, for a trip even if you can't paddle a canoe.''

How does a person gain enough courage to float white water?

''I don't know. I always think I am a little crazy when I hit the water in March—even with a wet suit. I think it must be part of your makeup. Though I know some very experienced paddlers who will admit their fright, most won't—at least not until after the run. Some paddlers are braver than others; some reckless; and a few are not very bright. Myself, I'm not very bold. Class IV (difficult rating where high skill is demanded) is where I quit with an open canoe. I know other paddlers who take Class IV in stride with open canoes, but they frequently tear their boats up. And once in awhile, they tear their bodies up too. I'm not prepared to do that. I'm always apprehensive when I enter a tough pitch—maybe even scared—but as soon as we hit the rapid, I'm too busy doing my thing to worry about being scared. I just paddle. The canoe does the rest.''

What makes a good canoeist or kayaker?

''A good boater is a safe boater. I know some mechanically excellent hotshots who think they can run anything. I know others who are more cautious who damage their boats and their bodies less frequently. I think anyone can be a good boater by this definition. You need some strength to paddle a canoe or kayak, of course, but mostly you need the right paddle skills. Also, I think you need a good sense of balance. Without that, you probably won't even be able to paddle a raft well.''

Pat Simmons

Pat Simmons owns and operates a canoe sales and rental operation, the Creek Canoe Company, in Dickinson, Texas. ''Racing stimulates me the most,'' he says, ''as I feel very capable and fit when I am racing, even if I don't win which is important when you are over 40.'' Simmons paddles for pleasure, as well as competitively, and is presently Vice-President of the United States Canoe Association and Vice-President of the Texas Canoe Racing Association. He is a past President of the Houston Canoe Club. An avid canoeist, kayaker, and surf-kayaker, his comments are based on a great deal of experience.

How did Pat Simmons first get interested in canoeing and kayaking?

''I started out in my teen years in a canoe, paddling and poling around in Mobile Bay, Alabama. I really didn't get super-interested in canoes until some years later in Texas after making canoe trips with the Boy Scouts. I was exposed to racing and that did it. I then learned about all the refinements that make canoes go better and I was hooked.''

What was the first lesson you learned that no one could have taught you?

''I honestly can't think of anything I've learned on the river that could not have been taught by someone beforehand. I believe I have been guilty of the same things that many others are. We were told, but it didn't sink in until we actually experienced it for ourselves.''

What advice can you offer beginners?

''Get to know some canoeists in your area who will give you good, sound advice. Read all that you can about the sport. With your reading and the help of capable paddlers, you'll progress faster with your own skills. Take a course in canoeing, kayaking or both. Even if you feel you never want to kayak, try it. Later the skills you picked up in kayaking will pay off by making you a better canoeist. For example, many canoeists never think about using a brace when they get into a situation that warrants it. That kayak technique would make simple correction strokes almost second nature and prevent many spills.

"One common problem for new canoeists is that they shy away from experienced paddlers at first because of the fear of 'looking bad.' This is exactly the time when they should lean on the knowledge of others so they can learn correctly, faster and safer. Bad habits, formed in the early stages of paddling, are hard to break."

How does a person gain enough courage to float white water?

"Fear, in my mind, is nothing more than not knowing. In the case of white water, it means that when you don't know the river, can't read it, or you don't trust yourself or your partner, then you will fear white water running. The best way to gain courage for any potentially dangerous situation, such as white water runs, is to prepare yourself by good instructions and by paddling with a capable partner. With the proper safety equipment precautions that are used by competent paddlers, you will succeed. When I overstep my known capabilities, I experience fear to the degree that I take extra precautions to keep myself cool."

What makes a good canoeist and kayaker?

"I think the biggest factor is the desire to do it. The type of person who desires the thrill of white water will have what it takes. A good boatman is one who is levelheaded, safety conscious, and courteous, as well as experienced on the river."

Pat
Simmons

John
Malo

John Malo

John Malo has been canoeing ever since he was a teenager. He is one of those gifted individuals who has been able to combine a genuine love and skill in the sport with the ability to write about its many benefits. Malo is an all-around outdoorsman and prolific journalist whose skills are reflected in his books, *Malo's Complete Guide to Canoeing and Canoe Camping; Wilderness Canoeing;* and *Canoeing* (for children).

How did John Malo first get interested in flat water canoeing and kayaking?

"I first became interested in canoeing as a teenage junior counselor at a summer camp on the Des Plaines River (Illinois). We decided to utilize the river in other ways besides swimming and fishing. So the camp bought a used wood/canvas 18-foot canoe from a store 40 miles downstream. We paddled that canoe all the way back to camp. That same canoe was used at camp for several summers until the interest in canoeing grew where more boats and new waters were needed. At the same camp, the supervisor of recreation a few years later came up with plans for a 2-seat, plywood frame, canvas-covered kayak. In time, 11 of these kayaks were handcrafted and a club was formed. The Illinois lakes and rivers were used for one-day and overnight experiences."

What was the first lesson you learned that no one could have taught you?

"When you sit high in a canoe, like on the thwart, the stability is nullified and falling overboard or capsizing is the result. Also, be aware of the winds and current. Have a vigilant eye open for nature's tantrums."

What advice can you offer beginners?

"The 'tippiness' of the canoe must be dispelled.

Keep the center of gravity low at all times. Begin elementary lessons in calm waters—with a knowledgeable canoeist nearby. Experiment, at first, with various strokes and sense the responsiveness of the streamlined craft. Good balance in the canoe gives a feeling of confidence. Physical conditioning is important and so is strength. Novices, however, often work 'too hard' at the paddles, rather than using clean, smooth strokes."

How does a person gain enough courage to float white water?

"All water-oriented sports call for a compatibility with water. It is important to learn to relax and float without exertion. Mastering body floating skills will build up confidence. The gradation of white water experience, from gentle to rough, along with good coaching and tandem paddling with an experienced partner, yields confidence and courage."

What makes a good canoeist or kayaker?

"There are several points I'd like to make here. Learn the rhythmic coordinations of paddling. Toughen up the hands gradually. Paddle with a partner. Have the desire to advance beyond basic techniques. Remember no great size nor strength is necessary. The French voyageurs were small, wiry, well-coordinated men. Men and women, youngsters and adults can be good paddlers if they want to be."

Robert Ferguson

Robert Ferguson has rafted for 6 years and has operated his own company, Zephyr River Expeditions, for the past 4. White water seems to bring out the poet in him. On his river trips, he offers the "paddle option." The guest may elect to paddle a neoprene raft along with five others under the professional guidance of a guide at the helm. In this way, guests may share in the thrill and excitement which can be lost to them in an oar boat.

How did Robert Ferguson first get interested in rafting?

"I was told by a friend in Berkeley, California, that a certain white water outfit was hiring guides. I was grabbed by the thought of such work—it hardly seemed like work — and went for the interview. I was hired and flowed with the current to my present endeavor."

What was the first lesson you learned that no one could have taught you?

"That white water rafting is learned from experience. And there are many ways to run a rapid. Experts can give pointers and quote theories. But in the final analysis, it's one on one, only you on the river."

How does a person gain enough courage to float white water?

"Admittedly, a premier white water raft trip on a major river makes not only the novice but also the expert a bit nervous. In fact, usually it is the expert who is more 'up-tight' than the novice, as we know the possibilities that exist for dangerous situations. Rafting is essentially safe if done right. All it takes is going down a few times and becoming entranced with the beauty of it all."

What advice can you offer beginners?

"As with riding a motorcycle, do not become overconfident. Always respect and protect the river and it will do the same for you. Do not attempt an unknown river. And bring plenty of food."

What makes a good rafter?

"A person who really enjoys what he or she is doing and is humbled and cleansed after each trip. A person who respects the river and does not take it for granted."

Manufacturers and Suppliers

IN THE BOOMING business of float boat production and supply there is a stable of old name manufacturers as well as an ever-fluctuating crop of newcomers. In April of 1973, *Boating Industry Magazine* predicted a canoe sales growth rate of 25 percent per year. That estimate, given a slight decline in 1975, has run pretty much true to form. In addition, canoeists spend about $25,000,000 a year on boats, equipment and accessories. Include kayaking and rafting advocates, and we can see that river running *is* big business. Small manufacturers and suppliers come and go. The ones that stay have good products, a sound business operation, and successful advertising. The current emphasis on active, do-it-yourself outdoor sports that are environmentally sound and compatible can only make the forecast even brighter for boat and equipment manufacturers and suppliers.

CANOE MANUFACTURERS

Alumacraft, 315 W. St. Julien St., St. Peter, MN 56082

Dolphin Canoes, Wabasha, MN 55981

Eskay Plastics, Ltd., 2565 Blvd. Le Courbusier, Chomedey, Laval, Quebec, Canada

Fiberglass Boat Co., P.O. Box 88108, Seattle, WA 98188

Grumman Boats, Marathon, NY 13803

Jensen Canoes (racing), 308 78th Ave. N, Minneapolis, MN 55444

Keewaydin Canoes, Box 66, Forest Dale, VT 05745

Lincoln Canoes (racing), Waldoboro, ME 04572

Lowe Line, Lebanon, MO 65536

Lund American, Inc., Box 10, New York Mills, MN 56567

Mad River Canoe, Box 363, Waitsfield, VT 05673

Michi-Craft Corp., 19995 19 Mile Rd., Big Rapids, MI 49307

Midwestern Fiberglass Products, Breezy Acres, Box 247, Winona, MN 55987

Mohawk Canoes, Box 668, Longwood, FL 32750

Mon Ark Boats, Box 210, Monticello, AR 71655

Noah Co. (racing), 3461 Wilson Ave., Bronx, NY 10469

Nona, 997 W. 19th St., Costa Mesa, CA 92627

Old Town Canoe Co., Old Town, ME 04468

Pinetree Canoes, Ltd., Box 824, Orillia, Ontario, Canada

Ranger Canoes (racing), Allen St., Clinton, MA 01510

Sawyer Canoe Co., Box 452, Oscoda, MI 48750

Sea Nymph, Box 298, Syracuse, IN 46567

Seda Products, Box 41, San Ysidio, CA 92173

Smoker-Craft, Inc., New Paris, IN 46553

Sportspal, Industrial Park Rd., Johnstown, PA 15904

Wilderness Boats, Inc. (racing), Route 1, Box 101, Carlton, OR 97111

KAYAK MANUFACTURERS

Folbot Corp. (folding kayaks), Charleston, SC 29405

Hyperform, Industrial Park Rd., Hingham, ME 02043

Klepper (folding & rigid kayaks), 35 Union Square West, New York, NY 10003

Nona, 977 W. 19th St., Costa Mesa, CA 92627

Old Town Canoe Co., Old Town, ME 04468

Phoenix Products, Tymer, KY 40486

Seda Products, Box 41, San Ysidio, CA 92173

White Water Boats by Dick Held, Box 483, Cedar City, UT 84720

INFLATABLE BOATS

Avon Rubber, Seagull Marine (U.S. distributors), 1851 McGaw, Irvine, CA 92714

Bonair Boats, 1550 W. 109th St., Lenexa, KS 66219

Camp-Ways River Boats, 12915 S. Spring St., Los Angeles, CA 90061

Gladding (pack boats), 20 Whitesboro St., Utica, NY 13502

Leisure Imports, 104 Arlington Ave., St. James, NY 11780

Sears Roebuck, stores and boating catalog, nationwide

Zodiac of North America, 11 Lee St., Annapolis, MD 21401

PADDLES (canoes—c; kayak—k)

Azzali Paddles, RFD I, Box 186, Carlton Rd., Keene, NH 03431 (k)

Cannon Products, Inc., 2345 N.W. 8th Ave., Faribault, MN 55021 (c&k)

Carlisle Ausable Paddle Co., 110 State St., Grayling, MI 49738 (c&k)

Clement, 1625 Broadway, Miles, MI 49120, (c)

Feather Brand, Caviness Woodworking Co., Box 710, Calhoun City, MS 38916 (c)

Grabber Paddles, Box T, Mantua, OH 44255 (c&k)

Hurka Paddles, 1 Charles St., Newbury Port, MA 01950 (c&k)

Iliad, 170 Circuit St., Norwell, MA 02061 (c&k)

L. L. Bean, Freeport, ME 04033 (c)

Mitchell Paddles, Canaan, NH 03741 (k)

Mohawk Paddles, Box 668, Longwood, FL 32750 (c)

Nona Paddles, 977 W. 19th St., Costa Mesa, CA 92627 (c&k)

Old Town Canoe Co., Old Town, ME 04468 (c&k)

Sawyer Woodworking, 8891 Rogue River Highway, Rogue River, OR 97537 (c)

Seda, Box 41, San Ysidio, CA 92173 (c&k)

POLES

Sylvester Aluminum Poles, Mackenzie River Co., Box 9301, Richmond Heights, MO 63117

OARS

Camp-Ways River Equipment, 12915 S. Spring St., Los Angeles, CA 90061

Shaw & Penney Co. (manufacturer—ash and spruce oars), 20 Water St., Orono, ME 04473

(*Note:* Generally speaking, good spruce oars are best in deep, powerful rivers where strength and *flex* is important. Ash oars, have little flex, but are stronger than spruce for shallow, rocky bottoms. Cheaper oars are usually made of pine and don't last long under tough use.)

CARGO BAGS-BOAT PACKS

Camp-Ways, 12915 S. Spring St., Los Angeles CA 90061

Canoe California, Box 61, Kentfield, CA 94904

Great World, West Simsbury, CT 06092

Holubar, Box 7, Boulder, CO 80302

L.L. Bean, Freeport, ME 04033 (woven ash pack baskets)

Medalist/Universal, 11525 Sorrento Valley Rd., San Diego, CA 92121

Old Town Canoe Co., Old Town, ME 04468

Phoenix Products, Inc., U.S. Route 421, Tymer, KY 40486

Recreation Creations, Inc., Silver Lake Rd., Dingmans Ferry, PA 18328

Rec-Pak, 1159 Suarte Rd., Duarte, CA 91010

Recreational Equipment, Inc., Box 22090, Seattle, WA 98122

Voyageur Enterprises, Box 512, Shawnee Mission, KS 66201

Ultimate Experience (specialized foam padded camera packs) P.O. Box 2118, Santa Barbara, CA 93120

LIFE VESTS

Grumman Boat Company, Marathon, NY 13803

Medalist Water Sports, 11525 Sorrento Valley Rd., San Diego, CA 92121

Old Town Canoe Co., Old Town, ME 04468

Omega, 266 Border St., East Boston, MA 02128

Stearns Mfg. Co., Box 1498, St. Cloud, MN 56301

WET SUITS

Bayley Suit, Inc., 900 South Fortuna Blvd., Fortuna, CA 95540

Old Town Canoe Co., Old Town, ME 04468

Sears Roebuck, stores and boating catalog, nationwide

Wilderness Wet Suits, 837 W. 18th St., Costa Mesa, CA 92627

(*Note:* Local dive shops and some sporting goods stores carry wet suits.)

HELMETS

Nona, 997 W. 19th St., Costa Mesa, CA 92627

Old Town Canoe Co., Old Town, ME 04468

(*Note:* Most sporting goods stores carrying team sports equipment have hockey helmets that serve as white water headgear.)

BOAT RACKS

L.L. Bean, Freeport, ME 04033

Grumman Boat Company, Marathon, NY 13803

Old Town Canoe Co., Old Town, ME 04468

Rubber Rope Co., 412 See Gwun Ave., Mt. Prospect, IL 60056

Sears Roebuck, stores and boating catalog centers, nationwide

CANOE TRAILERS

MO Trailer Corp. (trailers for hauling 6, 8, 10, 16, 20, 30, & 36 canoes), 1030 S. Tenth St., Goshen, IN 46526

Sears, Roebuck, stores and boating catalog centers, nationwide

Glossary

Abeam — At right angle to the centerline of the boat.

Aft — Toward the stern.

Ahead — Ahead of the boat.

Air Chamber — A chamber of an inflatable boat that receives and holds air.

Amidships — The middle of the boat.

Astern — Behind the boat.

Back Rowing — Basic control and maneuver stroke in rafting to work boat away from obstacles into good position by rowing against the current. Similar to Side Rowing across the current.

Back Wave — The uphill slope found at the bottom of strong chutes or falls.

Bailing Bucket — Emergency plastic bucket kept on board for heavy white water trips where water is taken in and should be bailed out.

Bay — Interior spaces between thwarts or seats.

Beam — The transverse measurement at a boat's widest part.

Beavertail — Type of paddle which is broadest at the tip for maximum drive.

Bellows — Foot pump used to inflate boats.

Bilge — The point of greatest curvature between the bottom and the side in the cross section of a hull. Also, the lower interior areas of the hull.

Boatman — A person who handles the oars of an inflatable boat.

Boil — A water current upswelling into a convex mound.

Bow — The forward part of a boat.

Bow Cover (Bow Dodger) — Covers bow of boat to lessen chances of taking in water. Used mainly on high performance boats.

Bowman — Person who paddles from the bow or forward position.

Brace — A paddle stroke that provides stability against a capsizing force of a lateral current. Can also be used for turning.

Braking — Using oars or paddle to brake the boat to a stop by holding them against the current.

Broach — An out-of-control canoe that turns sideways in a fast current.

Buttocks — The bottom sections of the hull to either side of the keel.

C-1, C-2 — Racing one- or two-person canoes in which canoeists use a single paddle.

Canoe — As officially defined by the International Canoe Federation: a craft lower in the middle than at the ends along the gunwales or deck with a minimum beam of .80-meter and minimum length of 4.00 meters for a single canoe and 4.59 meters for a double canoe.

Carabiner — A mountain climber's hook used by boaters for snapping gear in and out of the boat.

Cartop Carrier — A system of wooden or aluminum crossbars, tie-downs and ropes used to carry small or lightweight boats on top of vehicles.

Channel — A canoeable route through a river section.

Chute — A channel through a drop or gap in a rapid that is steeper and faster than the surrounding water.

Coaming — The lip surrounding a cockpit used for securing a spray cover or skirt.

Cockpit — The sitting area or cockpit of a kayak.

Control Blade or Hand — That which stays firm, as opposed to the rotating hand on a double kayak paddle.

Deck — A rigid or semi-rigid covering over the hull of a boat.

Draft — The amount of water displaced by a boat. Shallow draft means a boat displaces very little water and is good in shallow water.

Drag — The slowing effect of an inflatable boat's hull on the water surface caused by inflatable design and construction.

Draw — A paddle stroke which involves pulling directly in toward the canoe to move sideways.

D-Rings — Come in various sizes. Found on larger, better boats to contain and support lifelines and to sometimes secure seats and rowing frames.

Drop — A place where the river bottom pitches most steeply.

Dry Pack — A waterproof pack for keeping gear and clothing dry.

Duffek Stroke — A high brace stroke, first used by kayaker, Milovan Duffek of Czechoslovakia.

Eddy — A portion of a stream or river that appears calm compared to the rest of the river, but where the flow is reversed or circular.

Eddy Line — A sharp boundary between two currents of different velocities and directions.

Eskimo Roll — A 360-degree boat roll with kayaker in boat and performed with paddle strokes and body positioning. Used to complete runs instead of beaching boat.

Falls — A rather abrupt vertical or semi-vertical drop where water *falls* or drops free.

Feathered Paddles — The blades of a double kayak paddle that are set at 90-degree angles to each other.

Ferry — Moving laterally across the current by paddling upstream, either backward or forward at an angle to the current.

Flat Blade — Paddles with flat, non-curving blades.

Float Trip — Paddling or rowing on stream or river, sometimes for the express purpose of fishing.

Floor — The entire bottom of the canoe.

Floorboards — Sectioned marine plywood floorboards used in high performance inflatables to help eliminate floor bounce.

Folding Kayak — A kayak-designed boat that can be disassembled and packed into carrying bags.

Forward — Toward the bow.

Forward Control Stroke — A forward checking stroke used to retain position or for minor course change.

Freeboard — The distance from the water surface to the top of the gunwales.

Gradient — The average rate of river drop or descent measured in feet per mile.

Grip — The extreme upper end of the canoe paddle shaped to fit in the palm of the hand.

Gunwales — The uppermost portion of the sides of the canoe.

Hanging Strokes — High bracing strokes for kayak and canoe so named because paddler's weight is hung on the high paddle.

Haystack — Smooth hump of water over a rock or obstruction, or standing wave at the bottom of a chute.

High Performance Inflatable Boats — Designed primarily for use with outboard motors, with floorboard and rigid transoms.

Hole — A depression in the water at the bottom of a chute.

Hypalon — A synthetic rubber by Du Pont that has proven tougher and longer wearing than rubber for boat use. Currently used in Hypalon-nylon layers in better inflatable boats.

Hypothermia — Sometimes called exposure. Caused when the body loses heat faster than it produces it. Shivering, exhaustion and stumbling are symptoms. Can cause death.

Inflatable Boat — Raft or canoe-shaped boat made of an inflatable material that can be deflated for packing and storage.

J-Stroke — Finishing a power stroke off by turning the paddle edge up or "J'd" like a rudder.

K-1, K-2 — Racing one- or two-person kayaks utilizing double-bladed paddles.

Kayak — As officially defined by the International Canoe Federation: a craft paddled with a double paddle from a sitting position with a minimum beam of .60-meter and a minimum length of 4.00 meters.

Keel — A projecting strip of various sizes along the bottom of the canoe's outside hull that cuts down side slipping.

Kevlar — Du Pont's registered trademark for a family of aramid fibers that is used to reinforce plastics. Used for boats and paddles. Yields high strength and light weight.

Lake Canoe — A canoe better suited for lakes because of deeper keel and better tracking ability and not as much freeboard design.

Landing — A place along river or lake to put in or take out boats. Points of ingress (entering) or egress (leaving).

Ledge — Exposed edge of rock stratum that produces small falls or acts as a low dam.

Leeward — Downwind side. The direction toward which the wind is blowing.

Lifelines — Those lines found around the outside chambers of inflatable boats.

Life Preservers — Vests or jackets, filled with a buoyant insulation that keeps wearers above water in case of capsizing. Proper fit is important and preservers should be U. S. Coast Guard approved for all types of boating uses.

Lining — The use of ropes, at bow and stern, to work boats upstream or downstream.

Marina Boat (Dingy) — Inflatable boat best suited for flat water marina use due to design and construction. Not generally suited for white water river running.

Motor Mount — A wood or aluminum bracket that can be attached to the stern or gunwales to mount outboard motor.

Pack Boat — A small, lightweight plastic or polyethylene boat used for small lakes or ponds. Can be deflated and packed on a pack frame. Generally unsuitable for white water use on rivers.

Paddle — The instrument used to hand-propel a boat, made of grip, shaft and blade.

Paddle Floating — Passengers use paddles, instead of single oarsman, to run river.

Painter — A line attached to bow or stern of a boat.

Pawlata Roll — The kayak roll done with the paddle in the extended position. Named after an Australian paddler who first learned it from the Eskimos.

Pitch — A section of rapid that is steeper than the surrounding sections.

Pitch-Pole — A boat pitches up on end and falls over on its side. Usually caused by a dam or steep chute.

Pool — A river section slower and deeper than the surrounding sections.

Port — To the left.

Portage — (Verb) To carry a boat overland. (Noun) The place where the carry is performed.

Portside — Left side of the boat when facing forward.

Power Face — The face of a paddle that faces the water in a normal stroke as opposed to the non-power face of the blade.

Push-Over — A sideways paddle stroke that is opposite of the draw stroke.

Rafting — Using inflatable boat or "raft" to negotiate rivers and streams.

Rapid — Steep river gradient with increased water speed that causes fast or "rapid" white water.

Rib — Lateral interior bottom reinforcing members of a canoe or kayak.

Riffle — Light, choppy water characterized by small waves. Usually over shallow water.

River Cruising — Touring with canoe, kayak or raft in a rather leisurely manner as opposed to racing.

River Rating — Based on a grading system from one (very easy) through six (extraordinarily difficult).

River Running — The sport or business of negotiating white water rivers.

Rocker — The longitudinal curvature of the bottom of a boat at the center line of the hull.

Rowing Frame — A frame made from wood, aluminum or steel where the rower and passengers sit in an inflatable boat.

Rubber Raft — Somme boats are made of rubberized fabric or nylon. However, the term often incorrectly used to describe inflatable boats. Modern inflatables are seldom built with rubber but rather a combination of nylon and new synthetics such as Hypalon.

Runoff — Snow melt or rain in the spring that causes extremely high, turbulent water that can be treacherous for inexperienced river runners.

Sculling — Using oar or paddle blade against current to propel or turn boat from stern position.

Send — The length of a paddle stroke.

Setting — Ferrying a boat with the bow downstream.

Setting Pole — A pole 10 to 12 feet in length of wood or aluminum used to pole (snub or push) canoe in shallow water.

Sheer — The upward curve of the sides of a hull from amidship to the ends.

Shoe Keel — A keel with minimal lateral area for maneuverability in white water.

Sideslipping — The positioning maneuver used for inflatables by which a dominant oar is used to sideslip across current, while still maintaining control with subordinate oar.

Slalom Course — Pairs of poles (gates) suspended above the water to mark a slalom canoe or kayak competition course in an appropriate water grade. Hence, the term slalom kayak, used for running slalom downstream or upstream courses.

Souse Hole — The area just downstream of a large underwater obstruction in a powerful current.

Splash Cover — Covers entire canoe for rough water and bad weather to keep boat and cargo dry.

Spoon Blade — Paddles that are spoon-shaped or curved for more power.

Spray Skirt (Spray Cover) — A waterproof fabric designed to close the cockpit space. Worn by the paddler.

Standing Wave — A wave which accompanies deceleration of the current. A haystack wave.

Starboard — To the right.

Starboard Side — Right side of the boat when facing forward.

Stern — The rear portion of the boat.

Sternman — Person who paddles from the stern or rear position.

Straking — Rubber bumpers (fenders) around inflatable boats that protect from rubbing or colliding.

Strokes — Paddle or oar techniques or motion by which boats are controlled.

Tandem — Referring to paddling position of crew of two, one behind the other (sometimes on opposite sides of the boat for weight distribution) in paddling a canoe.

Throat — The section of paddle shaft just above the blade.

Thwart — Transverse braces or seats attached from gunwale to gunwale in canoes.

Tracking — Paddling a straight course on smooth water such as a lake. A boat that tracks well is easy to keep in line or track.

Transom — A fixed panel or board at the stern of the boat on which a motor can be mounted.

Trim — The angle to the plane of the water at which a boat rides. Boat can be trimmed at bow, stern or trimmed level.

Tumblehome — Recurvature of the hull inward from the vertical at the gunwale line.

Upturn — Upsweep of the sheerline bow and stern of a canoe in imitation of Indian styling. Used for the purpose of holding canoe's mid-section off the ground to provide sleeping shelter. Too much upturn is affected by wind and makes canoe difficult to turn.

Wet Suit — Snug-fitting neoprene pants, tunic, gloves, boots and hood which uses a thin layer of trapped water as insulation against the cold.

White Water — Water characterized by swift current and obstacles, such as rocks, that produce 'white' chops or waves.

White Water Canoe — A canoe with adequate freeboard, shallow-draft keel and sometimes extra ribs for rugged white water use.

Windward — The direction from which the wind is blowing.

Yoke — A padded shoulder brace, either made from lashing paddles to thwarts or purchased commercially, that is used to carry a canoe upside down.